Study Guide

EIGHTH EDITION

SCOTT, JR.

MARTIN

PETTY

KEOWN

Basic Financial Management

Prentice Hall, Upper Saddle River, New Jersey 07458

Acquisitions editor: *Paul Donnelly*
Associate editor: *Gladys Soto*
Project editor: *Theresa Festa*
Manufacturer: *Victor Graphics, Inc.*

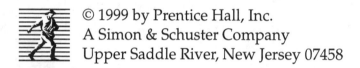

© 1999 by Prentice Hall, Inc.
A Simon & Schuster Company
Upper Saddle River, New Jersey 07458

Printed in the United States of America

10 9 8 7 6 5 4 3 2

ISBN 0-13-083375-4

Prentice-Hall International (UK) Limited, *London*
Prentice-Hall of Australia Pty. Limited, *Sydney*
Prentice-Hall Canada Inc., *Toronto*
Prentice-Hall Hispanoamericana, S.A., *Mexico*
Prentice-Hall of India Private Limited, *New Delhi*
Prentice-Hall of Japan, Inc., *Tokyo*
Simon & Schuster Asia Pte. Ltd., *Singapore*
Editora Prentice-Hall do Brasil, Ltda., *Rio de Janeiro*

CONTENTS

Supplementary Materials

PREFACE

The objective of this *Study Guide* is to provide a student-oriented supplement to *Basic Financial Management*. There are several ways in which we have attempted to accomplish that end, these being:

1. A condensation of each chapter in the form of a detailed sentence outline. This overview of the key points of the chapter can serve both as a preview and quick survey of the chapter content and as a review.

2. Problems (with detailed solutions) and self-tests which can be used to aid in the preparation of outside assignments and in studying for examinations. The problems were keyed to the end-of-chapter problems in the text in order to provide direct and meaningful student aid. Also, both multiple-choice and true-false questions are used to provide a self-test over the descriptive chapter material.

3. A tutorial on capital budgeting. The tutorial helps the student work through this important topic on an individual basis at his or her own pace.

4. We provide worked-out solutions to selected end-of-chapter problems from Set B in the text. These problems are identical to Problem Set A problems, except the names and numbers have been changed. The list of these problems appears following this preface.

5. In addition to the tables giving compound sum and present value interest factors, we provide tables showing how to compute the interest factors using a financial calculator.

The foregoing material provides what we believe is a valuable learning tool for the student of financial management. The response of the students who have used the *Study Guide* has been most favorable.

LIST OF PROBLEM SOLUTIONS APPEARING IN THE STUDY GUIDE

The solutions to the following end-of-chapter problems in the text (Set B only) are provided in the respective chapters of this Study Guide.

Chapter	Problem Solutions Appearing in the Study Guide
Chapter 1:	3B, 5B, 7B, 9B, 11B, and 13B
Chapter 2:	2B
Chapter 3:	3B, 7B, and 9B
Chapter 4:	4B and 8B
Chapter 5:	14B, 16B, 20B, 21B, 23B, 25B, 29B, 31B, and 33B
Chapter 6:	1B, 4B, and 10B
Chapter 7:	1B, 3B, 7B, and 10B
Chapter 8:	3B, 5B, 8B, and 10B
Chapter 9:	1B, 5B, 7B, and 9B
Chapter 10:	3B, 6B, 7B, 9B, 11B, and 13B
Chapter 11:	3B, 5B, and 7B
Chapter 12:	3B, 13B, 14B, and 16B
Chapter 13:	3B, 7B, 10B, 13B, 17B, 21B, and 25B
Chapter 14:	3B, 6B, 10B, 13B, and 15B
Chapter 15:	2B, 4B, 5B, 8B, 11B, and 12B
Chapter 16:	3B, 5B, and 6B
Chapter 17:	3B, 6B, 10B, 14B, and 18B
Chapter 18:	1B, 5B, 7B, 9B, and 11B
Chapter 19:	4B and 7B
Chapter 20:	None
Chapter 21:	1B and 4B
Chapter 22:	1B, 3B, and 5B

CHAPTER 1

An Introduction to Financial Management

<u>Orientation</u>: This chapter lays a foundation for what will follow. First, it focuses on the goal of the firm, followed by a review of the legal forms of business organization, and a discussion of the tax implications relating to financial decisions. Ten axioms that form the foundations of financial management then follow.

I.   Goal of the firm

    A.   In this book we will designate maximization of shareholder wealth, by which we mean maximization of the total market value of the firm's common stock, to be the goal of the firm. To understand this goal and its inclusive nature it is first necessary to understand the difficulties involved with the frequently suggested goal of profit maximization.

    B.   While the goal of profit maximization stresses the efficient use of capital resources, it assumes away many of the complexities of the real world and for this reason is unacceptable.

        1.   One of the major criticisms of profit maximization is that it assumes away uncertainty of returns. That is, projects are compared by examining their expected values or weighted average profit.

        2.   Profit maximization is also criticized because it assumes away timing differences of returns.

    C.   Profit maximization is unacceptable and a more realistic goal is needed.

II.   Maximization of shareholder wealth

    A.   We have chosen the goal of shareholder wealth maximization because the effects of all financial decisions are included in this goal.

    B.   In order to employ this goal we need not consider every price change to be a market interpretation of the worth of our decisions. What we do focus on is the effect that our decision should have on the stock price if everything were held constant.

    C.   The agency problem is a result of the separation between the decision makers and the owners of the firm. As a result managers may make decisions that are not in line with the goal of maximization of shareholder wealth.

III.   Legal forms of business organization

    A.   The significance of different legal forms

        1.   The predominant form of business organization in the United States in pure numbers is the sole proprietorship.

    B.   Sole proprietorship: A business owned by a single person and that has a minimum amount of legal structure.

        1.   Advantages

            a.   Easily established with few complications

            b.   Minimal organizational costs

            c.   Does not have to share profits or control with others

        2.   Disadvantages

            a.   Unlimited liability for the owner

            b.   Owner must absorb all losses

            c.   Equity capital limited to the owner's personal investment

  d. Business terminates immediately upon death of owner

C. Partnership: An association of two or more individuals coming together as co-owners to operate a business for profit.

  1. Two types of partnerships

    a. General partnership: Relationship between partners is dictated by the partnership agreement.

      1. Advantages

        a. Minimal organizational requirements

        b. Negligible government regulations

      2. Disadvantages

        a. All partners have unlimited liability

        b. Difficult to raise large amounts of capital

        c. Partnership dissolved by the death or withdrawal of general partner

    b. Limited partnership

      1. Advantages

        a. For the limited partners, liability limited to the amount of capital invested in the company

        b. Withdrawal or death of a limited partner does not affect continuity of the business

        c. Stronger inducement in raising capital

2. Disadvantages

    a. There must be at least one general partner who has unlimited liability in the partnership

    b. Names of limited partners may not appear in the name of the firm

    c. Limited partners may not participate in the management of the business

    d. More expensive to organize than general partnership, as a written agreement is mandatory

D. The corporation: An "impersonal" legal entity having the power to purchase, sell, and own assets and to incur liabilities while existing separately and apart from its owners.

  1. Ownership is evidenced by shares of stock

  2. Advantages

    a. Limited liability of owners

    b. Ease of transferability of ownership, i.e., by the sale of one's shares of stock

    c. The death of an owner does not result in the discontinuity of the firm's life

    d. Ability to raise large amounts of capital is increased

  3. Disadvantages

    a. Most difficult and expensive form of business to establish

b. Control of corporation not guaranteed by partial ownership of stock

IV. Federal income taxation

A. Objectives of federal income taxation

1. Provide government revenues

2. Achieve socially desirable goals

3. Stabilize the economy

B. Income taxes for sole proprietorship

1. All income and expenses for the business are reported on the owner's personal income tax forms.

2. Taxation of the business income is the same as for the owner's personal income.

C. Income taxes for partnerships

1. Partnership tax return reports every transaction that has a tax consequence and allocates the transactions as specified by the partnership agreement.

2. The individual partners report their portions of the partnership income within their personal tax returns.

D. Income taxes for corporations

1. A tax return must be filed and the resulting taxes paid by the corporation.

2. Taxable income is basically determined as income less allowable exclusions and tax deductible expenses.

3. Seventy percent of any dividends received from another corporation are tax exempt.

4. Dividends paid by the corporation to its stockholders are not tax deductible.

5. Corporate rate structure:

15%	$0 - $50,000
25%	$50,001 - $75,000
34%	$75,001 - 10,000,000
35%	over $10,000,000

Additional surtaxes:

There is an added tax of 5 percent for income between $100,000 and $335,000.

There is an additional added tax of 3 percent on income between $15 and $18 and 1/3 million.

6. It may be that some of a firm's income originates in a foreign country. If so, the tax rates, and the method of taxing the firm, frequently vary. The financial manager would obviously want to minimize the firm's taxes by reporting as much income in the low tax-rate countries and as little as possible in the high tax-rate countries. Of course, other factors, such as political risk, may discourage your efforts to minimize taxes across national borders.

7. Depreciation

   a. For assets acquired prior to 1981, two depreciation methods, among others, may be used for tax purposes.

      (1) Straight-line
      (2) Double-declining balance

b. For assets acquired in 1981 or later, the Modified Accelerated Cost Recovery System (MACRS) should be used.

8. Net operating loss: If a corporation has an operating loss in any year, the loss may be applied against the profits in the 3 prior years. If the loss has not been completely absorbed by the profits in these 3 years, the loss may be carried forward to each of the 15 following years.

9. If after deducting all capital gains and capital losses the company has a net capital loss, such losses may be carried back for 3 years and forward for 5 years to offset any capital gains occurring during those periods.

10. Accumulated earnings tax is a penalty surtax assessed on the corporation on any accumulation of earnings by a corporation for the purpose of avoiding taxes by its shareholders.

11. Subchapter S corporation

a. Subchapter S of the Internal Revenue Code permits the owners of a small corporation with 35 or fewer stockholders to use the corporation organizational form but be taxed as though the firm were a partnership.

b. This treatment eliminates the double taxation normally associated with the corporate entity, yet provides limited personal liability and other favorable features of the corporate structure.

c. This provision became even more important in 1987 when individual tax rates fell below corporate tax rates.

E.   Implications of taxes in financial decision making

   1.   Taxes and capital investment decisions

      a.   When a plant or equipment acquisition is being considered, the returns from the investment should be measured on an after-tax basis using the marginal not average tax rate in the computations.

      b.   The depreciation method will have an impact on the timing of taxes.

      c.   The estimated salvage value also may have a tax impact; the greater the anticipated salvage value, the less the amount of annual depreciation charges.

   2.   Taxes and the firm's capital structure: The tax deductibility of interest payments gives debt financing a definite cost advantage over preferred and common stock financing.

   3.   Taxes and corporate dividend policies: The differential tax treatment for the firm's common stockholders might influence the firm's preference between stock price appreciation, i.e., capital gains for the investor, and dividends, i.e., ordinary income for the investor.

V.   Ten Axioms that form the foundations of financial management.

   A.   Axiom 1: The risk-return tradeoff - we won't take additional risk unless we expect to be compensated with additional return.

      1.   Almost all financial decisions involve some sort of risk- return trade off.

   B.   Axiom 2: The time value of money - a dollar received today is worth more than a dollar received in the future.

C.   Axiom 3: Cash -- Not Profits -- is King. In measuring value we will use cash flows rather than accounting profits because it is only cash flows that the firm receives and is able to reinvest.

D.   Axiom 4: Incremental cash flows - it's only what changes that counts. In making business decisions we will only concern ourselves with what happens as a result of that decision.

E.   Axiom 5: The curse of competitive markets - why it's hard to find exceptionally profitable projects. In competitive markets, extremely large profits cannot exist for very long because of competition moving in to exploit those large profits. As a result, profitable projects can only be found if the market is made less competitive, either through product differentiation or by achieving a cost advantage.

F.   Axiom 6: Efficient Capital Markets - The markets are quick and the prices are right.

G.   Axiom 7: The agency problem - managers won't work for the owners unless it's in their best interest. The agency problem is a result of the separation between the decision makers and the owners of the firm. As a result managers may make decisions that are not in line with the goal of maximization of shareholder wealth.

H.   Axiom 8: Taxes bias business decisions.

I.   Axiom 9: All risk is not equal since some risk can be diversified away and some cannot. The process of diversification can reduce risk, and as a result, measuring a project or an asset's risk is very difficult.

J.   Axiom 10: Ethical behavior is doing the right thing, and ethical dilemmas are everywhere in finance. Ethical behavior is important in financial management, just as it is important in everything we do. Unfortunately, precisely how we define what is and what is not ethical behavior is sometimes difficult. Nevertheless, we should not give up the quest.

Study Problems

1. A corporation had $145,000 in taxable earnings. What is the tax liability?

SOLUTION

Income		Marginal Tax Rate		Tax Liability
$ 50,000	x	15%		$ 7,500
25,000	x	25%		6,250
25,000	x	34%		8,500
45,000	x	39%		17,550
$145,000		Total tax liability	=	$39,800

2. A corporation has earnings before interest and taxes of $86,000, dividend income of $5,333, and interest expenses of $9,000. Also, a contribution to a university was made in the amount of $1,000. What is the corporation's (a) taxable income and (b) tax liability?

SOLUTION

(a)
Operating income		$86,000
Dividend income	$5,333	
Dividend exclusion 70% x $5,333	(3,733)	
Taxable dividend income		1,600
Interest expense		(9,000)
Contribution		(1,000)
Taxable income		$77,600

(b)
15%	x	$50,000	=	$ 7,500		
25%	x	25,000	=	6,250		
34%	x	2,600	=	884		
		$77,600		$14,634	=	Tax liability

3. The M. M. Roscoe Corporation is a regional truck dealer. The firm sells new and used trucks and is actively involved in the parts business. During the most recent year the company generated sales of $4 million. The combined cost of goods sold and the operating expenses were $3.2 million. Also, $300,000 in interest expense was paid during the year. The firm received $5,000 during the year in dividend income from 1,000 shares of common stock that had been purchased three years previously. However, the stock

was sold toward the end of the year for $100 per share; its initial cost was $80 per share. The company also sold land that had been recently purchased and had been held for only four months. The selling price was $55,000; the cost was $45,000. Calculate the corporation's tax liability.

SOLUTION

M.M. Roscoe Corp. - Corporate Income Tax

Sales		$4,000,000
Cost of Goods Sold + Operating Expenses		(3,200,000)
Operating Profits		$800,000
Dividend Income	$5,000	
Less 70% Exclusion	(3,500)	1,500
Interest Expense		(300,000)
S-T Capital Gain		
Selling Price	$55,000	
Cost	(45,000)	10,000
L-T Capital Gain		
Selling Price		
(#Shares)(Price/Share)		
1,000 x $100	$100,000	
Cost		
(#Shares)(Price/Share)		
1,000 x $80	(80,000)	20,000
Taxable Ordinary Income		$531,500

Tax liability:

$50,000	x	.15	=	$7,500
25,000	x	.25	=	6,250
456,500	x	.34	=	155,210

Surtax:				
$235,000	x	.05	=	11,750
Total taxes due			=	$180,710

4.   The A.K.U. Corporation had sales of $5.5 million this past year. The cost of goods sold was $4.6 million and operating expenses were $125,000. Dividend income totaled $5,000. The firm sold land for $150,000 that had cost $100,000 five months ago. The firm received $140 per share from the sale of 1,000 shares of stock. The stock was purchased for $100 per share three years ago. Determine the firm's tax liability.

SOLUTION

A.K.U. Corporation - Corporate Income Tax

Sales		$5,500,000
Cost of Goods Sold		(4,600,000)
Gross Profits		$900,000
Operating Expenses		(125,000)
Dividend Income	$5,000	
Less 70% Exclusion	(3,500)	1,500
Ordinary Income		$776,500
Plus Capital Gains		
Land:		
Sales Price	$150,000	
Selling Price	(100,000)	50,000
Stock:		
Selling Price		
(#Shares)(Price/Share)		
1,000 x $140	$140,000	
Cost		
(#Shares)(Price/Share)		
1,000 x $100	(100,000)	40,000
Taxable income		$866,500

Tax Liability:

$50,000	x	0.15	=	$7,500
$25,000	x	0.25	=	6,250
$25,000	x	0.34	=	8,500
$235,000	x	0.39	=	91,650
$531,500	x	0.34	=	180,710
$866,500				$294,610

Self-Tests

TRUE-FALSE

_____ 1. Profit maximization is considered to be a more appropriate goal than shareholder wealth maximization because it considers the timing of the expected returns of the firm.

_____ 2. Shareholder wealth maximization considers the effects of the riskiness of a prospective earnings stream.

_____ 3. Many businesses are formed as corporations because of the ease of establishment.

_____ 4. Two major criticisms of the profit maximization goal are that it does not deal adequately with the uncertainty and the timing of returns.

_____ 5. The income from a partnership is reported by the partners on their personal tax returns.

_____ 6. Interest and dividend payments made by a corporation are both tax deductible by the paying corporation.

_____ 7. In general, the less risk a firm is willing to assume, the higher the expected return will be from a given course of action.

_____ 8. Ethical considerations are not relevant in the financial management.

_____ 9. Product differentiation helps reduce competition and thereby allows for larger profits.

_____ 10. In order to employ the goal of shareholder wealth maximization, every stock price change should be considered to be a market interpretation of the worth of our financial decisions.

_____ 11. The agency problem is a result of a separation of management and the owners of the firm.

MULTIPLE CHOICE

1. The long-run goal of the firm is to

    a. Hold large quantities of cash.
    b. Increase sales regularly.
    c. Maximize earnings per share.
    d. Maximize shareholder wealth.

2. Maximizing shareholder wealth means maximizing the

    a. Value of the firm's assets.
    b. Value of the firm's cash.
    c. Value of the firm's investments.
    d. Value of the firm's profits.
    e. Market value of the firm's common stock.

3. Advantages of the corporation include:

    a. Transferability of ownership.
    b. Unlimited liability.
    c. Ability of the corporation to raise capital.
    d. Double taxation of dividend income.
    e a and c.
    f. a and b.

4. Disadvantages of the partnership are:

    a. Expense of formation.
    b. Lack of permanence.
    c. Double taxation on income.
    d. Unlimited liability.
    e. b and d.
    f. a and d.

5. Profit maximization is not the proper objective of a firm because

    a. It is not as inclusive a goal as the maximization of shareholder wealth.
    b. It does not consider the uncertainty of the return.
    c. It does not consider the timing of the returns.
    d. All of the above.
    e. None of the above.

6. The market price of a share of stock is determined by

    a. The New York Stock Exchange.
    b. The Federal Reserve.
    c. The company's management.
    d. Individuals buying and selling the stock.

7. Which of the following forms of business organization is the largest in number?

    a. Corporation.
    b. Partnership.
    c. Sole proprietorship.

8. The agency problem is:

    a. Associated with insuring the firm.
    b. No longer important.
    c. Invalidates the goal of maximization of shareholder wealth.
    d. Is a result of the separation of the decision makers and the owners of the firm.
    e. All of the above.

1-3B. Carter B. Daltan - Corporate Income Tax

Sales		$3,500,000
Cost of Goods Sold		(2,000,000)
Gross Profits		$1,500,000
Cash Operating Expenses		(500,000)
Depreciation Expense		(100,000)
Operating Profits		$1,000,000
Dividend Income	$55,000	
Less 70% Exclusion	(38,500)	16,500
Interest Expense		(165,000)
Taxable Ordinary Income		$751,500

Tax Liability

$50,000	x	0.15	=	$	7,500
25,000	x	0.25	=		6,250
25,000	x	0.34	=		8,500
235,000	x	0.39	=		91,650
416,500	x	0.34	=		141,610
$751,500					$255,510

1-5B. Burgess Corporation - Corporate Income Tax

Sales		$2,500,000
Cost of Goods Sold		(700,000)
Gross Profits		$1,800,000
Cash Operating Expenses		(150,000)
Depreciation Expense		(150,000)
Dividend Income	$50,000	
Less 70% Exclusion	(35,000)	15,000
Interest Expense		(200,000)
Taxable Ordinary Income		$1,315,000

Tax Liability:

$50,000	x	0.15	=	$ 7,500
25,000	x	0.25	=	6,250
25,000	x	0.34	=	8,500
235,000	x	0.39	=	91,650
980,000	x	0.34	=	333,200
$1,315,000				$447,100

1-7B. Phil Schubert, Inc. - Corporate Income Tax

Sales		$5,000,000
Cost of Goods Sold		(3,800,000)
Gross Profits		$1,200,000
Cash Operating Expenses		(500,000)
Depreciation Expenses		(400,000)
Operating Profits		$300,000
Dividend Income	$15,000	
Less 70% Exclusion	(10,500)	4,500
Taxable Income		$304,500

Tax Liability:

$50,000	x	0.15	=	$7,500
25,000	x	0.25	=	6,250
25,000	x	0.34	=	8,500
204,500	x	0.39	=	79,755
$304,500				$102,005

1-9B. J. Johnson, Inc. - Corporate Income Tax

Sales	$7,000,000
Cost of Goods Sold	(4,000,000)
Gross Profits	$3,000,000
Operating Expenses	(2,600,000)
Interest Expense	(40,000)
Taxable Income	$360,000

Tax Liability:

$50,000	x	0.15	=	$7,500
$25,000	x	0.25	=	6,250
$25,000	x	0.34	=	8,500
$235,000	x	0.39	=	91,650
$25,000	x	0.34	=	8,500
$360,000				$122,400

1-11B.   Martinez, Inc. - Corporate Income Tax

Sales		$8,300,000
Cost of goods sold and cash operating expenses		(6,391,000)
Depreciation expense		(79,000)
Operating profit		$1,830,000
Interest expense		(150,000)
Dividend Income	$72,000	
Less 70% Exclusion	(50,400)	21,600
Long term gain:		
Selling price	$375,000	
Purchase price	(350,000)	125,000
Taxable Income		$1,826,600

Tax Liability:

$50,000	x	0.15	=	$7,500
25,000	x	0.25	=	6,250
25,000	x	0.34	=	8,500
235,000	x	0.39	=	91,650
1,491,600	x	0.34	=	507,144
$1,826,600				$621,044

1-13B.   Tetsua Corporation - Carryforward - Carryback

Year	Taxable Income	Tax Payment	Carry Back	Carry Forward	Tax Refund
1987	$60,000	$10,000			
1988	(90,000)		$60,000('87)		$10,000[a]
1989	80,000	7,500[b]		$30,000('88)	
1990	110,000	26,150			
1991	80,000	15,450			
1992	(150,000)			50,000('89) 100,000('90)	32,150[c]
1993	75,000	13,750			
1994	(100,000)			80,000('91) 20,000('93)	20,450[d]

(a) Refund: $10,000 from 1987.
(b) Taxes based on $50,000 taxable income ($80,000 income in 1989 - $30,000 carryforward from 1988).
(c) Refund: $7,500 from 1989; $24,650 from 1990.
(d) Refund: $15,450 from 1991; $5,000 from 1993.

CHAPTER 2

The Role of Financial Markets and Interest Rates in Financial Management

Orientation: This chapter considers the market environment in which long-term capital is raised. The underlying rationale for the existence of security markets is presented, investment banking services and procedures are detailed, private placements are discussed, and security market regulation is reviewed. Further discussions cover rates of return over long periods and recent periods, interest rate determinants, and theories of the term structure of interest rates.

I.   The mix of corporate securities sold in the capital market.

    A.   When corporations raise cash in the capital market, what type of financing vehicle is most favored? The answer to this question is corporate bonds. The corporate debt markets clearly dominate the corporate equity markets when new (external) funds are being raised.

    B.   We will learn from our discussion on the cost of capital and planning the firm's financing mix that the U.S. tax system inherently favors debt as a means of raising capital. Over the 1981-96 period, bonds and notes accounted for about 75.6 percent of new corporate securities sold for cash.

II.   Why financial markets exist

    A.   Financial markets consist of institutions and procedures that facilitate transactions in all types of financial claims.

B.   Some economic units spend more during a given period of time than they earn. Some economic units spend less than they earn. Accordingly, a mechanism is needed to facilitate the transfer of savings from those economic units that have a savings surplus to those that have a savings deficit. Financial markets provide such a mechanism.

C.   The function of financial markets, then, is to allocate savings in an economy to the ultimate demander (user) of the savings.

D.   If there were no financial markets, the wealth of an economy would be lessened. Savings could not be transferred to economic units, such as business firms, which are most in need of those funds.

III.   Financing business: The movement of funds through the economy.

A.   In the financing process, financial institutions play a major role in bridging the gap between savers and borrowers in the economy.

B.   In a normal year the household sector is the largest net supplier of funds to the financial markets. We call the household sector, then, a savings-surplus sector.

C.   In contrast, the nonfinancial business sector is a savings-deficit sector. In recent years the federal government has become a "quasi-permanent" savings deficit sector.

D.   All in all, within the domestic economy, the nonfinancial business sector is dependent on the household sector to finance its investment needs.

E.   The financial market system includes a complex network of intermediaries that assist in the transfer of savings among economic units.

F. The <u>movement of savings</u> through the economy occurs in three distinct ways:

    1.   The direct transfer of funds.

    2.   Indirect transfer using the investment banker.

    3.   Indirect transfer using the financial intermediary.

IV. Components of the U.S. financial market system.

A. <u>Public offerings</u> can be distinguished from <u>private placements</u>.

    1.   The public (financial) market is an impersonal market in which both individual and institutional investors have the opportunity to acquire securities.

        a.   A public offering takes place in the public market.

        b.   The security-issuing firm does not meet (face-to-face) the actual investors in the securities.

    2.   In a private placement of securities only a limited number of investors have the opportunity to purchase a portion of the issue.

        a.   The market for private placements is more personal than its public counterpart.

        b.   The specific details of the issue may actually be developed on a face-to-face basis among the potential investors and the issuer.

B. <u>Primary markets</u> can be distinguished from <u>secondary markets</u>.

    1.   Securities are first offered for sale in a primary market. For example, the sale of a new bond issue, preferred stock issue, or common stock issue takes place in the primary market. These transactions increase the total stock of financial assets in existence in the economy.

2.   Trading in currently existing securities takes place in the secondary market. The total stock of financial assets is unaffected by such transactions.

C.   The <u>money market</u> can be distinguished from the <u>capital market</u>.

    1.   The money market consists of the institutions and procedures that provide for transactions in short-term debt instruments which are generally issued by borrowers who have very high credit ratings.

        a.   "Short-term" means that the securities traded in the money market have maturity periods of not more than 1 year.

        b.   Equity instruments are not traded in the money market.

        c.   Typical examples of money market instruments are (1) U.S. Treasury bills, (2) federal agency securities, (3) bankers' acceptances, (4) negotiable certificates of deposit, and (5) commercial paper.

    2.   The capital market consists of the institutions and procedures that provide for transactions in long-term financial instruments. This market encompasses those securities that have maturity periods extending beyond 1 year.

D.   <u>Organized security exchanges</u> can be distinguished from <u>over-the-counter markets</u>.

    1.   Organized security exchanges are tangible entities whose activities are governed by a set of bylaws. Security exchanges physically occupy space and financial instruments are traded on such premises.

a. Major stock exchanges must comply with a strict set of reporting requirements established by the Securities and Exchange Commission (SEC). These exchanges are said to be <u>registered</u>.

b. Organized security exchanges provide several benefits to both corporations and investors. They (1) provide a continuous market, (2) establish and publicize fair security prices, and (3) help businesses raise new financial capital.

c. A corporation must take steps to have its securities <u>listed</u> on an exchange in order to directly receive the benefits noted above. Listing criteria differ from exchange to exchange.

2. Over-the-counter markets include all security markets <u>except</u> the organized exchanges. The money market is a prominent example. Most corporate bonds are traded over-the-counter.

V. The investment banker

A. The investment banker is a financial specialist who acts as an intermediary in the selling of securities. He or she works for an investment banking firm (house).

B. Three basic functions are provided by the investment banker:

1. He or she assumes the risk of selling a new security issue at a satisfactory (profitable) price. This is called <u>underwriting</u>. Typically, the investment banking house, along with the underwriting syndicate, actually buys the new issue from the corporation that is raising funds. The syndicate (group of investment banking firms) then sells the issue to the investing public at a higher (hopefully) price than it paid for it.

2. He or she provides for the <u>distribution</u> of the securities to the investing public.

3.　He or she <u>advises</u> firms on the details of selling securities.

C.　Several distribution methods are available for placing new securities into the hands of final investors. The investment banker's role is different in each case.

　　1.　In a <u>negotiated purchase</u> the firm in need of funds contacts an investment banker and begins the sequence of steps leading to the final distribution of the securities that will be offered. The price that the investment banker pays for the securities is "negotiated" with the issuing firm.

　　2.　In a <u>competitive-bid purchase</u> the investment banker and underwriting syndicate are selected by an auction process. The syndicate willing to pay the greatest dollar amount per new security to the issuing firm wins the competitive bid. This means that it will underwrite and distribute the issue. In this situation, the price paid to the issuer is not negotiated; instead, it is determined by a sealed-bid process much on the order of construction bids.

　　3.　In a <u>commission</u> (or <u>best-efforts</u>) offering the investment banker does not act as an underwriter. He or she attempts to sell the issue in return for a fixed commission on each security that is actually sold. Unsold securities are simply returned to the firm hoping to raise funds.

　　4.　In a privileged <u>subscription</u> the new issue is not offered to the investing public. It is sold to a definite and limited group of investors. Current stockholders are often the privileged group.

　　5.　In a <u>direct sale</u> the issuing firm sells the securities to the investing public without involving an investment banker in the process. This is not a typical procedure.

D. The negotiated purchase is most likely to be the distribution method used by the private corporation. It consists of several steps.

1. The security-issuing firm selects an investment banker.

2. A series of pre-underwriting conferences take place. Discussions center on (1) the amount of capital to be raised, (2) the possible receptiveness of the capital markets to a specific mode of financing, and (3) the proposed use of the new funds. These conferences are consummated by the signing of a <u>tentative underwriting agreement</u>. The approximate price to be paid for each security is identified in this agreement.

3. An underwriting syndicate is formed. The syndicate is a temporary association of investment bankers formed to purchase the security issue from the corporation. The syndicate's objective is to resell the issue at a profit.

4. Most new public issues must be registered with the SEC before they can be sold to final investors. This involves filing a lengthy technical document called a <u>registration statement</u> with the SEC. This document aims to disclose relevant facts about the issuing firm and the related security to potential investors. Another document, the <u>prospectus</u>, is also filed with the SEC for examination. It is a shortened version of the official registration statement. Once both documents are approved, the prospectus becomes the official advertising vehicle for the security offering.

5. A selling group is formed to distribute the new securities to final investors. Securities dealers who are part of the selling group are permitted to purchase a portion of the new issue at a price to the public. A <u>selling-group agreement</u> binds the syndicate and the members of the selling group.

6. A due diligence meeting is held to finalize all details prior to taking the offering to the public. The price at which the issuing firm will sell the new securities to the syndicate is settled. Usually, the offering is made to the public on the day after this meeting.

7. The syndicate manager (from the investment banking house that generated the business) is permitted to mitigate downward price movements in the secondary market for the subject offering. This is accomplished by the syndicate managers placing buy orders for the security at the agreed upon public offering price.

8. A contractual agreement among the syndicate members terminates the syndicate. In the most pleasant situations this agreement is made when the issue is fully subscribed (sold).

VI. Private placements

A. Each year billions of dollars of new securities are privately (directly) placed with final investors. In a private placement a small number of investors purchases the entire security offering. Most private placements involve debt instruments.

B. Large financial institutions are the major investors in private placements. These include (1) life insurance firms, (2) state and local retirement funds, and (3) private pension funds.

C. The advantages and disadvantages of private placements as opposed to public offerings must be carefully evaluated by management.

1. The advantages include (1) greater speed than a public offering in actually obtaining the needed funds, (2) lower flotation costs than are associated with a public issue, and (3) increased flexibility in the financing contract.

2. The disadvantages include (1) higher interest costs than are ordinarily associated with a comparable public issue, (2) the imposition of several restrictive covenants in the financing contract, and (3) the possibility that the security may have to be registered some time in the future at the lender's option.

VII. Flotation costs

A. The firm raising long-term capital typically incurs two types of flotation costs: (1) the underwriter's spread and (2) issuing costs. The former is typically the larger.

1. The underwriter's spread is the difference between the gross and net proceeds from a specific security issue. This absolute dollar difference is usually expressed as a percent of the gross proceeds.

2. Many components comprise issue costs. The two most significant are (1) printing and engraving and (2) legal fees. For comparison purposes, these, too, are usually expressed as a percent of the issue's gross proceeds.

B. SEC data reveal two relationships about flotation costs.

1. Issue costs (as a percent of gross proceeds) for common stock exceed those of preferred stock, which exceed those of bonds.

2. Total flotation costs per dollar raised decrease as the dollar size of the security issue increases.

VIII. Regulation

A. The primary market is governed by the Securities Act of 1933.

1. The intent of this federal regulation is to provide potential investors with accurate and truthful disclosure about the firm and the new securities being sold.

2.   Unless exempted, the corporation selling securities to the public must register the securities with the SEC.

3.   Exemptions follow from a variety of conditions. For example, if the size of the offering is small enough (less than $1.5 million), the offering does not have to be registered. If the issue is already regulated or controlled by some other federal agency, registration with the SEC is not required. Railroad issues and public utility issues are examples.

4.   If not exempted, a registration statement is filed with the SEC containing particulars about the security-issuing firm and the new security.

5.   A copy of the prospectus, a summary registration statement, is also filed. It will not yet have the selling price of the security printed on it; it is referred to as a red herring and called that until approved by the SEC.

6.   If the information in the registration statement and prospectus is satisfactory to the SEC, the firm can proceed to sell the new issue. If the information is not satisfactory, a stop order is issued which prevents the immediate sale of the issue. Deficiencies have to be corrected to the satisfaction of the SEC before the firm can sell the securities.

7.   The SEC does not evaluate the investment quality of any issue. It is concerned, rather, with the presentation of complete and accurate information upon which the potential investor can act.

B.   The secondary market is regulated by the Securities Exchange Act of 1934. This federal act created the SEC. It has many aspects.

1.   Major security exchanges must register with the SEC.

2.   Insider trading must be reported to the SEC.

2-10

3. Manipulative trading that affects security prices is prohibited.

4. Proxy procedures are controlled by the SEC.

5. The Federal Reserve Board has the responsibility of setting margin requirements. This affects the proportion of a security purchase that can be made via credit.

C. The Securities Act Amendments of 1975 touched on three important issues.

1. Congress mandated the creation of a national market system (NMS). Implementation details of the NMS were left to the SEC. Agreement on the final form of the NMS is yet to come.

2. Fixed commissions (also called fixed brokerage rates) on public transactions in securities were eliminated.

3. Financial institutions, like commercial banks and insurance firms, were prohibited from acquiring membership on stock exchanges where their purpose in so doing might be to reduce or save commissions on their own trades.

D. In March, 1982, the SEC adopted "Rule 415." This process is now known as a shelf registration or a shelf offering.

1. This allows the firm to avoid the lengthy, full registration process each time a public offering of securities is desired.

2. In effect, a master registration statement that covers the financing plans of the firm over the coming two years is filed with the SEC. After approval, the securities are sold to the investing public in a piecemeal fashion or "off the shelf."

3.   Prior to each specific offering a short statement about the issue is filed with the SEC.

IX.   Rates of return in the financial markets. Ibbotson and Sinquefield examine the realized rates of return for a wide variety of securities spanning the period 1926-1996. They have found the following:

    A.   The average inflation rate (the "inflation-risk premium") was 3.2 percent for the period.

    B.   The default-risk premium for long-term corporate bonds was 0.6 percent.

    C.   Common stocks earned 6.7 percent more than the rate earned on long-term corporate bonds (12.7%-6.0%), and small firms earned 5% more than the total population of common stocks.

X.   Interest rate levels over recent periods

    A.   According to the logic of financial-economics, investors will *require* a <u>nominal</u> rate of interest that <u>exceeds</u> the inflation rate or else their realized *real* return will be negative. Earning a negative return over long periods of time is not very wise.

    B.   Accordingly, investors will demand an (1) inflation-risk premium and a (2) default-risk premium across various financial instruments. Specific, observed values for these premiums can be observed in the text of Chapter 2 by inspecting Table 2-7. This would be a good thing to do--right now.

    C.   Notice in Table 2-7 that the implied inflation-risk premium demanded on three-month Treasury bills was 3.06 percent over the 1981-1996 time period.

    D.   Other factors that affect interest rate levels are called the (1) maturity premium and the (2) liquidity premium.

    E.   If you will refer to equation number (2-1) in Chapter 2, you will see how these various risk premiums can be arrayed to allow you to estimate the <u>nominal</u> (observed) rate of interest on a specific fixed-income security.

XI.   Estimating specific interest rates using risk premiums: An Example

    A.   By making use of our knowledge of various risk premia as contained in equation (2-1) the financial manager can generate useful information for the firm's financial planning process.

    B.   For instance, if the firm is about to offer a new issue of corporate bonds to the investing marketplace, it is possible for the financial manager or analyst to estimate what interest rate (yield) will satisfy the markets and help ensure that the bonds are actually bought by investors.

    C.   A Problem Situation is provided in this section of the text that provides for a reasonable estimate of the nominal interest rate expected for a new issue of highly-rated corporate bonds. Various risk premia estimates have to be computed to generate the "built-up" nominal interest rate. The solution is found in the text discussion.

XII.   The effects of inflation on rates of return

    A.   The real rate of interest is the difference in the nominal rate and the anticipated rate of inflation.

    B.   The notion of a real rate of interest can be thought of as the "price for deferring consumption."

    C.   Letting the nominal rate of interest be represented by K_{rf}, the anticipated rate of inflation by IRP, and the real rate of interest by K^*, we can express the result by the following equation:

$$1 + K_{rf} = (1 + K^*)(1 + IRP)$$

$$\text{or} \quad K_{rf} = K^* + IRP + IRP \ K^*$$

For example, if the real rate, K^*, is five percent and the expected inflation rate, IRP, is four percent, the nominal rate, K_{rf}, would then be 9.2 percent, computed as follows:

$$K_{rf} = .05 + .04 + (.05)(.04)$$

$$= .092 \text{ or } 9.2\%$$

2-13

XIII. Inflation and real rates of return" The financial analyst's approach

    A.   This section simplifies the discussion of the "Fisher Effect" and puts it into a format more familiar and widely used by practicing financial analysts and managers.

    B.   This discussion revolves around this common method of presentation:
(Nominal interest rate) – (inflation rate) = real interest rate

    C.   An example using observable yields on Treasury bills, Treasury bonds, and corporate bonds is used and put into the risk premia format discussed earlier in the chapter.

Study Problem

1.   If the expected inflation rate is four percent, and the real rate of interest is eight percent, what is the nominal interest rate?

SOLUTION

$$\text{Nominal rate, } K_{rf} = \left(\begin{array}{c}\text{Real} \\ \text{rate}\end{array}\right) + \left(\begin{array}{c}\text{Inflation} \\ \text{rate}\end{array}\right) + \left(\begin{array}{c}\text{Real} \\ \text{rate}\end{array}\right)\left(\begin{array}{c}\text{Inflation} \\ \text{rate}\end{array}\right)$$

$$= \quad 8\% + 4\% + (4\%)(8\%) = 12.32\%$$

Self-Tests

TRUE-FALSE

_____ 1.   A share of IBM common stock is a real asset.

_____ 2.   Capital formation in underdeveloped countries might be assisted if those countries' financial market systems were more extensively developed.

_____ 3.   General Motors is a typical example of a financial intermediary.

_____ 4. The Money Market is housed at 11 Wall Street, New York City.

_____ 5. Common stocks are money market instruments.

_____ 6. Price quotations on organized security exchanges have been facilitated by the existence of NASDAQ.

_____ 7. The Banking Act of 1933 separated the activities of commercial banking and investment banking.

_____ 8. In a negotiated purchase, the price the investment banker pays the security-issuing firm for the new issue is negotiated between these parties.

_____ 9. Underwriting syndicates are prohibited by the Securities Act of 1933.

_____ 10. Life insurance companies are major purchasers of privately placed securities.

_____ 11. Secondary markets reduce the risk of investing in financial claims.

_____ 12. Equity instruments are traded in the money market.

_____ 13. The capital market includes those securities that have maturity periods extending beyond one year.

_____ 14. Trading in currently existing securities takes place in the primary market.

_____ 15. When new funds are being raised in a typical year, corporate equity markets are favored over corporate debt markets, in terms of dollar volume.

_____ 16. The U.S. tax system favors debt as a method of raising capital in comparison to equity instruments.

_____ 17. A life insurance company is an example of a financial intermediary.

_____ 18. "Crowding out" refers to the use of debt vs. the use of common stock to raise new funds.

_____ 19. Flotation costs for debt generally exceed those of common stock.

_____ 20. In general, flotation costs are inversely related to the size of the security issue.

_____ 21. Inventories represent a category of financial assets.

_____ 22. Financial markets allocate savings in the economy to demanders of those funds.

_____ 23. Financial intermediaries issue their own financial claims called direct securities, and invest the money obtained in indirect securities, the financial claims of other economic units.

_____ 24. The U.S. government is the largest savings surplus sector in the economy.

_____ 25. Financial markets provide a mechanism to facilitate the transfer of savings from those economic units that have a savings surplus to those that have a savings deficit.

_____ 26. The New York Stock Exchange, American Stock Exchange, and Midwest Stock Exchange are the only three national exchanges in the U.S.

_____ 27. There is an inverse relationship between the total flotation cost per dollar of funds raised and the amount of the security issue.

_____ 28. The primary objective of the Securities Act of 1933 is to provide potential investors with accurate and truthful disclosure about the firm and the new securities being sold.

_____ 29. Long-term corporate bonds are more risky than common stocks from the investor's point of view.

MULTIPLE CHOICE

1. Which of the following is <u>not</u> a benefit provided by the existence of organized security exchanges?

   a. A continuous market.
   b. Helping business raise new capital.
   c. Keeping long-term bond prices below 8%.
   d. Establishing and publicizing fair security prices.

2. What is it called when an investment banker agrees to sell only as many securities as he or she can at an established price?

   a. A private placement.
   b. A direct placement.
   c. A privileged subscription.
   d. A best-efforts agreement.
   e. An upset agreement.

3. Which of the following security distribution methods is least profitable to the investment banker?

   a. Negotiated purchase.
   b. Competitive-bid purchase.
   c. Commission basis.
   d. Privileged subscription.
   e. Direct sale.

4. A prospectus resembles most closely

   a. A registration statement.
   b. A red herring.
   c. A selling group agreement.
   d. A letter of credit.

5. The purpose of financial markets is to

   a. Lower bond yields.
   b. Allocate savings efficiently.
   c. Raise stock prices.
   d. Employ stock brokers.

6. The maturity boundary dividing the U.S. money and capital markets is

   a. An arbitrary classification system.
   b. Set by the Federal Reserve Board.
   c. Periodically reviewed and altered by the SEC.
   d. Determined by the U.S. Treasury.

7. Flotation costs are highest on

   a. Bonds.
   b. Preferred stock.
   c. Common stock.

8. Insider trading is regulated by

   a. The Banking Act of 1933.
   b. The Glass-Steagall Act of 1933.
   c. The Securities Act of 1933.
   d. The Securities Exchange Act of 1934.

9. Which of the following methods for the distribution of securities bypasses the use of an investment banker?

   a. Negotiated purchase.
   b. Competitive-bid purchase.
   c. Direct sales.
   d. Best-efforts basis.
   e. Privileged subscriptions.

10. The difference between the gross and net proceeds from a given security issue expressed as a percent of the gross proceeds is known as:

    a. Issue costs.
    b. Flotation costs.
    c. Underwriter's spread.
    d. Legal fees.

11. Which of the following is generally <u>not</u> an advantage of private placements?

    a. Speed.
    b. Reduced flotation costs.
    c. Financing flexibility.
    d. Interest costs.

12. Which of the following is <u>not</u> an example of a money market instrument?

    a. U.S. Treasury bills.
    b. Common stock.
    c. Federal agency securities.
    d. Commercial paper.

13. An agreement which obligates the investment banker to underwrite securities that are not accepted by privileged investors is known as a:

    a. Privileged subscription.
    b. Standby agreement.
    c. Negotiated purchase.
    d. Best-efforts basis.

14. The demand for funds by the federal government puts upward pressure on interest rates causing private investors to be pushed out of the financial markets. This is called:

    a. The big squeeze.
    b. The efficient market hypothesis.
    c. The crowding out effect.
    d. Liquidity preference.
    e. Government intervention.

15. Insurance companies invest in the "long-end" of the securities market. In which of the following instruments would an insurance company be least likely to invest most of its funds in?

   a. Mortgages.
   b. Corporate Bonds.
   c. Commercial Paper.
   d. Corporate Stocks.

16. Which of the following is/are NYSE listing requirements?

   a. Profitability.
   b. Market Value.
   c. Public Ownership.
   d. All of the above.
   e. None of the above.

17. The indirect method of transferring savings in which securities are not transformed, but passed through to other purchasers, most frequently involves:

   a. An established relationship between buyer and issuer.
   b. A finance company.
   c. A commercial bank.
   d. An investment banker.
   e. All of the above.

18. Which of the following does not describe an organized security exchange?

   a. It occupies physical space as opposed to being strictly communication links among traders.
   b. It is strictly regional in scope.
   c. It is regulated by the Securities and Exchange Commission.
   d. Its trades are conducted strictly by exchange members.

19. Shelf registration refers to the process of:

    a.   Registering single issues with the SEC through the use of SEC-prepared, standardized forms.

    b.   Selecting and seeking SEC approval for an investment banker from their approved or "shelf" list of investment bankers.

    c.   Registering a chosen underwriting syndicate with the SEC.

    d.   Receiving a blanket order approval from the SEC to issue securities periodically over the next two years.

20. Primary markets are distinguished from secondary markets by the fact that:

    a.   Primary markets sell securities for corporations with assets over $2 million, while secondary markets sell securities for corporations with assets less than $2 million.

    b.   Primary markets are more developed than the secondary markets.

    c.   Primary markets trade new securities issues while secondary markets trade existing securities.

    d.   Primary markets enjoy higher trading volume than the secondary markets.

21. How many registered stock exchanges are there in the U.S.?

    a.   4
    b.   5
    c.   more than 5
    d.   none

22. What is the correct <u>sequence</u> of steps for the negotiated purchase distribution method? The key steps follow each Roman numeral, below.

    I.   File a registration statement and prospectus with SEC.

    II.   Hold a due diligence meeting.

    III.   Form an underwriting syndicate.

    IV.   Form a contractual agreement among syndicate members to terminate the syndicate.

    V.   Form a selling group to distribute new securities.

    a.   I, II, III, IV, V

    b.   II, III, I, V, IV

    c.   III, I, V, II, IV

    d.   IV, I, II, III, V

23.   The primary market is governed by:

    a.   The Banking Act of 1933.

    b.   The Glass-Steagall Act of 1933.

    c.   The Securities Act of 1933.

    d.   The Securities Exchange Act of 1934.

24.   In terms of risk, it is correct to say:

    a.   Government securities are less risky than common stocks, but more risky than corporate bonds.

    b.   Corporate bonds are less risky than common stocks.

    c.   Long-term government securities are less risky than short-term government securities.

    d.   Common stocks of large companies are more risky than the common stocks of small firms.

SOLUTIONS TO SELECTED SET B PROBLEMS (See text for problems.)

2-2B.

If k_{rf} = nominal rate

       k^* = real rate

       IRP = inflation rate

then, k_{rf} = $k^* + IRP + (IRP)(k^*)$

       k_{rf} = $.07 + .05 + (.05)(.07)$ = 12.4%

CHAPTER 3

Evaluating Financial Performance

Orientation: Financial analysis can be defined as the process of assessing the financial condition of a firm. The principal analytical tool of the financial analyst is the financial ratio. In this chapter, we provide a brief overview of a firm's basic financial statements followed by a survey of a set of key financial ratios and a discussion of their effective use.

I.   Basic Financial Statements

    A.   The Income Statement

        1.   The income statement reports the results from operating the business for a period of time, such as a year

        2.   It is helpful to think of the income statement as comprising four types of activities:

            a.   Selling the product

            b.   The cost of producing or acquiring the goods or services sold

            c.   The expenses incurred in marketing and distributing the product or service to the customer, along with administrative operating expenses

            d.   The financing costs of doing business, for example, interest paid to creditors and dividend payments to the preferred stockholders

3. An example of an income statement is provided in Table 3-1 for the Jamin Corporation.

B. The Balance Sheet

1. The balance sheet provides a snapshot of the firm's financial position at a specific point in time, presenting its asset holdings, liabilities, and owner-supplied capital.

   a. Assets represent the resources owned by the firm

      (1) Current assets--consisting primarily of cash, marketable securities, accounts receivable, inventories, and prepaid expenses

      (2) Fixed or long-term assets--comprising equipment, buildings, and land

      (3) Other assets--all assets not otherwise included in the firm's current assets or fixed assets, such as patents, long-term investments in securities, and goodwill

   b. The liabilities and owners' equity indicate how those resources are financed.

      (1) The debt consists of such sources as credit extended from suppliers or a loan from a bank.

      (2) The equity includes the stockholders' investment in the firm and the cumulative profits retained in the business up to the date of the balance sheet.

2. The balance sheet is not intended to represent the current market value of the company, but rather reports the historical transactions recorded at their cost.

3.   Balance sheets for the Jamin Corporation are presented in Table 3- 2

C.   The Cash Flow Statement

    1.   The Cash Flow Statement shows the actual cash flows generated by the firm for the year.

    2.   Cash Flow from Operations

        a.   A firm's cash flow from operations consists of collections from customers and payments to suppliers for the purchase of materials.

        b.   Also included are other operating cash outflows, such as marketing and administrative expenses and interest payments, and cash tax payments.

    3.   Cash Flows--Investment Activities
        This section includes such transactions as the purchase (or sales) of fixed assets, land, and patents.

    4.   Cash Flows--Financing Activities
        This section deals with financing activities, including any cash inflows or outflows to or from the firm's investors, both lenders of debt and owners. Examples include dividends paid, payments on debt, or issuing new shares of stock.

II.   Financial Ratio Analysis

A.   Financial ratios help us identify some of the financial strengths and weaknesses of a company.

B.   The ratios give us a way of making meaningful comparisons of a firm's financial data at different points in time and with other firms.

C.   We could use ratios to answer some important questions about a firm's operations.

1.	Question 1: How liquid is the firm?

	a.	The liquidity of a business is defined as its ability to meet maturing debt obligations. That is, does or will the firm have the resources to pay the creditors when the debt comes due?

	b.	There are two ways to approach the liquidity question.

		(1)	We can look at the firm's assets that are relatively liquid in nature and compare them to the amount of the debt coming due in the near term.

		(2)	We can look at how quickly the firm's liquid assets are being converted into cash.

2.	Question 2: Is management generating adequate operating profits on the firm's assets?

	a.	We want to know if the profits are sufficient relative to the assets being invested.

	b.	We have several choices as to how we measure profits: gross profits, operating profits, or net income. Gross profits is not acceptable because it overlooks important information such as marketing and distribution expenses. Net income includes the unwanted effects of the firm's financing policies. This leaves operating profits as our best choice in measuring the firm's operating profitability.

3.	Question 3: How is the firm financing its assets?
	Here we are concerned with the mix of debt and equity capital the firm is using. Two primary ratios used to answer this question are the debt ratio and times interest earned. The debt ratio is the proportion of total debt to total assets. Times interest earned compares operating income to interest expense for a crude measure of the firm's capacity to service its debt.

4.   Question 4: Are the owners (stockholders) receiving an adequate return on their investment?

a.   We want to know if the earnings available to the firm's owners or common equity investors are attractive when compared to the returns of owners of similar companies in the same industry.

b.   Return on equity (ROE) $= \dfrac{\text{net income}}{\text{common equity}}$

c.   The Effect of Using Debt on Net Income: An Example.
Shows how the use of debt affects the return on equity.

d.   Return on equity is a function of:

(1)   the operating income return on investment less the interest rate paid, and

(2)   the amount of debt used in the capital structure relative to the equity

e.   Return on equity may be expressed as follows:
$$\begin{matrix}\text{return} \\ \text{on equity}\end{matrix} = \left(\begin{matrix}\text{operating income} \\ \text{return on investment}\end{matrix}\right)$$
$$+ \left(\left(\begin{matrix}\text{operating income} \\ \text{return on investment}\end{matrix} - \begin{matrix}\text{interest} \\ \text{rate}\end{matrix}\right) \times \dfrac{\text{debt}}{\text{equity}}\right)$$

D.   An Integrative Approach to Ratio Analysis: The DuPont Analysis
The DuPont Analysis is another approach used to evaluate a firm's profitability and return on equity. Its graphic technique may be helpful in seeing how ratios relate to one another and the account balances.

E.   Limitations of Ratio Analysis

This list warns of the many pitfalls that may be encountered in computing and interpreting financial ratios. Ratio users should be aware of these concerns prior to making decisions based solely on ratio analysis.

III. Measuring Firm Performance: The EVA Way

A.   In using financial ratios, we are considering firm performance purely from an accounting perspective. However, the ratios used are not linked directly to the financial goal of the firm, that of creating shareholder value.

B.   Shareholder value is a function of:

1.   The financial return earned on the firm's capital relative to the investor's required rate of return, and

2.   The amount of capital invested in the firm.

C.   Shareholder value is created when a firm generates returns in excess of its investors' required rate of return.

D.   While several techniques have been developed for assessing whether management is creating shareholder value, the one seeming to capture the most attention at the present is Economic Value Added (EVA).

E.   EVA is computed as follows:

$$\text{EVA} = (r - k) \times C$$

where r = the firm's operating income return on investment.
      k = the opportunity cost of all capital, both debt and equity.
      C = the amount of capital (total assets) invested in the firm.

<u>Study</u> <u>Problems</u>

1. Prepare a balance sheet for the A. R. Peterson Mfg. Co. from the scrambled list of items below. The owner's equity balance is not given but it can be determined as a balancing figure.

Building	$49,100	Office equipment	4,100
Accounts receivable	21,600	Land	22,000
Machinery	2,950	Notes payable	14,000
Cash	9,200	Owner's equity	
Accounts payable	16,500		

SOLUTION

A. R. Peterson Mfg. Co.
Balance Sheet

Cash	$ 9,200	Accounts payable	16,500
Accounts receivable	21,600	Notes payable	14,000
Land	22,000	Owner's equity	78,450
Building	49,100		
Machinery	2,950		
Office equipment	4,100	Total liabilities	
Total assets	$108,950	& owner's equity	$108,950

2. By studying the successive balance sheets for AMP, Inc. found below, determine what transactions have occurred. Prepare a list of the transactions and the corresponding balance-sheet dates. For example, on March 31, 1998, the firm's owners invested $200,000 in AMP, Inc. and started the business.

(a)

AMP, Inc.
Balance Sheet
March 31, 1998

Assets		Owner's Equity	
Cash	$200,000	Owner's equity	$200,000

(b)

AMP, Inc.
Balance Sheet
April 2, 1998

Assets		Owner's Equity	
Cash	$100,000	Owner's equity	$200,000
Land	100,000		
	$200,000		$200,000

(c)

AMP, Inc.
Balance Sheet
April 15, 1998

Assets		Owner's Equity	
Cash	$ 50,000	Owner's equity	$200,000
Building	50,000		
Land	100,000		
	$200,000		$200,000

(d)

AMP, Inc.
Balance Sheet
May 2, 1998

Assets		Liabilities & Owner's Equity	
Cash	$50,000	Accounts payable	$25,000
Inventories	25,000	Owner's equity	200,000
Building	50,000		
Land	100,000		
	$225,000		$225,000

(e)

AMP, Inc.
Balance Sheet
May 15, 1998

Assets		Liabilities & Owner's Equity	
Cash	$60,000	Accounts payable	$25,000
Inventories	25,000	Notes payable	25,000
Equipment	15,000	Owner's equity	200,000
Building	50,000		
Land	100,000		
	$250,000		$250,000

SOLUTION

(a) On March 31, 1998, the firm's owners invested $200,000 in AMP, Inc. and started the business.

(b) On April 2, 1998, $100,000 of the original investment by the owners was used to acquire land.

(c) On April 15, 1998, $50,000 of the original cash was used to acquire a building.

3-9

(d)   On May 2, 1998, $25,000 of inventory was purchased on account (credit).

(e)   On May 15, 1998, a $25,000 loan was obtained and $15,000 of the proceeds used to purchase equipment.

3.   Balance sheets for Marion Mfg. Co. and the Sterlington Corp. are found below. Both firms are involved in the manufacture of electrical components used in small electronic calculators and digital wristwatches. Since both firms are less than 3 years old, their book values are reasonably close to actual market value.

Marion Mfg. Co.
Balance Sheet
November 30, 1998

Assets		Liabilities & Equity	
Cash	$ 50,000	Notes payable	$ 520,000
Accounts receivable	90,000	(due in 30 days)	
Building	225,000	Accounts payable	420,000
Machinery	350,000	Owner's equity	150,000
Land	375,000		
	$1,090,000		$1,090,000

Sterlington Co.
Balance Sheet
November 30, 1998

Assets		Liabilities & Equity	
Cash	$ 50,000	Notes payable	$120,000
Accounts receivable	200,000	(due in 30 days)	
Land	10,000	Accounts payable	150,000
Machinery	350,000	Owner's equity	640,000
Building	300,000		
	$910,000		$910,000

(a)   Assume the role of a commercial banker who has been approached by both of the previous firms with a request for a 90-day loan for $200,000. For which of the firms are you most likely to approve the loan? Why?

(b)   If you were considering the purchase of one of these firms and assuming the liabilities of each, for which one would you be willing to pay the higher price? (Obviously, you would want more information in order to make a complete analysis, but make your evaluation based on the balance sheets above.)

SOLUTION

(a)   Sterlington Corp. In reviewing requests for short-term loans, the commercial loan officer is most interested in the liquidity of the subject firm. The current ratio of Marion Mfg. Co. is a very weak 0.15 while Sterlington Corp.'s current ratio is .93. In addition, a quick glance at the balance sheet of Marion Mfg. shows that a very substantial note of $520,000 comes due in 30 days which the company may have difficulty paying.

(b)   Sterlington Corp. If it is assumed that book values are reasonably close to actual market values, the difference between Sterlington's total assets and assumed debt is $640,000, as opposed to Marion's net difference of $150,000.

4.   Burruss Inc. had the following condensed balance sheet at the end of operation for 1997:

Burruss, Inc.
Balance Sheet
December 31, 1997

Cash	$ 24,000	Current liabilities	$ 30,000
Other current assets	51,000	Long-term notes	
Total current assets	$ 75,000	payable	33,000
Investments	40,000	Bonds	40,000
Fixed assets(net)	125,000	Capital stock	150,000
Land	62,000	Retained earnings	49,000
	$302,000		$302,000

During 1998 the following occurred:

(a)   Burruss, Inc. sold some of its investments for $20,600 which resulted in a gain of $600.

(b)   Additional land for a plant expansion was purchased for $12,000.

(c)   Bonds were paid in the amount of $10,000.

(d)   An additional $ 20,000 in capital stock was issued.

(e)   Dividends of $15,000 were paid to stockholders.

(f)   Net income for 1998 was $42,000 after allowing for $18,000 in depreciation.

(g)   A second parcel of land was purchased through the issuance of $12,000 in bonds, $6,000 in long-term notes payable, and internally generated funds.

Required:

(a)   Using the indirect method, prepare a cash flow statement for 1998.

(b)   Prepare a condensed balance sheet for Burruss, Inc. at December 31, 1998.

Assume that current liabilities (including accounts payable and accruals) remain unchanged and other current assets did not change during the year.

SOLUTION

Burruss, Inc.
Statement of Cash Flow
For the Year Ended December 31, 1998

Cash flows from operating activities:

Net Income (from the statement of income)	$42,000
Add (deduct) to reconcile net income to net cash flow	
Depreciation Expense	18,000
Gain from the sale of investments (included in sales price below)	
	(600)
Net cash inflow from operating activities	$59,400

Cash flows from investing activities:

Sale of Investments	20,600
Purchase of Land	(30,000)

Cash flows from financing activities:

Issuance of capital stock	20,000
Issuance of bonds	12,000
Issuance of notes payable	6,000
Repayment of bonds	(10,000)
Dividends	(15,000)
Net increase (decrease) in cash during the period	$63,000

Burruss, Inc.
Balance Sheet
December 31, 1998

Cash	$ 87,000	Current liabilities	$ 30,000
Other current assets	51,000	Long-term notes	39,000
Total Current Assets	$138,000	payable	
Investments	20,000	Bonds	42,000
Fixed assets (net)	107,000	Capital stock	170,000
Land	92,000	Retained earnings	76,000
	$357,000		$357,000

5. The financial manager of Sudhop, Inc. has just hired you (a recent finance graduate). Now he wishes to test your familiarity with financial ratios and your overall ability to work with financial statements. He gives you the following incomplete year-end balance sheet:

Sudhop, Inc.
Balance Sheet
December 31, 1998

Cash	$	Accounts payable	$
Accounts receivable		Long-term debt	
Inventory	_____	Total Debt	$
Total Current Assets	$	Common Stock	125,000
Fixed assets	400,000	Retained earnings	275,000
	$		$

He then gives you the following additional information and asks you to complete the above balance sheet.

Average collection period (assume a 360-day year)	30 days
Interest paid on long-term debt (10% rate)	$5,000
Debt-to-equity ratio	75%
Sales to total assets	2.0 times
Quick ratio	1.1
Current ratio	1.2

SOLUTION

Sudhop, Inc.
Balance Sheet
December 31, 1998

Cash	$158,333	Accounts payable	$250,000
Accounts receivable	116,667	Long-term debt	50,000
Inventory	25,000	Total Debt	$300,000
Total current assets	$300,000	Common stock	125,000
Fixed assets	400,000	Retained earnings	275,000
Total assets	$ 700,000	Total debt and equity	$700,000

3-14

Computations:

a. Since debt to equity is 0.75, then debt must be $300,000 (0.75 x $400,000 equity).

b. Debt plus equity equals total debt and equity and total assets, which comes to $700,000.

c. Current assets equal total assets less fixed assets ($700,000 - $400,000).

d. Since current assets ÷ current liabilities equals 1.20, then current liabilities equal $250,000 ($300,000 ÷ current liabilities = 1.2).

e. Sales ÷ total assets = 2.0; so, sales ÷$700,000 = 2.0; and sales = $1,400,000

f. Accounts receivable may be determined to be $116,667 as follows:

$$\text{Average collection period} = \frac{\text{accounts receivable}}{\text{daily credit sales}}$$

From what we already know and assuming all sales are on credit,

$$30 = \frac{\text{accounts receivable}}{\$1,400,000 \div 360}$$

g. Given a quick ratio of 1.1, then inventory must be $25,000:

$$\frac{\$300,000 - \text{inventories}}{\$250,000} = 1.1.$$

h. Cash equals current assets minus accounts receivable and inventory.

6. The balance sheet and income statement for Miller Company are given for the year 1998 in addition to various financial ratios for the industry in which Miller operates.

Miller Company
Balance Sheet
December 31, 1998
(000 's)

Cash	$ 230	Notes payable	$ 1,015
Accounts receivable	9,380	Accounts payable	3,545
Inventories	7,515	Accrued taxes	225
Current assets	17,125	Current liabilities	4,785
Fixed assets (net)	34,125	Long-term debt	18,035
Total Assets	$51,250	Deferred income taxes	2,840
		Total Debt	$20,875
		Common stock-par	575
		Paid in capital	7,945
		Retained earnings	17,070
		Common equity	25,590
		Total liabilities	
		& net worth	$51,250

Miller Company
Income Statement
Year Ended December 31, 1998

Net sales (credit)	$46,235
Cost of sales	33,167
Gross profit	13,068
General and administrative expense	9,590
Operating income	3,478
Interest expense	1,120
Net income before taxes	2,358
Income taxes	1,130
Net income	$ 1,228

Industry Ratios

	Industry
Current ratio	4.02
Acid-test ratio	3.00
Inventory turnover	7.50
Average collection period	63.1
Operating profit margin	6.0%
Total asset turnover	2.0
Fixed asset turnover	3.0
Debt ratio	38.0%
Times interest earned	3.90
Return on equity	4.0%

Required:

Evaluate Miller's financial performance, using the "four-question approach" presented in Chapter 3 of the text.

SOLUTION

(a)

	Industry	Miller
Current ratio	4.02	3.58
Acid-test ratio	3.00	2.01
Inventory turnover	7.50	4.41
Average collection period	63.1	74.1
Operating profit margin	6.0%	7.5
Total asset turnover	2.0	0.9
Fixed asset turnover	3.0	1.4
Debt ratio	38.0%	40.7%
Times interest earned	3.90	3.11
Return on equity	4.0%	4.8%

(b) Miller's liquidity ratios are well below the industry averages. The most serious problem is with inventory turnover which is almost one-half the industry norm.

The operating income return on investment, OIROI, for Miller and the industry are determined as follows:

$$\text{OIROI} = \frac{\text{operating}}{\text{profit margin}} \times \frac{\text{total asset}}{\text{turnover}}$$

Miller: 7.5% x 0.9 = 6.8%

Industry: 6.0% x 2.0 = 12%

Thus, Miller's management is not generating satisfactory operating profits on the firm's assets. However, Miller's operating profit margin exceeds the industry, which suggests that they are better than the average firm at some combination of:

1. Receive above-average prices for their products.

2. Sell more units of their products.

3. Lower cost of goods sold.

4. Lower operating expenses (general and administrative and marketing).

However, the firm is clearly not using its assets efficiently, as suggested by all the turnover ratios and collection period, to generate sales.

The net effect of the operating profit margin and the asset turnovers is a low OIROI.

The firm uses slightly more debt to finance its assets, as reflected by the higher debt ratio and the lower times interest earned. The low times interest earned is also due to the lower OIROI, which affects the numerator of the ratio.

Miller's stockholders received an above-average return on their investment (return on equity), but it was accomplished by using more debt, which exposes the investors to greater financial risk.

Self-Tests

TRUE-FALSE

_____ 1. The balance sheet is a statement of the firm's financial position over a specified time interval.

_____ 2. Noncurrent assets are those which are not expected to be converted into cash within the firm's operating cycle.

_____ 3. The income statement represents an attempt to measure the net results of the firm's operations on a given date.

_____ 4. The owner's equity represents the book value of the owner's investment in the assets of the firm.

_____ 5. A firm attempts to match sales from the period's operations with the expenses incurred in generating those revenues by compiling the income statement on an accrual basis.

_____ 6. Reported sales and expenses must represent actual cash flows for the period when the income statement is prepared on an accrual basis.

_____ 7. Investments in securities are always considered to be current assets.

_____ 8. Payments to suppliers for the purchase of materials is a component of the financing activities section of a cash flow statement.

_____ 9. Because fixed assets are used in operations, any purchases of fixed assets belong in the cash flow operating activities section.

_____ 10. Financial ratios help us identify financial strengths and weaknesses of companies by way of being able to make meaningful comparisons of firm's financial data at different points in time and with other firms.

_____ 11. A firm's cash account is not considered in determining its liquidity.

_____ 12. The current ratio is more conservative than the acid-test ratio.

_____ 13. Inventory turnover and the average collection period may be used to measure the same thing-- operating profitability.

_____ 14. Return on equity measures the dividends investors received in the current year.

_____ 15. The DuPont Analysis is another approach frequently used to evaluate a firm's liquidity and financing decisions.

MULTIPLE CHOICE

1. Which of the following is generally considered to be the most important financial statement for judging the economic well-being of a firm?

   a. Income statement.
   b. Balance sheet.
   c. Cash Flow Statement.
   d. All of the above.
   e. None of the above.

2. The most important section of the cash flow statement for a firm as far as its ability to continue as a going concern is the _____.

   a. operations section.
   b. investment activities section.
   c. financing activities section.
   d. all the sections are equally important.

3. Collections from customers and payments to suppliers should be included as part of the _____ section of a cash flow statement.

   a. financing activities
   b. investment activities
   c. working capital
   d. operating

4. Interest expense is considered a(n) _____ on the income statement and a(n) _____ on the cash flow statement.

   a. operating expense, operating activities item
   b. financing expense, financing activities item
   c. operating expense, financing activities item
   d. financing expense, operating activities item

5. The difference between the current ratio and the quick ratio is____
   _____.

   a. inventories.
   b. inventories is subtracted from the numerator.
   c. inventories is subtracted from the denominator.
   d. the current ratio is more conservative.

6. The ratio of total debt over total assets is _____.

   a. the current ratio.
   b. the debt ratio.
   c. a measure of a firm's liquidity.
   d. referred to as the quick ratio because it is so easily determined.

7. Robert Morris Associates and other published industry averages are_____.

   a. offered for every industry.
   b. scientifically determined averages.
   c. only approximations.
   d. good for many years.

8. An industry average is best used as _____.

   a. a desirable target or norm for the firm
   b. a guide to the financial position of the average firm in the industry.
   c. a scientifically determined average of the ratios of a representative sample of firms within an industry.
   d. a point or rule with which to measure profitability.

9. Operating income return on investment is affected by _____.

   a. depreciation expense
   b. interest expense
   c. income tax
   d. all of the above

10. The direct method beginning with _____ and the indirect method beginning with _____ are two approaches for determining __ _on the cash flow statement.

   a. net sales, operating income, cash flows from operations
   b. net income, cash collected from the firm's customers, cash flows from operations
   c. net income, cash collected from the firm's customers, total cash flows
   d. cash collected from the firm's customers, net income, cash flows from operations

3-3B.

Allendale's present current ratio of 2.0 to 1 in conjunction with its $3.0 million investment in current assets indicates that its current liabilities are presently $1.09 million. Letting x represent the additional borrowing against the firm's line of credit (which also equals the addition to current assets) we can solve for that level of x which forces the firm's current ratio down to 2 to 1, i.e.,

$$2 = (\$3.0 \text{ million} + x) / (\$1.09 \text{ million} + x)$$

or   x = $.82 million

3-7B.
(a)

RATIO	1997	1998	Industry Norm	Evalu- ation
Liquidity:				
Current Ratio	5.00	5.35	5.00	Satis.
Acid-test(Quick) Ratio	2.70	2.63	3.00	Poor
Average Collection Period	131.40	108.24	90.00	Poor
Inventory Turnover	1.22	1.40	2.20	Poor
Operating profitability:				
Operating Income return on investment	12.24%	12.97%	15.00%	Poor
Operating Profit Margin	24.00%	22.76%	20.00%	Good
Total Asset Turnover	.51	.57	.75	Poor
Average Collection Period	131.40	108.24	90.00	Poor
Inventory Turnover	1.22	1.40	2.20	Poor
Fixed Asset Turnover	1.04	1.12	1.00	Satis.

Financing:

Debt Ratio	34.69%	32.81%	33.00%	Satis.
Times Interest Earned	6.00	5.50	7.00	Poor

Rate of return on common stockholders' investment:

Return on Common Equity	9.38%	9.53%	13.43%	Poor

b. Regarding the firm's liquidity, the acid-test (quick) ratios are below the industry average and has decreased from the prior year. Also, the average collection period and inventory turnover are well below the industry averages, which suggests that inventories are not of equal quality of these assets in other firms in the industry. Since the current ratio is satisfactory, the problem apparently lies in the management of inventories. So, we may reasonably conclude that Chavez is less liquid than the average company in its industry because they have a greater investment in inventories than the industry average.

c. Operating profitability

In evaluating Chavez's operating profitability relative to the average firm in the industry, we must first determine the operating income return on investment (OROI) both for Chavez and the industry. From the information given, this computation may be made as follows:

Operating income return on investment	=	Operating profit margin	x	Total asset turnover

Industry: 20% x 0.75 = 15%

Chavez 1997:   24.00% x 0.51 = 12.24%

Chavez 1998:   22.76% x 0.57 = 12.97%

Thus, given the low operating income return on investment for Chavez relative to the industry, we must conclude that management is not doing an adequate job on generating operating profits on the firm's assets. However, they did improve between 1997 and 1998. The problem lies not with the operating profit margin, which addresses the operating costs and expenses relative to sales. Instead the problem arises from Chavez's management not using the firm's assets efficiently, as indicated by the low asset turnover ratios. Here the problem occurs in managing accounts receivable and inventories, where we see the low turnover ratios. The firm does appear to be using the fixed assets reasonably well--note the satisfactory fixed assets turnover.

d.   Financing decisions

A balance-sheet perspective:

The debt ratio for Chavez in 1998 is around 33 percent, a decrease from 34.7 percent in 1997; that is, they finance about one-third of their assets with debt and a little less than two-thirds with common equity. Also, the average firm in the industry uses about the same amount of debt per dollar of assets as Chavez.

An income-statement perspective:

Chavez's times interest earned is below the industry norm--6.0 and 5.5 in 1997 and 1998, respectively, compared to 7.0 for the industry average. In thinking about why, we should remember that a company's times interest earned is affected by (1) the level of the firm's operating profitability (EBIT), (2) the amount of debt used, and (3) the interest rate. (Items 2 and 3 determine the amount of interest paid by the company. Here is what we know about Chavez:

1.   The firm's operating profitability is below average, but improving. Thus, we would expect this fact to contribute to a lower operating income return on investment (OIROI). The evidence is consistent with this thought.

2.   Chavez uses about the same amount of debt as the average firm, which should mean that its times interest earned, all else equal, would be about the same as for the average firm. Thus, Chavez's low times interest earned is not the consequence of using more debt.

3-25

3.   We do not have any information about Chavez's interest rate. So we cannot make any observation about the effect of the interest rate. But we know if Chavez is paying a higher interest rate that its competitor, such a situation would also be contributing to the problem.

e.   The return on common equity

Chavez has improved its return on common equity from 9.38 percent in 1997 to 9.53 percent in 1998, compared to an industry norm of 13.43 percent. The improvement has come from an increase in the firm's operating income return on investment, despite a slight decrease in the use of debt financing. Thus, Chavez has enhanced the returns to its owners, and with a small decline of financial risk (slightly lower debt ratio) in the process.

3-9B.

Instructor's Note: This problem provides an exercise in preparing a realistic cash flow statement. Many students have difficulty with the decrease in the "patent" account. It is included in the cash flow statement here as an amortization of patents rather than a sale.

(a)

Cramer, Inc.
Statement of Cash Flows
For Year Ended December 31,1998

Cash flows from operations (direct method)

Cash inflows received from customers	
Net sales	$190,000
Less change in accounts receivable	9,000
Cash inflows from customers	$199,000
Less cash paid to suppliers	
Cost of goods sold (excluding depreciation)	($51,500)
Plus change in inventory	5,000
Less change in accounts payable	(29,500)
Cash paid to suppliers	($76,000)

Less other operating cash outflows and interest payments

Cash operating and interest expenses (excluding the amortization of patents)	($34,500)
Plus increase in prepaid expenses	(2,000)
Less change in accrued expenses	0
Less change in interest payable	0
Other operating cash outflows and interest payments	($36,500)

Less cash tax payments

Provision for taxes	($24,000)
Less change in taxes payable	7,500
Cash tax payments	($16,500)

Total cash flows from operations	$70,000

Cash Flow from Investing Activities:

Purchase of Fixed Assets	($124,500)	
Net Cash Proceeds from Investing Activities		(124,500)

Cash Flow from Financing Activities:

Issue of Preferred Stock	$231,000	
Mortgages Payable Reduced	(150,000)	
Payment of Dividend	(20,000)	
Net Cash Proceeds from Financing Activities		$61,000

Net Change in Cash	$ 6,500

Cash Flow from Operating Activities (Indirect method)

Net Income		$ 36,500
Adjustments to Reconcile		
Depreciation	$34,500	
Amortization of Patents	9,000	
Decrease in Accounts Receivable	9,000	
Decrease in Inventory	5,000	
Increase in Prepaid Expenses	(2,000)	
Decrease in Accounts Payable	(29,500)	
Increase in Taxes Payable	7,500	33,500
Net Cash Proceeds from Operating Activities		$ 70,000

(b) The firm's primary sources of cash were from the sale of preferred stock and its profitable operations. Uses were composed of retirement of mortgages and purchase of fixed assets.

CHAPTER 4

Financial Forecasting, Planning, and Budgeting

Orientation: In this chapter we develop predictions of the firm's future financing needs based on a sales forecast. This entails construction of a pro forma income statement and balance sheet. We also discuss the concept of a firm's sustainable Rate of Growth. This is the maximum rate at which sales can grow and the firm's financial ratios remain unchanged with no new common stock being issued. The chapter also reviews the preparation and use of the cash budget as an essential tool of financial planning.

I.   Financial forecasting and planning

    A.   The need for forecasting in financial management arises whenever the future financing needs of the firm are being estimated. There are three basic steps involved in predicting financing requirements.

        1.   Project the firm's sales revenues and expenses over the planning period.

        2.   Estimate the levels of investment in current and fixed assets which are necessary to support the projected sales level.

        3.   Determine the financing needs of the firm throughout the planning period.

    B.   The key ingredient in the firm's planning process is the sales forecast. This forecast should reflect (1) any past trend in sales that is expected to continue and (2) the effects of any events which are expected to have a material effect on the firm's sales during the forecast period.

C.	The traditional problem faced in financial forecasting begins with the sales forecast and involves making forecasts of the impact of predicted sales on the firm's various expenses, assets, and liabilities. There are a number of techniques that can be used to make these forecasts.

II.	Financial planning and budgeting

A.	In general, a business will use four types of budgets: physical, cost, profit, and cash.

1.	Physical budgets include budgets for unit sales, personnel or manpower, unit production, inventories, and actual physical facilities. They are also used as a basis for generating cost and profit budgets.

2.	Cost budgets are prepared for every major expense category of the firm, such as manufacturing or production cost, selling cost, and administrative cost.

3.	The profit budget is prepared based upon information generated from the sales budget and cost budget.

4.	The cash budget is generated by converting all budget information previously discussed into a cash basis.

B.	The cash budget represents a detailed plan of future cash flows and can be broken down into four components: cash receipts, cash disbursements, net change in cash for the period, and new financing needed. Cash budgets can also be either fixed or variable.

1.	In a fixed cash budget, cash flow estimates are made for a single set of sales estimates.

2.	The variable cash budget involves the preparation of several budgets with each budget corresponding to a different set of sales estimates. This budget fulfills the two following basic needs:

a. The variable budget gives management more information on the range of possible financing needs of the firm.

b. Management is provided with a standard against which it can measure the performance of subordinates responsible for various cost and revenue items contained in the budget.

C. Although no strict rules exist, as a general rule, the budget period shall be long enough to show the effect of management policies, yet short enough so that estimates can be made with reasonable accuracy. For instance, the capital expenditure budget may be properly developed for a 10-year period while a cash budget may only cover 12 months.

D. The development of pro forma financial statements represents the final stage of the budgeting process.

1. A pro forma income statement represents a statement of planned profit or loss for the future period and is based primarily on information generated in the cash budget.

2. The pro forma balance sheet for a future date is developed by adjusting present balance-sheet figures for projected information found primarily within the cash budget and pro forma income statement.

Study Problems

1. The most recent balance sheet for the Parino Manufacturing Co. is shown in the table below. The company is about to embark on an advertising campaign, which is expected to raise sales from the present level of $10 million to $12 million by the end of next year. The firm is presently operating at full capacity and will have to increase its investment in both current and fixed assets to support the projected level of new sales. In fact, the firm estimates that both categories of assets will rise in direct proportion to the projected increase in sales. The firm's net profits were 4 percent of current year's sales but are expected to rise to 5 percent of next year's sales.

To help support its anticipated growth in asset needs next year, the firm has suspended plans to pay cash dividends to its stockholders. In past years a $1.50 per share dividend has been paid annually.

Parino Manufacturing Co., Inc. ($ millions)

	Present Level	Percent of Sales	Projected Level
Current assets	$2.0		
Net fixed assets	3.0		
Total	$5.0		
Accounts payable	$0.5		
Accrued expenses	0.5		
Notes payable	- -		
Current liabilities	$1.0		
Long-term debt	$2.0		
Common stock	0.5		
Retained earnings	1.5		
Common equity	$2.0		
Total	$5.0		

Parino's payables and accrued expenses are expected to vary directly with sales. In addition, notes payable will be used to supply the funds needed to finance next year's operations that are not forthcoming from other sources.

Fill in the table and project the firm's needs for discretionary financing. Use notes payable as the balancing entry for future discretionary financing needed.

SOLUTION

($ millions)

	Current Sales	$10		
	Predicted Sales	12		
	Net Profit Margin	5%		

	Present Level	Percent of Sales	Projected Level
Current assets	$2.00	0.20	$2.40
Net fixed assets	3.00	0.30	3.60
Total	5.00	0.50	6.00
Accounts payable	0.50	0.05	0.60
Accrued expenses	0.50	0.05	0.60
Notes payable	___		___
Current liabilities	1.00	0.10	1.20
Long-term debt	2.00	No Change	2.00
Common stock	0.50	No Change	0.50
Retained earnings	1.50	Ret. Earnings + NI	2.10
Common equity	2.00		2.60
Total	$5.00		
	Total Financing Provided		$5.80
	Discretionary Financing Needed		$ .20

2. The Horn Corporation's projected sales for the first 8 months of 1998 are as follows:

January	$300,000	May	$1,200,000
February	450,000	June	1,000,000
March	540,000	July	900,000
April	960,000	August	700,000

Twenty percent of Horn's sales are for cash, another 40% is collected in the month following sale, and 40% is collected in the second month following sale. November and December sales for 1997 were $800,000 and $650,000, respectively.

Horn purchases raw materials equal to 60% of sales and it makes its purchases 2 months in advance of sales. The supplier is paid 1 month after the purchase. For example, purchases for April sales are made in February and are paid for in March.

Furthermore, Horn pays $42,000 per month for rent and $90,000 per month for other expenditures. Finally, tax deposits of $85,000 are made each quarter, beginning in March.

The company's cash balance at December 31, 1997, was $80,000 and a minimum balance of $50,000 must be maintained at all times. Assume that any short-term financing needed to maintain the minimum cash balance would be paid off in the month following the month of financing with interest paid at a 12% annual rate.

Prepare a cash budget for Horn covering the first 6 months of 1998.

SOLUTION

	January	February	March	April	May	June	July
Sales	$300,000	$450,000	$540,000	$960,000	$1,200,000	$1,000,000	$900,000
Cash sales	60,000	90,000	108,000	192,000	240,000	200,000	180,000
Collections 1 month later	260,000	120,000	180,000	216,000	384,000	480,000	400,000
2 months later	320,000	260,000	120,000	180,000	216,000	384,000	480,000
Total collections from sales	640,000	470,000	408,000	588,000	840,000	1,064,000	1,060,000
Purchases	324,000	576,000	720,000	600,000	540,000	420,000	
Payments on purchases	270,000	324,000	576,000	720,000	600,000	540,000	420,000
Cash Receipts:							
Collections from sales	640,000	470,000	408,000	588,000	840,000	1,064,000	1,060,000
Cash disbursements:							
Payments on purchases	270,000	324,000	576,000	720,000	600,000	540,000	420,000
Other expenditures	90,000	90,000	90,000	90,000	90,000	90,000	90,000
Rent	42,000	42,000	42,000	42,000	42,000	42,000	42,000
Tax deposits			85,000			85,000	
Total disbursements	402,000	456,000	793,000	852,000	732,000	757,000	552,000
Net change for the month	238,000	14,000	(385,000)	(264,000)	108,000	307,000	
Beginning cash balance	80,000	318,000	332,000	50,000	50,000	50,000	
Plus: net change	238,000	14,000	(385,000)	(264,000)	108,000	307,000	
Borrowing	-----	-----	103,000	265,030	(104,320)	(263,710)	
Interest for prior month's borrowing	-----	-----	-----	1,030*	3,680	2,637	
Ending cash balance	$318,000	$332,000	$ 50,000	$ 50,000	$ 50,000	$ 90,653	
Cumulative borrowing	-----	-----	-----	$368,030	$263,710		

*0.12 x 103,000 x 1/2 = $1,030

4-7

Self-Tests

TRUE-FALSE

_____ 1. Budgets perform the basic functions of (1) providing the basis for taking corrective action and (2) providing the basis for performance evaluation.

_____ 2. The Financial planning process begins with a sales forecast.

_____ 3. Depreciation expense is an essential element in the cash budget.

_____ 4. Performance evaluation is a principal function that can be performed through the use of budgets.

_____ 5. The cash budget can be used to project future cash requirements of the firm.

_____ 6. The sustainable rate of growth represents the rate at which a firm's sales can grow if it wants to maintain its present capital structure and does not want to sell new equity.

_____ 7. As a general rule, all budgets of the firm should project no longer than one year in the future so that estimates can be made with reasonable accuracy.

_____ 8. The plowback ratio reflects the proportion of a firm's earnings that are paid in dividends.

_____ 9. If projected cash receipts are $50,000 and cash disbursements equal $40,000 then the net charge in cash for the period is ($10,000).

_____ 10. The percent-of-sales method is used to develop a forecast of a firm's financing needs.

MULTIPLE CHOICE

1. The most important element in determining the accuracy of most cash budgets is the:

    a. Forecast of cash disbursements.
    b. Forecast of collection schedule.
    c. Forecast of sales.
    d. Cannot be determined.
    e. None of the above.

2. The discretionary financing needed model includes:

    a. Forecasts of future cash requirements of the firm.
    b. Forecasts of all assets and liabilities.
    c. Forecasts of the firm's personnel requirements.
    d. All of the above.
    e. a and b only.

3. Which of the following items would be included in the cash budget?

    a. Depreciation charges.
    b. Accumulated depreciation.
    c. Accounts receivable bad debt allowance.
    d. All of the above.
    e. None of the above.

4. The cash budget provides the following information:

    a. The exact amount of borrowing needed for the budget interval.
    b. The type of loan which should be obtained to meet the cash needs for the time interval.
    c. A point estimate of the borrowing needs for the budget interval.
    d. An estimate of the cash needed for depreciation expense
    e. None of the above.

5. In general, a budget is simply

    a. a forecast of future events.
    b. another name for the balance sheet.
    c. a tool for analyzing cash requirements.
    d. both a and c.
    e. None of the above.

6. Which of the following would <u>not</u> fall under the physical budget classification?

    a. Unit sales budget.
    b. Physical facilities budget.
    c. Production cost budget.
    d. Unit production budget.
    e. None of the above.

CHAPTER 5

The Time Value of Money

Orientation: In this chapter the concept of a time value of money is introduced, that is, a dollar today is worth more than a dollar received a year from now. Thus if we are to logically compare projects and financial strategies, we must either move all dollar flows back to the present or out to some common future date.

I.   Compound interest results when the interest paid on the investment during the first period is added to the principal and during the second period the interest is earned on the original principal plus the interest earned during the first period.

A.   Mathematically, the future value of an investment if compounded annually at a rate of i for n years will be

$$FV_n = PV (1+i)^n$$

where n   =   the number of years during which the compounding occurs

i   =   the annual interest (or discount) rate

PV   =   the present value or original amount invested at the beginning of the first period

FV_n =   the future value of the investment at the end of n years

1.   The future value of an investment can be increased by either increasing the number of years we let it compound or by compounding it at a higher rate.

5-1

2.   If the compounded period is less than one year, the future value of an investment can be determined as follows:

$$FV_n = PV \left(1 + \frac{i}{m}\right)^{mn}$$

where m = the number of times compounding occurs during the year

II.   Determining the present value, that is, the value in today's dollars of a sum of money to be received in the future, involves nothing other than inverse compounding. The differences in these techniques come about merely from the investor's point of view.

A.   Mathematically, the present value of a sum of money to be received in the future can be determined with the following equation:

$$PV = FV_n \left(\frac{1}{(1 + i)^n}\right)$$

where n = the number of years until payment will be received,

i = the opportunity rate or discount rate

PV = the present value of the future sum of money

FV_n = the future value of the investment at the end of n years

1.   The present value of a future sum of money is inversely related to both the number of years until the payment will be received and the opportunity rate.

5-2

III. An annuity is a series of equal dollar payments for a specified number of years. Because annuities occur frequently in finance, for example, bond interest payments, we treat them specially.

    A. A compound annuity involves depositing or investing an equal sum of money at the end of each year for a certain number of years and allowing it to grow.

        1. This can be done by using our compounding equation and compounding each one of the individual deposits to the future or by using the following compound annuity equation:

$$FV_n \;=\; PMT \left(\sum_{t=0}^{n-1} (1+i)^t \right)$$

            where PMT = the annuity value deposited at the end of each year

            i = the annual interest (or discount) rate

            n = the number of years for which the annuity will last

            FV_n = the future value of the annuity at the end of the nth year

    B. Pension funds, insurance obligation, and interest received from bonds all involve annuities. To compare these financial instruments we would like to know the present value of each of these annuities.

1. This can be done by using our present value equation and discounting each one of the individual cash flows back to the present or by using the following present value of an annuity equation:

$$PV = PMT \left(\sum_{t=1}^{n} \frac{1}{(1+i)^t} \right)$$

where PMT = the annuity withdrawn at the end of each year

i = the annual interest or discount rate

PV = the present value of the future annuity

n = the number of years for which the annuity will last

C. This procedure of solving for PMT, the annuity value when i, n, and PV are known, is also the procedure used to determine what payments are associated with paying off a loan in equal installments. Loans paid off in this way, in periodic payments, are called amortized loans. Here again we know three of the four values in the annuity equation and are solving for a value of PMT, the annual annuity.

IV. A perpetuity is an annuity that continues forever, that is every year from now on this investment pays the same dollar amount.

A. An example of a perpetuity is preferred stock which yields a constant dollar dividend infinitely.

B.   The following equation can be used to determine the present value of a perpetuity:

$$PV = \frac{pp}{i}$$

where PV $=$ the present value of the perpetuity

pp $=$ the constant dollar amount provided by the perpetuity

i $=$ the annual interest or discount rate

V.   Bond valuation illustrates a combination of several discounting techniques and procedures including an annuity, a single cash flow and semiannual periods. When a bond is purchased the owner receives two things: interest payments, which are generally made semiannually and at maturity repayment of the full principal, regardless of how much the bond was purchased for.

A.   The present value of a bond can be illustrated as follows:

$$\text{Bond value} = \begin{array}{c}\text{Present}\\\text{value of}\\\text{interest}\\\text{payments}\end{array} + \begin{array}{c}\text{present value}\\\text{of return of}\\\text{principal}\end{array}$$

$$= PMT \left(\sum_{t=1}^{n \cdot m} \frac{1}{(1+\frac{i}{m})^t} \right) + FV_{n \cdot m} \left(\frac{1}{(1+\frac{i}{m})^{n \cdot m}} \right)$$

VI.   To aid in the calculations of present and future values, tables are provided at the back of <u>Basic Financial Management</u> (<u>BFM</u>).

A.   To aid in determining the value of FV_n in the compounding formula

$$FV_n = PV(1+i)^n = PV(FVIF_{i,n})$$

tables have been compiled for values of $FVIF_{i,n}$ or $(i+1)^n$ in Appendix B, "Compound Sum of $1," in BFM.

B.   Thus to determine the value of:

$$FV_{10} = \$1,000(1+0.08)^{10}$$

we need merely to look up the value of $FVIF_{8\%,10\,yr.}$ in Appendix B and substitute it in. The table value given in the $n = 10$ row and 8% column of Appendix B is 2.159. Substituting this in the equation, we get

$$FV_{10} = \$1,000(2.159)$$

$$FV_{10} = \$2,159$$

C.   To aid in the computation of present values

$$PV = FV_n \frac{1}{(1+i)^n} = FV_n(PVIF_{i,n})$$

tables have been compiled for values of

$$\frac{1}{(1+i)^n} \quad or \quad PVIF_{i,n}$$

and appear in Appendix C in the back of BFM.

D.   Because of the time-consuming nature of compounding an annuity,

$$FV_n = PMT \sum_{t=0}^{n-1}(1+i)^t = PMT(FVIFA_{i,n})$$

Tables are provided in Appendix D of <u>BFM</u> for

$$\sum_{t=0}^{n-1} (1+i)^t \quad \text{or} \quad FVIFA_{i,n}$$

for various combinations of n and i.

E. To simplify the process of determining the present value of an annuity

$$PV \quad = \quad PMT \left(\sum_{t=1}^{n} \frac{1}{(1+i)^t} \right) \quad = PMT\ (PVIFA_{i,n})$$

tables are provided in Appendix E of <u>BFM</u> for various combinations of n and i for the value

$$\sum_{t=1}^{n} \frac{1}{(1+i)^t} \quad \text{or} \quad PVIFA_{i,n}$$

<u>Study</u> <u>Problems</u>

1. What will $1,000 invested for 10 years at 10% compounded annually accumulate to?

SOLUTION

Substituting into the compound value formula, we get:

$$FV_n \quad = \quad PV(1+i)^n$$

$$FV_{10} \quad = \quad \$1,000(1+0.10)^{10}$$

$$FV_{10} \quad = \quad \$1,000(2.594)$$

$$FV_{10} \quad = \quad \$2,594$$

2. How many years will it take $500 to grow to $1,586 if it is invested at 8% compounded annually?

SOLUTION

From the compound value formula we know:

$$FV_n = PV(1+i)^n$$

Substituting in the values that we know, we get:

$$\$1,586 = \$500(1+0.08)^n$$

or using table values, we get:

$$\$1,586 = \$500 \; (FVIF_{8\%, \; n \; yr.})$$

Dividing both sides by $500, we get:

$$3.172 = FVIF_{8\%, \; n \; yr.}$$

Looking in the 8% column, we find a value of 3.172 in the 15-year row. Thus, it will take 15 years.

3. At what annual rate would $1,000 have to be invested in order to grow to $4,046 in 10 years?

SOLUTION

From the compound value formula we know:

$$FV_n = PV(1+i)^n = PV(FVIF_{i,n})$$

Substituting the table value given in Appendix B of <u>BFM</u> for $(1 + i)^n$, we get:

$$FV_n \quad = \quad PV \ (FVIF_{i,n})$$

Substituting in the given values, we get:

$$\$4,046 \quad = \quad \$1,000 \ (FVIF_{i, \ 10 \ yr.})$$

$$4.046 \quad = \quad FVIF_{i, \ 10 \ yr.}$$

Thus, we are looking for a table value of 4.046 in the 10-year row of Appendix B. This appears in the 15% column; thus, 15% is the annual rate we are looking for.

4.   What is the present value of $1,000 to be received 8 years from now discounted back to present at 10%?

SOLUTION

Substituting in the present value formula we get:

$$PV \quad = \quad FV_n \left(\frac{1}{(1 \ + \ i)^n} \right) = FV_n \ (PVIF_{i,n})$$

$$PV \quad = \quad \$1,000 \left(\frac{1}{(1 \ + \ 0.10)^8} \right)$$

$$PV \quad = \quad \$1,000[0.467]$$

$$PV \quad = \quad \$467$$

5. What is the accumulated sum of the following streams of payments, $1,000 per year for 5 years compounded annually at 5%?

SOLUTION

Substituting into the compound annuity formula, we get:

$$FV_n = PMT \sum_{t=0}^{n-1} (1+i)^t = PMT(FVIFA_{i,n})$$

$$FV_5 = \$1,000 \sum_{t=0}^{5-1} (1+0.05)^t$$

$$FV_5 = \$1,000(5.526)$$

$$FV_5 = \$5,526$$

6. What is the present value of $100 a year for 15 years discounted back to the present at 15%?

SOLUTION

Substituting into the present value of an annuity formula:

$$PV = PMT \left(\sum_{t=1}^{n} \frac{1}{(1+i)^t} \right) = PMT \, (PVIFA_{i,n})$$

$$PV = \$100 \left(\sum_{t=1}^{15} \frac{1}{(1+0.15)^t} \right)$$

$$PV = \$100(5.847)$$

$$PV = \$584.70$$

7. If you receive a 9 percent $100,000 loan that has annual payments of $14,695.08, how many loan payments must you make in order to pay off the loan?

SOLUTION

Substituting into the present value of an annuity formula:

$$PV = PMT \left(\sum_{t=1}^{n} \frac{1}{(1+i)^t} \right)$$

$100,000 = $14,695.08 \; PVIFA_{9\%, \; n \; yr.}$

$6.805 = PVIFA_{9\%, \; n \; yr.}$

Looking down the 9% column of Appendix E we find a value of 6.805 in the 11 year row. Thus, in 11 years the loan will be paid off.

8. At what annual rate would the following have to be invested?

   a. $550 to grow to $1,898.60 in 13 years

   b. $275 to grow to $406.18 in 8 years

   c. $60 to grow to $279.66 in 20 years

   d. $180 to grow to $486.00 in 6 years

SOLUTION

   (a) $FV_n = PV(1+i)^n$

   $$\$1,898.60 = \$550 \; (1+i)^{13}$$

$3.452 \quad = \quad FVIF_{i\%,\ 13\ yr.}$

Thus, i $\quad = \quad$ 10% (because the Appendix B value of 3.452 occurs in the 12 year row in the 10 percent column)

(b) $\quad FV_n \quad = \quad PV\,(1+i)^n$

$\$406.18 \quad = \quad \$275\ (1+i)^8$

$1.477 \quad = \quad FVIF_{i\%,\ 8\ yr.}$

Thus, i $\quad = \quad$ 5%

(c) $\quad FV_n \quad = \quad PV\,(1+i)^n$

$\$279.66 \quad = \quad \$60\ (1+i)^{20}$

$4.661 \quad = \quad FVIF_{i\%,\ 20\ yr.}$

Thus, i $\quad = \quad$ 8%

(d) $\quad FV_n \quad = \quad PV\,(1+i)^n$

$\$486.00 \quad = \quad \$180\ (1+i)^6$

$2.700 \quad = \quad FVIF_{i\%,\ 6\ yr.}$

Thus, i $\quad = \quad$ 18%

9. What is the accumulated sum of each of the following streams of payments?

a. $500 a year for 10 years compounded annually at 6 percent

b. $150 a year for 5 years compounded annually at 11 percent

c. $35 a year for 8 years compounded annually at 7 percent

d. $25 a year for 3 years compounded annually at 2 percent

SOLUTION

(a) FV_n = $PMT \left(\sum_{t=0}^{n-1} (1+i)^t \right)$

      FV = $\$500 \left(\sum_{t=0}^{10-1} (1+0.06)^t \right)$

      FV_{10} = $\$500 (13.181)$

      FV_{10} = $\$6,590.50$

(b) FV_n = $PMT \left(\sum_{t=0}^{n-1} (1+i)^t \right)$

      FV_5 = $\$150 \left(\sum_{t=0}^{5-1} (1+0.11)^t \right)$

      FV_5 = $\$150 (6.228)$

      FV_5 = $\$934.20$

(c) FV_n = $PMT \left(\sum_{t=0}^{n-1} (1+i)^t \right)$

      FV_7 = $\$35 \left(\sum_{t=0}^{8-1} (1+0.07)^t \right)$

      FV_7 = $\$35 (10.260)$

$$FV_7 \quad = \quad \$359.10$$

(d) $FV_n \quad = \quad PMT \left(\sum_{t=0}^{n-1} (1+i)^t \right)$

$$FV_3 \quad = \quad \$25 \left(\sum_{t=0}^{3-1} (1+0.02)^t \right)$$

$$FV_3 \quad = \quad \$25 \, (3.060)$$

$$FV_3 \quad = \quad \$76.50$$

10. Stefani Moore purchased a new house for $150,000. She paid $30,000 down and agreed to pay the rest over the next 25 years in 25 equal annual payments that include principal payments plus 10 percent compound interest on the unpaid balance. What will these equal payments be?

SOLUTION

$$PV \quad = \quad PMT \left(\sum_{t=1}^{n} \frac{1}{(1+i)^t} \right)$$

$$\$120,000 \quad = \quad PMT \left(\sum_{t=1}^{25} \frac{1}{(1+0.1)^t} \right)$$

$$\$120,000 \quad = \quad PMT(9.077)$$

Thus, PMT $= \quad \$13.220.23$ per year for 25 years

11. How much do you have to deposit today so that beginning 11 years from now you can withdraw $10,000 a year for the next five years (periods 11 through 15) plus an *additional* amount of $15,000 in that last year (period 15)? Assume an interest rate of 7 percent.

SOLUTION

The Present value of the $10,000 annuity over years 11-15.

$$PV = PMT \left(\left(\sum_{t=1}^{15} \frac{1}{(1+.07)t} \right) - \left(\sum_{t=1}^{10} \frac{1}{(1+.07)t} \right) \right)$$

$$= \$10,000(9.108 - 7.024)$$

$$= \$10,000(2.084)$$

$$= \$20,840$$

The present value of the $15,000 withdrawal at the end of year 15:

$$PV = FV_{15} \left(\frac{1}{(1+.07)^{15}} \right)$$

$$= \$15,000(.362)$$

$$= \$5,430$$

Thus, you would have to deposit $20,840 + $5,430 or $26,270 today.

TRUE/FALSE

_____ 1.   The fact that there is an opportunity cost to money brings on the concept of the time value of money.

_____ 2.   The higher the rate used to compound a given sum, the larger it will be at some future date.

_____ 3.   The future value of an investment can be increased by reducing the number of years we let it compound.

_____ 4.   There is an inverse relationship between the present value of a future cash flow and the discount rate.

_____ 5.   More frequent compounding (for example, daily compounding as opposed to annual compounding) allows money to grow faster (assuming a no change in the interest rate) because it allows interest to be earned on interest more frequently.

_____ 6.   Determining present value is merely the inverse of compounding.

_____ 7.   A compound annuity involves depositing or investing an equal sum of money at the end of each year for a certain number of years and allowing it to grow.

_____ 8.   A perpetuity is an annuity that continues for 30 years or more.

_____ 9.   The present value of an annuity increases as the discount rate decreases.

_____ 10. An example of perpetuity is the interest received on long-term bonds.

MULTIPLE CHOICE

1. To determine the present value of a future sum we need only multiply it by:

    a. $\dfrac{1}{(1+i)^n}$

    b. $\dfrac{1}{(1+n)^1}$

    c. $(1+n)^i$

    d. $(1+i)^n$

2. The present value of a $100 perpetuity discounted back to present at 6% is:

    a. $6,000.00.
    b. $6,666.66.
    c. $1,666.67.
    d. $1,200.00.

3. If we place $100 in a savings account that yields 6% compounded semiannually, what will our investment grow to at the end of 5 years?

    a. $133.80.
    b. $130.00.
    c. $125.00.
    d. $134.40.

4. The future value of an investment compounded continuously is calculated by the formula:

   a. $FV_n = PV/e^{in}$

   b. $FV_n = PVe^{-in}$

   c. $FV_n = PVe^{in}$

   d. $FV_n = PVe(1+i)^n$

5. A bond maturing in 10 years pays $80 each year and $1,000 upon maturity. Assuming 10 percent to be the appropriate discount rate, the present value of the bond is:

   a. $1,010.84
   b. $925.74
   c $877.60
   d. $1,000.00

6. The Fuller Company has received a $50,000 loan. The annual payments are $6,202.70. If the Fuller Company is paying 9 percent interest per year, how many loan payments must the company make?

   a. 15
   b. 13
   c. 12
   d. 19

5-14B. FV_n $=$ $PMT \left(\sum_{t=0}^{n-1} (1+i)^t \right)$

$25,000 $=$ $PMT \left(\sum_{t=0}^{15} (1+0.07)^t \right)$

$25,000 $=$ $PMT(25.129)$

Thus, PMT $=$ $994.87

5-16B.   The value of the home in 10 years

FV_{10} $=$ $PV (1+.05)^{10}$

          $=$ $125,000(1.629)$

          $=$ $203,625

How much must be invested annually to accumulate $203,625?

$203,625 $=$ $PMT \left(\sum_{t=0}^{10} (1+.10)^t \right)$

$203,625 $=$ $PMT(15.937)$

PMT $=$ $12,776.87

5-20B.   PV $= FV_n \left(\dfrac{1}{(1 + i)^n} \right)$

PV $= \$1{,}000 \left(\dfrac{1}{(1 + .09)^8} \right)$

$= \$1{,}000(.502)$

$= \$502$

5-21B.

(a)   PV $= \dfrac{PP}{i}$

PV $= \dfrac{\$400}{0.09}$

PV $= \$4{,}444$

(b)   PV $= \dfrac{PP}{i}$

PV $= \dfrac{\$1{,}500}{0.13}$

PV $= \$11{,}538$

(c)   PV $= \dfrac{PP}{i}$

PV $= \dfrac{\$150}{0.10}$

PV $= \$1{,}500$

$$\text{(d)} \quad PV = \frac{PP}{i}$$

$$PV = \frac{\$100}{0.06}$$

$$PV = \$1,667$$

5-23B.
$$FV_n = PV\left(1 + \frac{i}{m}\right)^{m \cdot n}$$

$$7 = 1\left(1 + \frac{0.10}{2}\right)^{2 \cdot n}$$

$$7 = (1 + 0.05)^{2 \cdot n}$$

$$7 = FVIF_{5\%, \, 2n \text{ yr.}}$$

A value of 7.040 occurs in the 5 percent column and 40-year row of the table in Appendix B. Therefore, $2n = 40$ years and $n =$ approximately 20 years.

5-25B.

The Present value of the $10,000 annuity over years 11-15.

$$PV = PMT\left[\left(\sum_{t=1}^{15}\frac{1}{(1+.07)t}\right) - \left(\sum_{t=1}^{10}\frac{1}{(1+.07)t}\right)\right]$$

$$= \$10,000(9.108 - 7.024)$$

$$= \$10,000(2.084)$$

$$= \$20,840$$

The present value of the $15,000 withdrawal at the end of year 15:

$$PV = FV_{15}\left(\frac{1}{(1+.07)^{15}}\right)$$

$$= \$15,000(.362)$$

$$= \$5,430$$

Thus, you would have to deposit $20,840 + $5,430 or $26,270 today.

5-29B.
$$PV = PMT\left(\sum_{t=1}^{n}\frac{1}{(1+i)^t}\right)$$

$$\$30,000 = PMT\left(\sum_{t=1}^{4}\frac{1}{(1+.13)^t}\right)$$

$$\$30,000 = PMT(2.974)$$

$$PMT = \$10,087$$

5-31B.
$$FV_n = PMT\left(\sum_{t=0}^{n-1}(1+i)^t\right)$$

$$\$30,000 = PMT\left(\sum_{t=0}^{5-1}(1+.10)^t\right)$$

$$\$30,000 = PMT(6.105)$$

$$PMT = \$4,914$$

5-33B.   This problem can be subdivided into (1) the compound value of the $150,000 in the savings account, (2) the compound value of the $250,000 in stocks, (3) the additional savings due to depositing $8,000 per year in the savings account for 10 years, and (4) the additional saving due to depositing $2,000 per year in the savings account at the end of years 6-10. (Note the $10,000 deposited in years 6-10 is covered in parts (3) and (4).)

(1)   Future value of $150,000

$$FV_{10} = \$150,000 (1 + .08)^{10}$$

$$FV_{10} = \$150,000 (2.159)$$

$$FV_{10} = \$323,850$$

(2)   Future value of $250,000

$$FV_{10} = \$250,000 (1 + .12)^{10}$$

$$FV_{10} = \$250,000 (3.106)$$

$$FV_{10} = \$776,500$$

(3)   Compound annuity of $8,000, 10 years

$$FV_{10} = PMT \left(\sum_{t=0}^{n-1} (1+i)^t \right)$$

$$= \$8,000 \left(\sum_{t=0}^{10-1} (1+.08)^t \right)$$

$$= \$8,000\ (14.487)$$

$$= \$115,896$$

(4)   Compound annuity of $2,000 (years 6-10)

$$FV_5 = \$2,000 \left(\sum_{t=0}^{5-1} (1+.08)^t \right)$$

$$= \$2,000\ (5.867)$$

$$= \$11,734$$

At the end of ten years you will have $323,850 + $776,500 + $115,896 + $11,734 = $1,227,980.

$$PV = PMT \left(\sum_{t=1}^{20} \frac{1}{(1+.11)^t} \right)$$

$$\$1,227,980 = PMT\ (7.963)$$

$$PMT = \$154,210.72$$

CHAPTER 6

Risk and
Rates of Return

Orientation: This chapter introduces the concepts that underlie the valuation of securities and their rates of return. We are specifically concerned with common stock, preferred stock, and bonds. We also look at the concept of the investor's expected rate of return on an investment.

I.   Expected Return

    A.   The expected benefits or returns to be received from an investment come in the form of the cash flows the investment generates.

    B.   Conventionally, we measure the expected cash flow, $\bar{X}$, as follows:

$$\bar{X} = \sum_{1}^{N} X_i P(X_i)$$

    where N =   the number of possible states of the economy.

                    X_i =   the cash flow in the ith state of the economy.

                    $P(X_i)$ =   the probability of the ith cash flow.

II.   Riskiness of the cash flows

    A.   Risk can be defined as the possible variation in cash flow about an expected cash flow.

    B.   Statistically, risk may be measured by the standard deviation about the expected cash flow.

C.   Risk and diversification

    1.   Total variability can be divided into:

        a.   The variability of returns unique to the security (diversifiable or unsystematic risk)

        b.   The risk related to market movements (nondiversifiable or systematic risk)

    2.   By diversifying, the investor can eliminate the "unique" security risk. The systematic risk, however, cannot be diversified away.

    3.   The **characteristic line** tells us the average movement in a firm's stock price in response to a movement in the general market, such as the S&P 500 Index. The slope of the characteristic line, which has come to be called **beta**, is a measure of a stock's systematic or market risk. The slope of the line is merely the ratio of the "rise" of the line relative to the "run" of the line.

    4.   If a security's beta equals one, a 10 percent increase (decrease) in market returns will produce on average a 10 percent increase (decrease) in security returns.

    5.   A security having a higher beta is more volatile and thus more risky than a security having a lower beta value.

    6.   A portfolio's beta is equal to the average of the betas of the stocks in the portfolio.

III.   Required rate of return

A.   The required rate of return is the minimum rate necessary to compensate an investor for accepting the risk he or she associates with the purchase and ownership of an asset.

B. Two factors determine the required rate of return for the investor:

    1. The risk-free rate of interest which recognizes the time value of money.

    2. The risk premium which considers the riskiness (variability of returns) of the asset and the investor's attitude toward risk.

C. Capital asset pricing model-CAPM

    1. The required rate of return for a given security can be expressed as

$$\begin{matrix} \text{Required} \\ \text{rate} \end{matrix} = \begin{matrix} \text{risk-free} \\ \text{rate} \end{matrix} + \text{beta} \times \left(\begin{matrix} \text{market} \\ \text{return} \end{matrix} - \begin{matrix} \text{risk-free} \\ \text{rate} \end{matrix} \right)$$

or

$$k_j = k_{rf} + b_j (k_m - k_{rf})$$

    2. Security market line

        a. Graphically illustrates the CAPM.

        b. Designates the risk-return trade off existing in the market, where risk is defined in terms of beta according to the CAPM equation.

    3. Criticism of CAPM

        a. It relies totally on a security's sensitivity to the market (b) for measuring risk.

        b. It is difficult to test empirically.

IV. Historical performance of portfolio returns

A. Data have been compiled by Ibbotson and Sinquefield on the actual returns for various portfolios of securities from 1926-1990.

6-3

B.   The following portfolios were studied.

    1.   Common stocks of small firms
    2.   Common stocks of large companies
    3.   Long-term corporate bonds
    4.   Long-term U.S. government bonds
    5.   U.S. Treasury bills

C.   Investors historically have received greater returns for greater risk-taking with the exception of the U.S. government bonds.

D.   The only portfolio with returns consistently exceeding the inflation rate has been common stocks.

V.   Risk and diversification
A.   The market rewards diversification. We can lower risk without sacrificing expected return, and/or we can increase expected return without having to assume more risk.

B.   Diversifying among different kinds of assets is called asset allocation. Compared to diversification within the different asset classes, the benefits received are far greater through effective asset allocation.

VI.   Risk and being patient

A.   An investor in common stocks must often wait longer to earn the higher returns than those provided by bonds.

B.   The capital markets reward us not just for diversifying, but also for being patient. The returns tend to converge toward the average as we lengthen our holding period.

VII.   Arbitrage pricing theory (See the chapter appendix)

A.   Security returns vary from expected returns due to <u>unanticipated changes</u> in important economic forces, such as: industrial production, inflation and interest rate structures.

B.   The Arbitrage Pricing Model (APM) may be expressed as follows:

$$\bar{k} = k_{rf} + (S_{i1})(RP_1) + (S_{i2})(RP_{i2}) + \ldots + (S_{iN})(RP_N)$$

where $\bar{k}$ =   the expected return for asset i

k_f =   the risk-free rate

S_{ij} =   the sensitivity of stock returns to unexpected changes in economic force j

RP_i =   the market risk premium associated with an unexpected change in the jth economic force

N   =   the number of relevant economic forces

Study Problems

1.   Phillips Inc., is considering an investment in one of two common stocks. Given the information below, which investment is better, based on risk and return.

Common Stock A		Common Stock B	
Probability	Return	Probability	Return
0.10	-10%	0.30	5%
0.20	6	0.20	12
0.40	15	0.40	10
0.30	9	0.10	20

SOLUTION

Common Stock A

Expected Return

$$= 0.1(-10\%) + 0.2(6\%) + 0.4(15\%) + 0.3(9\%)$$

$$= -1\% + 1.2\% + 6\% + 2.7\% = 8.9\%$$

Standard Deviation

$$= [(-10\% - 8.9\%)^2(0.10) + (6\% - 8.9\%)^2(0.2)$$
$$+ (15\% - 8.9\%)^2 (0.4) + (9\% - 8\ 9\%)^2(0\ 30)]^{1/2}$$

$$= (35.721\% + 1.682\% + 14.884\% + 0.003\%)^{1/2} = 7.23\%$$

Common Stock B

Expected Return

$$= 0.3(5\%) + 0.2(12\%) + 0.4(10\%) + 0.10(20\%)$$

$$= 1.5\% + 2\ .4\% + 4\% + 2\% = 9\ .9\%$$

Standard Deviation

$$= [(5\% - 9.9\%)^2(0.3) + (12\% - 9.9\%)^2(0.2)$$
$$+ (10\% - 9.9\%)^2(0.4) + (20\% - 9.9\%)^2(0.1)]^{1/2}$$

$$= (7.203\% + 0.882\% + 0.004\% + 10.201\%)^{1/2} = 4.28\%$$

Common stock B has both a higher expected return and a smaller standard deviation (less risk). Hence B is better.

2. Compute the annual holding-period return for the following stock.

Year	Stock Price
1991	$98
1992	105
1993	115
1994	100
1995	120

SOLUTION

Year	Return
1991	
1992	7.1%
1993	9.5%
1994	-13.0%
1995	20.0%

3. From the graph below, estimate Archie's beta.

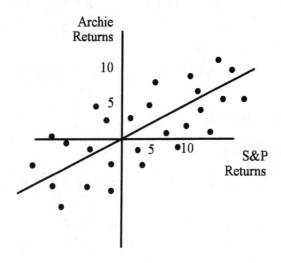

SOLUTION

Archie's beta is about 0.50, since Archie's returns change about 5 percent while the market's return changes 10 percent. Thus, 5 ÷ 10 = 0.50.

4. BC Incorporated, has a beta of 0.65. If the expected market return is 10 percent and the risk free rate is 5 percent, what is the appropriate expected return of BC Incorporated?

SOLUTION

Expected return of BC Incorporated

$$= \text{risk-free rate} + \text{Beta} \left(\begin{array}{ccc} \text{expected} & & \text{risk} \\ \text{market} & - & \text{free} \\ \text{return} & & \text{rate} \end{array} \right)$$

= 5% + 0.65(10%-5%)

= 5% + 3.25% = 8.25%

5.   (Appendix 6A) Using the results of the Bowers, Bowers, and Logue study given below, calculate the investor's required rate of return for the following stocks:

Economic factor	1	2	3	4
Market risk premium (BBL)	-185.5%	144.5%	12.4%	-274.4%
Stock sensitivity factor				
A	-0.040	0.010	0.020	0.004
B	-0.020	0.030	0.040	0.005
C	-0.050	-0.010	0.009	0.006

Assume that the risk-free rate is 7.3%

SOLUTION

A $E(k)$ = 7.3% - 185.5% (-0.040) + 144.5% (0.010) + 12.4% (0.020) - 274.4% (0.004)

= 15.32%

B $E(k)$ = 7.3% - 185.5% (-0.020) + 144.5% (0.030) + 12.4% (0.040) - 274.4% (0.005)

= 14.47%

C $E(k)$ = 7.3% - 185.5% (-0.050) + 144.5% (-0.010) + 12.4% (0.009) - 274.4% (0.006)

= 13.60%

Self Tests

TRUE-FALSE

_____ 1.   The investor's required rate of return is the minimum rate necessary to attract an investor to purchase or hold a security.

_____ 2. Risk, as defined in this chapter, is the variation in returns about an expected value.

_____ 3. Time value of money can be represented by a risk-free rate of return only for risk-free securities.

_____ 4. A proxy for the risk-free rate is the Corporate AA Bond rate.

_____ 5. An investor's required rate of return is always greater than the expected rate of return.

_____ 6. By proper diversification, an investor can eliminate the market-related (systematic) risk.

_____ 7. A security having a beta of 1 will move up (or down) on average with the market by the same percentage.

_____ 8. The addition of a security with a beta of 0 would not change the risk of a well-diversified portfolio.

_____ 9. The annual returns on common stocks have historically been greater than those of U.S. treasury bills on average.

_____ 10. A security with an expected return of 15.9% and a standard deviation of 9.8% is obviously better than a treasury bill earning 8%.

MULTIPLE CHOICE

1. Under the capital asset pricing model, the relevant risk is:

   a. Diversifiable risk.
   b. Systematic risk.
   c. Financial risk.
   d. Standard deviation.

2. If the required return for a security is 15% and the risk-free rate is 6%, the risk premium is:

   a. 0%.
   b. 6%.
   c. 10%.
   d. 9%.
   e. 15%.

3. In terms of the security market line, a security with a beta of 1.5 should provide a risk premium _____ times the risk premium existing for the market as a whole.

   a. 0%
   b. 1
   c. 1.5
   d. 2.5
   e. 0.5

4. The beta for a portfolio is determined by:

   a. Calculating the standard deviation of the betas of the individual stocks in the portfolio.
   b. Computing the unweighted average of the individual betas.
   c. Calculating a weighted average of the individual stock betas, where the weights equal the individual stocks' expected returns.
   d. Calculating a weighted average of the individual stock betas, where the weights equal the percentage invested in each stock.

5. A stock's holding period return represents:

   a. The dividend received each period.
   b. The rate of return that would be earned on a stock if bought at the beginning of the period and sold at the end of the period.
   c. The return received from diversifying one's portfolio.
   d. The return from a stock relative to the return of the portfolio.

6. An investor's required rate of return should be a function of:

   a. The riskiness of the investment being made without regard for the riskiness of other investments.
   b. The risk-free rate of return less the inflation rate.
   c. The risk-free rate of return plus the inflation rate.
   d. The risk-free rate of return plus a risk premium for the stock's systematic risk.

7. You should expect a higher rate of return from:

   a. Long-term corporate bonds than from common stocks.
   b. Small company stocks than from common stocks of large firms.
   c. U.S. Treasury Bills than from long-term government securities.
   d. None of the above are true.

SOLUTIONS TO SELECTED SET B PROBLEMS (See text for problems.)

6-1B.

(A) Probability $P(k_i)$	(B) Return (k_i)	(A) x (B) Expected Return $\bar{k}$	Weighted Deviation $(k_i - \bar{k})^2 P(k_i)$
.15	6%	0.90%	1.26
.30	5	1.50	4.56
.40	11	4.40	1.76
.15	14	2.10	3.90

$$\bar{k} = 8.9\% \qquad \sigma^2 = 11.48\%$$

$$\sigma = 3.39\%$$

No, Gautney should not invest in the security. The level of risk is excessive for a return which equals the rate offered on treasury bills.

6-4B.

(a) $$\left(\begin{array}{c}\text{Required rate}\\ \text{of return}\end{array}\right) = \left(\begin{array}{c}\text{Risk-free}\\ \text{rate}\end{array}\right) + \text{Beta}\left(\begin{array}{c}\text{Market Risk}\\ \text{Premium}\end{array}\right)$$

$$= 8\% + 1.5\,(16\% - 8\%)$$

$$= 20\%$$

(b)   The 20 percent "fair rate" compensates the investor for the time value of money and for assuming risk.   However, only nondiversifiable risk is being considered, which is appropriate.

6-10B.

a.

	Sugita		Market	
Month	kt	$(kt - \bar{k})^2$	kt	$(kt - \bar{k})^2$
1	1.80%	0.01%	1.50%	0.06%
2	-0.50	5.68	1.00	0.06
3	2.00	0.01	0.00	1.56
4	--2.00	15.08	-2.00	10.56
5	5.00	9.71	4.00	7.56
6	5.00	9.71	3.00	3.06
Sum	11.30	40.20	7.50	22.86

	Sugita	Market
Average monthly return (Sum ÷ 6)	1.88%	1.25%
Annualized average returns	22.60%	15.00%
Variance (Sum ÷ 5)	8.04%	4.58%
Standard deviation	2.84%	2.14%

b.

Required Rate of Return $=$ Risk-Free Rate $+$ (Market Return - Risk-Free Rate) X Beta

$\quad = \quad 8\% \quad + \quad [(15\% - 8\%) \text{ X } 1.18] = 16.26\%$

c. Sugita's historical return of 22.6 percent exceeds what we would consider a fair return of 16.26 percent, given the stock's systematic risk.

CHAPTER 7

Bond Valuation

Orientation: This chapter introduces the concepts that underlie asset valuation. We are specifically concerned with bonds. We also look at the concept of the bondholder's expected rate of return on an investment.

I.   Types of bonds

    A.   Debentures: unsecured long-term debt.

    B.   Subordinated debentures: bonds that have a lower claim on assets in the event of liquidation than do other senior debtholders.

    C.   Mortgage bonds: bonds secured by a lien on specific assets of the firm, such as real estate.

    D.   Zero and low coupon bonds allow the issuing firm to issue bonds at a substantial discount from their $1,000 face value with a zero or very low coupon.

        1.   The disadvantages are, when the bond matures, the issuing firm will face an extremely large nondeductible cash outflow much greater than the cash inflow they experienced when the bonds were first issued.

        2.   Discount bonds are not callable and can be retired only at maturity.

        3.   On the other hand, annual cash outflows associated with interest payments do not occur with zero coupon bonds.

    E.   Junk bonds: bonds rated BB or below.

F.   Eurobonds: bonds issued in a country different from the one in whose currency the bond is denominated; for instance, a bond issued in Europe or Asia that pays interest and principal in U.S. dollars.

II.   Bond Valuation

A.   Terminology and characteristics of bonds

1.   A bond is a long-term promissory note that promises to pay the bondholder a predetermined, fixed amount of interest each year until maturity. At maturity, the principal will be paid to the bondholder.

2.   In the case of a firm's insolvency, a bondholder has a priority of claim to the firm's assets before the preferred and common stockholders. Also, bondholders must be paid interest due them before dividends can be distributed to the stockholders.

3.   A bond's par value is the amount that will be repaid by the firm when the bond matures, usually $1,000.

4.   The contractual agreement of the bond specifies a coupon interest rate that is expressed either as a percent of the par value or as a flat amount of interest which the borrowing firm promises to pay the bondholder each year. For example: A $1,000 par value bond specifying a coupon interest rate of 9 percent is equivalent to an annual interest payment of $90.

5.   The bond has a maturity date, at which time the borrowing firm is committed to repay the loan principal.

6.   An indenture (or trust deed) is the legal agreement between the firm issuing the bonds and the bond trustee who represents the bondholders. It provides the specific terms of the bond agreement such as the rights and responsibilities of both parties.

7.   The current yield on a bond refers to the ratio of annual interest payment to the bond is market price.

8. Bond ratings

    a. Bond ratings are simply judgments about the future risk potential of the bond in question. Bond ratings are extremely important in that a firm's bond rating tells much about the cost of funds and the firm's access to the debt market.

    b. Three primary rating agencies exist-- Moody's, Standard and Poor's, and Fitch Investor Services.

    c. The different ratings and their implications are described.

III. Definitions of value

A. Book value is the value of an asset shown on a firm's balance sheet which is determined by its historical cost rather than its current worth.

B. Liquidation value is the amount that could be realized if an asset is sold individually and not as part of a going concern.

C. Market value is the observed value of an asset in the marketplace where buyers and sellers negotiate an acceptable price for the asset.

D. Intrinsic value is the value based upon the expected cash flows from the investment, the riskiness of the asset, and the investor's required rate of return. It is the value in the eyes of the investor and is the same as the present value of expected future cash flows to be received from the investment.

IV. Valuation: An Overview

A. Value is a function of three elements:

    1. The amount and timing of the asset's expected cash flow

    2. The riskiness of these cash flows

3.   The investors' required rate of return for undertaking the investment

B.   Expected cash flows are used in measuring the returns from an investment.

C.   Riskiness of the cash flows

   1.   Risk can be defined as the possible variation in cash flow about an expected cash flow.

   2.   Statistically, risk may be measured by the standard deviation about the expected cash flow.

D.   Procedure for asset valuation

$$V = \sum_{t=1}^{N} \frac{\$C_t}{(1+k)^t}$$

   where C_t =   the cash flow to be received at time t
   V   =   the intrinsic value or present value of an asset producing expected future cash flows, C_t, in years 1 through N
   k   =   the investor's required rate of return
   N   =   the number of periods

V.   Procedure for valuing a bond

A.   The value of a bond is simply the present value of the future interest payments and maturity value discounted at the bondholder's required rate of return. This may be expressed as:

$$V_b = \sum_{t=1}^{N} \frac{\$I_t}{(1+k_b)^t} + \frac{\$M}{(1+k_b)^N}$$

   where I_t =   the dollar interest to be received in each payment
   M   =   the par value of the bond at maturity

	k_b	=	the required rate of return for the bondholder
	N	=	the number of periods to maturity

In other words, we are discounting the expected future cash flows to the present at the appropriate discount rate (required rate of return).

B.   If interest payments are received semiannually (as with most bonds) the valuation equation becomes:

$$V_b = \sum_{t=1}^{N} \frac{\frac{\$I_t}{2}}{\left(1+\frac{k_b}{2}\right)^t} + \frac{\$M}{\left(1+\frac{k_b}{2}\right)^{2N}}$$

VI.   Bondholder's Expected Rate of Return

A.   The bondholder's expected rate of return is the rate the investor will earn if the bond is held to maturity, provided of course that the company issuing the bond does not default on the payments.

B.   We compute the bondholder's expected rate of return by finding the discount rate that gets the present value of the future interest payments and principal payment just equal to the bond's current market price.

VI.   Bond Value: Three Important Relationships

A.   First relationship

A decrease in interest rates (required rates of return) will cause the value of a bond to increase; an interest rate increase will cause a decrease in value. The change in value caused by changing interest rates is called <u>interest rate risk</u>.

B.   Second relationship

1.   If the bondholder's required rate of return (current interest rate) equals the coupon interest rate, the bond will sell at par, or maturity value.

2. If the current interest rate exceeds the bond's coupon rate, the bond will sell below par value, or at a "discount."

3. If the current interest rate is less than the bond's coupon rate, the bond will sell above par value, or at a "premium."

C. Third relationship

As the maturity date approaches, the market value of a bond approaches its par value.

1. The premium bond sells for less as maturity approaches.

2. The discount bond sells for more as maturity approaches.

D. Fourth relationship

A bondholder owning a long-term bond is exposed to greater interest rate risk than when owning a short-term bonds.

E. Fifth relationship

The sensitivity of a bond's value to changing interest rates depends not only on the length of time to maturity, but also on the pattern of cash flows provided by the bond.

1. The duration of a bond is simply a measure of the responsiveness of its price to a change in interest rates. The greater the relative percentage change in a bond price in response to a given percentage change in the interest rate, the longer the duration.

2. Calculating duration

$$\text{duration} = \frac{\sum\limits_{t=1}^{n} \dfrac{tC_t}{(1+k_b)^t}}{P_0}$$

where
$$
\begin{aligned}
t &= \text{the year the cash flow is to be received} \\
n &= \text{the number of years to maturity} \\
C_t &= \text{The cash flow to be received in year } t \\
k_b &= \text{the bondholder's required rate of return} \\
P_0 &= \text{the bond's present value}
\end{aligned}
$$

Study Problems

1. Gents Clothiers, Inc. has bonds maturing in 6 years and pays 6 percent interest semiannually on a $1000 face value.

    a. If your required rate of return is 10 percent, what is the value of the bond?

    b. How would your answer change if the interest were paid annually?

    SOLUTION

    a. Value of bond if interest is paid semiannually:

        (1) Present value of interest payments:

             $= \$30 \ (PVIFA_{12,5\%}) = \$30 \ (8.863)$

             $= \$265 \ . \ 89$

        (2) Present value of principal:

             $= \$1,000 \ (PVIFA_{12,5\%}) = \$1,000(0.557)$

             $= \$557$

        (3) Present value of the interest and principal

Present value of the interest	$265.89
Present value of the principal	557.00
Value of the bond	$822.89

b.   Value of bond if interest is paid annually:

    (1)   Present value of the interest payments:

$$= \$60 \ (PVIFA_{6,10\%}) = \$60(4.355)$$

$$= \$261.30$$

    (2)   Present value of the principal:

$$= \$1,000 \ (PVIFA_{6,10\%}) = \$1,000(0.564)$$

$$= \$564$$

    (3)   Present value of the interest and principal

Present value of the interest	$261.30
Present value of the principal	564.00
Value of the bond	$825.30

2.   Edge Manufacturing Corporation's bonds are selling in the market for $1,193.96. These 15-year bonds pay 8 percent interest (annually) on a $1,000 par value. If they are purchased at the market price, what is the expected rate of return?

SOLUTION

Expected Rate of Return:

$$\$1,193.96 = \$80 \ (PVIFA_{15,k_b}) + \$1,000 \ (PVIF_{15,k_b})$$

where k_b is the expected rate of return to be solved for by trial and error. Try a 6 percent rate of return. At 6 percent the present value of the interest and principal is equal to

$$\$80(9.712) + \$1,000(0.417) = \$1,193.96$$

The expected rate of return is 6 percent.

(Note: With a financial calculator, there is no need to guess as to the rate. The rate may be determined by the calculator.)

3. The market price is $865.60 for a 5-year, 12 percent bond ($1000 face value) that pays interest semiannually. What is the expected rate of return?

SOLUTION

$865.60 = $60 \ (PVIFA_{10,k_b}) + $1,000 \ (PVIF_{10,k_b})$

where k_b is the expected rate of return (to be solved by trial and error).

Try 8 percent:

$60(6.710) + $1,000(0.463) = $865.60

The required rate of return is 8 percent (on a semiannual basis) or 16% (on an annual basis).

Self Tests

TRUE-FALSE

____ 1. The par value of a bond is essentially independent of the market value of a bond.

____ 2. The only variable that can cause at a particular moment in time the value of a bond to increase or decrease is a change in the bondholder's required rate of return.

____ 3. A bond's value equals the present value of interest and principal the owner will receive.

____ 4. In an efficient market place, the intrinsic value of a security will equal its market value.

____ 5. If the market price of a security is larger than the value assigned to the security by an investor, then the expected rate is greater than the required rate of return.

_____ 6. A bond that is issued at a premium has a coupon interest rate that is higher than the market rate.

_____ 7. The intrinsic value of an asset can be defined as the present value of the asset's expected future cash flows.

_____ 8. Debentures are unsecured long-term debt.

_____ 9. The yield to maturity of a bond is the current value of the bond.

_____ 10. The three items that directly affect the cash flows from owning a bond are the bond's par value, maturity date, and the coupon rate of interest.

MULTIPLE CHOICE

1. For a $1,000 par-value bond carrying an 8% coupon (interest paid quarterly) and having a 10% yield to maturity, the quarterly interest payments would be:

   a. $20.
   b. $30.
   c. $25.
   d. $50.
   e. $10.

2. The par value of a bond:

   a. never equals its market value
   b. is determined by the investor
   c. always equals $1,000
   d. is returned to the investor at maturity

3. The value of a security may be expressed as a function of:

   a. Expected cash flows.
   b. Riskiness of cash flows.
   c. The investor's required rate of return.
   d. a and b only.
   e. a, b, and c.

4. If the market is in equilibrium, the expected rate of return and the required rate of return:

    a. Will be the same.
    b. Will be different.
    c. Have no relationship to each other.

5. If everything else is assumed to be constant, as the investor's required rate of return decreases, the value of a security:

    a. Stays the same.
    b. Increases.
    c. Decreases.
    d. Has no relationship to the investor's required rate of return.

6. In the basic security valuation model

    $$V = \sum_{t=1}^{n} \frac{C_t}{(1+k)^t}$$

    C_t stands for:

    a. the investor's required rate of return
    b. cash flow to be received in year t.
    c. the intrinsic value of an asset producing expected future cash flows
    d. None of the above

7. A bond can be issued at:

    a. a discount.
    b. a premium
    c. par.
    d. all of the above.

8.   Kohr Company issued $1,000 par value bonds at 102. The bonds pay 12% interest annually and mature in 30 years. The market rate of interest is: (round to the nearest hundredth of a percent)

    a.   12.00%
    b.   11.76%
    c.   10.12%
    d.   11.29%
    e.   cannot be determined from information given

9.   Which of the following is generally not a characteristic of a bond?

    a.   voting rights
    b.   par value
    c.   claims on assets and income
    d.   indenture

SOLUTIONS TO SELECTED SET B PROBLEMS (See text for problems.)

7-1B.   Value (V_b)

$$= \sum_{t=1}^{10} \frac{\$90}{(1+.15)^t} + \frac{\$1,000}{(1+.15)^{10}}$$

$$= \$90(5.018) + \$1,000\,(.247)$$

$$= \$451.62 + \$247.00$$

$$= \$698.62$$

10	N
15	I/Y
90	PMT
1000	FV
CPT	PV

$\rightarrow$ ANSWER -698.87

7-3B. $$\$950 = \sum_{t=1}^{16} \frac{\$45}{(1+\bar{k}b/2)^t} + \frac{\$1,000}{(1+\bar{k}_b/2)^{16}}$$

At 5%: $45(10.838) + $1,000(0.458) = $945.71

At 4%: $45(11.652) + $1,000(0.534) = $1,058.34

Interpolation:

$$\text{Expected rate of return} = 4\% + \left(\frac{\$108.34}{\$112.63}\right)(1\%) = 4.96\%$$

16	N		
950	+/-	PV	
45	PMT		
1000	FV		
CPT	I/Y	→	ANSWER 4.96

The rate is equivalent to 9.92 percent annual rate, compounded semiannually or 10.17 percent ($1.0496^2 - 1$) compounded annually.

7-7B.

a. Value
Par Value	$1,000.00
Coupon	$ 80.00
Required Rate of Return	0.07
Years to Maturity	20
Market Value	$ 1,105.94

b. Value at Alternative Rates of Return
Required Rate of Return	0.10
Market Value	$ 829.73
Required Rate of Return	0.06
Market Value	$1,229.40

c.   As required rates of return change, the price of the bond changes, which is the result of "interest-rate risk." Thus, the greater the investor's required rate of return, the greater will be his/her discount on the bond. Conversely, the less his/her required rate of return below that of the coupon rate, the greater the premium will be.

d.   Value at Alternative Maturity Dates

Years to Maturity	10
Required Rate of Return	0.07
Market Value	$ 1,070.24
Required Rate of Return	0.10
Market Value	$ 877.11
Required Rate of Return	0.06
Market Value	$1,147.20

e.   The longer the maturity of the bond, the greater the interest-rate risk the investor is exposed to, resulting in greater premiums and discounts.

7-10B.

Value Bond A

Par Value	$1,000.00
Coupon	$ 90.00
Required Rate of Return	0.07
Years to Maturity	5
Market Value	$ 1,082.00

Value Bond B

Par Value	$1,000.00
Coupon	$ 60.00
Required Rate of Return	0.07
Years to Maturity	5
Market Value	$ 959.00

Value Bond C

Par Value	$1,000.00
Coupon	$ 120.00
Required Rate of Return	0.07
Years to Maturity	10
Market Value	$ 1,351.18

Value Bond D

Par Value	$1,000.00
Coupon	$ 90.00
Required Rate of Return	0.07
Years to Maturity	15
Market Value	$ 1,182.16

Value Bond E

Par Value	$1,000.00
Coupon	$ 75.00
Required Rate of Return	0.07
Years to Maturity	15
Market Value	$ 1,045.54

Bond	A		B		C		D		E	
Bond value	$1,082		$959		$1,351		$1,182		$1,046	
Years	Ct	*tPV(Ct)	Ct	t*PV(Ct)	Ct	t*PV(Ct)	Ct	t*PV(Ct)	Ct	t*PV(Ct)
1	$90	$84	$60	$56	$120	$112	$90	$84	$75	$70
2	90	157	60	105	120	210	90	157	75	131
3	90	220	60	147	120	294	90	220	75	184
4	90	275	60	183	120	366	90	275	75	229
5	1,090	3,886	1,060	3,779	120	428	90	321	75	267
6					120	480	90	360	75	300
7					120	523	90	392	75	327
8					120	559	90	419	75	349
9					120	587	90	441	75	367
10					1,120	5,694	90	458	75	381
11							90	470	75	392
12							90	480	75	400
13							90	486	75	405
14							90	489	75	407
15							1,090	5,926	1,075	5,844
Sum of t*PV(Ct)	4,622		4,270		9,252		10,977		10,053	
Duration	4.27		4.45		6.85		9.29		9.62	

CHAPTER 8

Valuation and Characteristics of Stock

Orientation: This chapter continues the introduction of concepts underlying asset valuation began in Chapter 6. We are specifically concerned with valuing preferred stock and common stock. We also look at the concept of a stockholder's expected rate of return on an investment.

I.   Preferred Stock

   A.   Features of preferred stock

      1.   Owners of preferred stock receive dividends instead of interest.

      2.   Most preferred stocks are perpetuities (non-maturing).

      3.   Multiple classes, each having different characteristics, can be issued.

      4.   Preferred stock has priority over common stock with regard to claims on assets in the care of bankruptcy.

      5.   Most preferred stock carries a cumulative feature that requires all past unpaid preferred stock dividends to be paid before any common stock dividends are declared.

      6.   Preferred stock may contain other protective provisions.

      7.   Preferred stock contain provisions to convert to a predetermined number of shares of common stock.

8. Some preferred stock contains provisions for an adjustable rate of return.

9. The participation feature allows preferred stockholders to participate in earnings beyond the payment of the stated dividend.

10. PIK preferred stands for pay-in-kind preferred stock, meaning the investor receives more preferred stock instead of dividends for a given period of time. Eventually cash dividends are paid.

11. Retirement features for preferred stock are frequently included.

    a. Callable preferred refers to a feature which allows preferred stock to be called or retired, like a bond.

    b. A sinking fund provision requires the firm periodically to set aside an amount of money for the retirement of its preferred stock.

B. Valuation of preferred stock (V_{ps}):
The value of a preferred stock equals the present value of all future dividends. If the stock is nonmaturing, where dividends are expected in equal amount each year in perpetuity, the value may be calculated as follows:

$$V_{ps} = \frac{\text{annual dividend}}{\text{required rate of return}} = \frac{D}{k_{ps}}$$

II. Common Stock

A. Features of Common Stock

1. As owners of the corporation, common shareholders have the right to the residual income and assets after bondholders and preferred stockholders have been paid.

2.   Common stock shareholders are generally the only security holders with the right to elect the board of directors.

3.   Preemptive rights entitles the common shareholder to maintain a proportionate share of ownership in the firm.

4.   Common stock shareholders liability as owners of the corporation is limited to the amount of their investment.

5.   Common stock's value is equal to the present value of all future cash flows expected to be received by the stockholder.

B.   Valuing common stock

      1.   Company growth occurs either by:

           a.   The infusion of new capital.

           b.   The retention of earnings, which we call internal growth. The internal growth rate of a firm equals:

$$\text{Return on equity} \times \binom{\text{Percentage of earnings}}{\text{retained within the firm}}$$

      2.   Although the bondholder and preferred stockholder are promised a specific amount each year, the dividend for common stock is based on the profitability of the firm and the management's decision either to pay dividends or retain profits for reinvestment.

      3.   The common dividend typically increases along with the growth in corporate earnings.

      4.   The earnings growth of a firm should be reflected in a higher price for the firm's stock.

5. In finding the value of a common stock (V_{cs}), we should discount all future expected dividends (D_1, D_2, D_3, ..., $D_{\bullet}$) to the present at the required rate of return for the stockholder (k_c). That is:

$$V_{cs} = \frac{D_1}{(1 + k_{cs})^1} + \frac{D_2}{(1 + k_{cs})^2} + ... + \frac{D_{\bullet}}{(1 + k_{cs})^{\bullet}}$$

6. If we assume that the amount of dividend is increasing by a constant growth rate each year,

$$D_t = D_0 (1 + g)^t$$

where g   = the growth rate

D_0 = the most recent dividend payment

If the growth rate, g, is the same each year and is less than the required rate of return, K_c, the valuation equation for common stock can be reduced to

$$V_{cs} = \frac{D_1}{k_{cs} - g} = \frac{D_0 (1 + g)}{k_{cs} - g}$$

III. Shareholder's Expected Rate of Return

A. The shareholder's expected rate of return is of great interest to financial mangers because it tells about the investor's expectations.

B. Preferred stockholder's expected rate of return.
    If we know the market price of a preferred stock and the amount of the dividends to be received, the expected rate of return from the investment can be determined as follows:

$$\text{expected rate of return} = \frac{\text{annual dividend}}{\text{market price of the stock}}$$

or

$$\bar{k}_{ps} = \frac{D}{P_0}$$

C. Common stockholder's expected rate of return

    1. The expected rate of return for common stock can be calculated from the valuation equations discussed earlier.

    2. Assuming that dividends are increasing at a constant annual growth rate (g), we can show that the expected rate of return for common stock, K_c is

$$\bar{k}_{cs} = \left(\frac{\text{dividend in year 1}}{\text{market price}}\right) + \left(\begin{array}{c}\text{growth}\\\text{rate}\end{array}\right)$$

$$= \frac{D_1}{P_0} = g$$

Since dividend ÷ price is the "dividend yield," the

$$\text{Expected rate of return} = \left(\begin{array}{c}\text{dividend}\\\text{yield}\end{array}\right) + \left(\begin{array}{c}\text{growth}\\\text{rate}\end{array}\right)$$

Study Problems

1. The preferred stock of Craft Company pays a $3 dividend. What is the value of the stock if your required rate of return is 8 percent?

SOLUTION

$$\text{Value of preferred stock} = \frac{\text{dividend}}{\text{required rate of return}}$$

$$P_0 = \frac{\$3}{0.08} = \$37.50$$

2. Universal Machines' common stock paid $1.50 in dividends last year and dividends are expected to grow indefinitely at an annual 6 percent rate. What is the value of the stock if you require a 12 percent return?

SOLUTION

$$\text{Value } (P_0) = \frac{\text{dividend in year 1}}{\text{required rate - growth rate}} = \frac{D_1}{k_{cs} - g}$$

where $D_1 = D_0(1+g) = \$1.50(1 + 0.06) = \$1.59$

Then,

$$P_0 = \frac{\$1.59}{0.12 - 0.06} = \$26.50$$

3. Texas Mining Company's common stock is selling for $35. The stock paid dividends of $2.50 last year and has a projected growth rate of 10 percent. If you buy the stock at the market price, what is the expected rate of return?

SOLUTION

Expected rate of return (k_{cs}):

$$k_{cs} = \frac{\text{dividend in year 1}}{\text{price}} + \frac{\text{growth}}{\text{rate}} = \frac{D_1}{P_0} + g$$

where $D_1 = D_0 (1+g) = \$2.50 (1 + 0.10) = \$2.75$

$P_0 = \$35$

$$k_{cs} = \frac{\$2.75}{\$35.00} + 0.10 = 0.1785$$

$$= 17.85\%$$

4. Idalou Power Company's preferred stock is selling for $25 in the market and pays $2.50 in dividends.

a. What is the expected rate of return on the stock?

b.   If your required rate of return is 12 percent, what is the fair value of the stock for you?

c.   Should you acquire the stock?

SOLUTION

a.   Expected rate of return $= \dfrac{\$\,2.50}{\$25.00} = 10\%$

b.   Value of the stock to you $= \dfrac{\$\,2.50}{0.12} = \$20.83$

c.   Since your required rate of return is higher than the expected rate of return, you should not acquire it.

5.   The market price of International Electric Corporation is $40. The price at the end of one year is expected to be $45. Dividends for next year should be $2.50. What is the expected rate of return for a single holding period of one year?

SOLUTION

current price (P$_0$) =

$$\dfrac{\text{dividend in year 1}}{1 + \text{expected rate of return}} + \dfrac{\text{price in year 1}}{1 + \text{expected rate of return}}$$

$$\dfrac{\text{expected}}{\text{return}} = \dfrac{\text{dividend in year 1} + \text{price in year 1}}{\text{current price}} - 1$$

$$\dfrac{\text{expected}}{\text{return}} = \dfrac{\$2.50 + \$45.00}{\$40.00} - 1 = 18.75\%$$

6.   The Rose Corporation expects to earn $4 per share this year, of which 50 percent will be retained within the firm for investment purposes and 50 percent paid in the form of dividends to the stockholders. Management expects to earn a 20-percent return on any funds retained. The investor's required rate of return is 14 percent. Using the PVDG model, calculate the value of the stock.

8-7

SOLUTION

Using equation (8A-6) in the text, which reads

$$V_c = \frac{EPS_1}{k_{cs}} + \frac{NPV_1}{k_{cs} - g}$$

where $NPV1 = \left(\frac{rEPS_1 ROE}{k_{cs}}\right) - rEPS_1,$

the value of the stock may be computed as follows:

$$NPV_1 = \left(\frac{(.5)(\$4)(.20)}{.14}\right) - (.5)(\$4) = \$2.86 - \$2.00 = \$.86$$

and, therefore:

$$V_c = \frac{\$4}{.14} + \frac{.86}{14 - (.50)(.20)} = \$28.57 + \$21.50$$

$$= \$50.07$$

Self Tests

TRUE-FALSE

_____ 1. Preferred stock has some characteristics of both common stock and bonds.

_____ 2. Cumulative preferred stockholders receive dividends only after common stock dividends are paid.

_____ 3. An assumption necessary in the model for common stock valuation

$$P_o = \frac{D_1}{k_{cs} - g}$$

is that the amount of the dividend increases by a constant percent each year.

_____ 4. Paid-in-kind preferred stock receives initial dividends of common stock.

_____ 5. A company may issue multiple classes of stock.

_____ 6. The term "growth" when used in the context of a valuation model includes growth from reinvesting profits and from issuing stock.

_____ 7. Preferred stock, unlike bonds, cannot be converted into common stock.

_____ 8. The value of a preferred stock is the future value of the stock at maturity.

_____ 9. Common stock represents a claim on residual income.

_____ 10. The constant-growth common stock valuation model is defined as:

$$\text{common stock value} = \frac{\text{required rate of return}}{\text{dividend in year 1}}$$

assuming the dividends grow each year at a constant rate.

MULTIPLE CHOICE

1. A company's preferred stock pays $5.00 in annual dividends. If your required rate of return is 13%, how much will you be willing to pay for one share?

    a. $38.46
    b. $26.26
    c. $65.46
    d. $46.38

2. The most recent dividend paid by Xeron on its common stock was $1.50 (annual). The required rate of return for the security is 6%. Growth is anticipated to be at 4% annually. The market price of the stock should be:

    a. $78.
    b. $100.
    c. $50.
    d. $150.
    e. $75.

3. Which of the following provisions is (are) unique to preferred stock and usually not available to common stockholders?

   a. the cumulative feature
   b. A claim on assets
   c. A claim on income
   d. All of the above are available to both common and preferred stockholders

4. The quarterly dividends for adjustable rate preferred stock may be determined by:

   a. the three-month Treasury bill rate
   b. the 10-year Treasury bond rate
   c. the 20 year Treasury bond rate
   d. All of the above

5. The income received by the holder of a preferred stock is similar to the income received from which other financial asset in terms of it being a constant amount each year?

   a. Common Stocks
   b. Bonds
   c. Both A and B
   d. None of the above

SOLUTIONS TO SELECTED SET B PROBLEMS (See text for problems.)

8-3B. $\text{Value}(V_{ps}) = \dfrac{.16 \times \$100}{.12}$

$= \dfrac{\$16}{.12}$

$= \$133.33$

8-5B. (a) Expected return $= \dfrac{\text{Dividend}}{\text{Price}} = \dfrac{\$3.25}{\$38.50} = .0844 = 8.44\%$

(b) Given your 8 percent required rate of return, the stock is worth $40.62 to you

$$\text{Value} = \dfrac{\text{Dividend}}{\text{Required Rate of Return}} = \dfrac{\$3.25}{.08} = \$40.625$$

Since the expected rate of return (8.44%) is greater than your required rate of return (8%) or since the current market price ($38.50) is less than $40.62, the stock is undervalued and you should buy.

8-8B. Value (V_{cs}) $= \dfrac{\text{Last Year Dividend (1 + Growth Rate)}}{\text{(Required Rate - Growth Rate)}}$

$$V_{cs} = \dfrac{\$3.75(1 + .06)}{.20 - .06}$$

$$V_{cs} = \$28.39$$

8-10B. Expected Rate of Return $(\bar{k}_c) =$

$$\dfrac{\text{Last Year Dividend (1 + Growth Rate)}}{\text{Price}} + \text{Growth Rate}$$

$$\bar{k}_{cs} = \dfrac{\$3.00(1.085)}{\$33.84} + 0.085 = 0.181 = 18.1\%$$

CHAPTER 9

Capital Budgeting Decision Criteria

<u>Orientation</u>: Capital budgeting involves the decision making process with respect to investment in fixed assets; specifically, it involves measuring the incremental cash flows associated with investment proposals and evaluating the attractiveness of these cash flows relative to the project's costs. This chapter focuses on the various decision criteria. It also examines how to deal with complications in the capital budgeting process including mutually exclusive projects and capital rationing.

I.   Methods for evaluating projects

      A.   The payback period method

            1.   The payback period of an investment tells the number of years required to recover the initial investment. The payback period is calculated by adding the cash flows up until they are equal to the initial fixed investment.

            2.   Although this measure does, in fact, deal with cash flows and is easy to calculate and understand, it ignores any cash flows that occur after the payback period and does not consider the time value of money within the payback period.

            3.   To deal with the criticism that the payback period ignores the time value of money some firms use the discounted payback period. The discounted payback period method is similar to the traditional payback period except that it uses discounted net cash flows rather than actual undiscounted net cash flows in calculating the payback period.

4. The discounted payback period is defined as the number of years needed to recover the initial cash outlay from the discounted net cash flows.

B. Present-value methods

1. The net present value of an investment project is the present value of the cash inflows less the present value of the cash outflows. By assigning negative values to cash outflows, it becomes

$$NPV = \sum_{t=1}^{n} \frac{ACF_t}{(1+k)^t} - IO$$

where ACF_t = the annual after-tax cash flow in time period t (this can take on either positive or negative values)

k = the required rate of return or appropriate discount rate or cost of capital

IO = the initial cash outlay

n = the project's expected life

a. The acceptance criteria are

accept if $NPV \geq 0$

reject if $NPV < 0$

b. The advantage of this approach is that it takes the time value of money into consideration in addition to dealing with cash flows.

2. The profitability index is the ratio of the present value of the expected future net cash flows to the initial cash outlay, or

$$\text{profitability index} = \frac{\sum_{t-1}^{n} \frac{ACF_t}{(1+k)^t}}{IO}$$

   a. The acceptance criteria are

   accept if PI $\geq$ 1.0

   reject if PI $<$ 1.0

   b. The advantages of this method are the same as those for the net present value.

   c. Either of these present-value methods will give the same accept-reject decisions to a project.

C. The internal rate of return is the discount rate that equates the present value of the project's future net cash flows with the project's initial outlay. Thus the internal rate of return is represented by IRR in the equation below:

$$IO = \sum_{t=1}^{n} \frac{ACF_t}{(1+IRR)^t}$$

   1. The acceptance-rejection criteria are:

   accept if IRR $\geq$ required rate of return

   reject if IRR $<$ required rate of return

   The required rate of return is often taken to be the firm's cost of capital.

2.   The advantages of this method are that it deals with cash flows and recognizes the time value of money; however, the procedure is rather complicated and time-consuming. The net present value profile allows you to graphically understand the relationship between the internal rate of return and NPV. A net present value profile is simply a graph showing how a project's net present value changes as the discount rate changes. The IRR is the discount rate at which the NPV equals zero.

3.   The primary drawback of the internal rate of return deals with the reinvestment rate assumption it makes. The IRR implicitly assumes that the cash flows received over the life of the project can be reinvested at the IRR while the NPV assumes that cash flows over the life of the project are reinvested at the required rate of return. Since the NPV makes the preferred reinvestment rate assumption it is the preferred decision technique. The modified internal rate of return (MIRR) allows the decision maker the intuitive appeal of the IRR coupled with the ability to directly specify the appropriate reinvestment rate.

      a.   To calculate the MIRR we take all the annual after tax cash **in**flow, $ACIF_t$'s, and find their future value at the end of the project's life - this is called the terminal value or TV. All cash **out**flows, $ACOF_t$, are then discounted back to present at the required rate of return. The MIRR is the discount rate that equates the present value of the cash outflows with the present value of the project's terminal value.

      b.   If the MIRR is greater than or equal to the required rate of return the project should be accepted.

1. The cost of new machinery for a given investment project will be $100,000. Incremental cash flows after taxes will be $40,000 in years 1 and 2 and will be $60,000 in year 3. What is the payback period for this project, and if acceptable projects must recover the initial investment in 2.5 years, should this project be accepted or rejected?

SOLUTION

After 2 years they will have recovered $80,000 of the $100,000 outlay and they expect to recover an additional $60,000 in the third year. Thus, the payback period becomes

$$2 \text{ years} + \frac{\$20,000}{\$60,000} = 2.33 \text{ years}$$

2.33 years $<$ 2.5 years. Therefore, accept the project.

2. A given investment project will cost $50,000. Incremental annual cash flows after taxes are expected to be $10,000 per year for the life of the investment, which is 5 years. There will be no salvage value at the end of the 5 years. The required rate of return is 14%. On the basis of the profitability index method, should the investment be accepted?

SOLUTION

PV of cash flow = $10,000(3.433) = $34,330

PV of cash outlay = $50,000

$$PI = \frac{\$34,330}{\$50,000} = 0.6866 < 1$$

Therefore, the project should be rejected.

3. Determine the internal rate of return on the following projects:

    a. An initial outlay of $10,000 resulting in a cash flow of $2,146 at the end of each year for the next 10 years

    b. An initial outlay of $10,000 resulting in a cash flow of $1,960 at the end of each year for the next 20 years

    c. An initial outlay of $10,000 resulting in a cash flow of $1,396 at the end of each year for the next 12 years

    d. An initial outlay of $10,000 resulting in a cash flow of $3,197 at the end of each year for the next 5 years

SOLUTION

(a) $IO = ACF_t [PVIFA_{IRR\%,t\ yrs}]$

    $\$10,000 = \$2,146 [PVIFA_{IRR\%,10\ yrs}]$

    $4.659 = PVIFA_{IRR\%,10\ yrs}$

    Thus, IRR $= 17\%$

(b) $\$10,000 = \$1,960 [PVIFA_{IRR\%,20\ yrs}]$

    $5.102 = PVIFA_{IRR\%,20\ yrs}$

    Thus, IRR $= 19\%$

(c) $\$10,000 = \$1,396 [PVIFA_{IRR\%,12\ yrs}]$

    $7.163 = PVIFA_{IRR\%,12\ yrs}]$

    Thus, IRR $= 9\%$

(d)　　$10,000　　=　　$3,197 $[\text{PVIFA}_{\text{IRR}\%,5 \text{ yrs}}]$

　　　　3.128　　=　　$\text{PVIFA}_{\text{IRR}\%,5 \text{ yrs}}$

　　　　Thus, IRR　=　18%

Self-Tests

TRUE/FALSE

_____ 1. The higher the discount rate, the more valued is the proposal with the early cash flows.

_____ 2. The net present value of a project will equal zero whenever the internal rate of return equals the required rate of return.

_____ 3. The net present value of a project will equal zero whenever the payback period of a project equals the required payback period.

_____ 4. The profitability index provides the same accept/reject decision result as the net present value method.

MULTIPLE CHOICE

1. Which of the following considers the time value of money?

　　a.　Payback method.
　　b.　Profitability index.
　　c.　None of the above.

2.	Which of the following is a non-discounted cash flow approach?

    a.	Payback period.
    b.	Profitability index.
    c.	Internal rate of return.
    d.	Net present value.

3.	The payback period method will always lead to the same accept or reject decision as will the:

    a.	Profitability index.
    b.	Net-present-value method.
    c.	Internal-rate-of-return method.
    d.	None of the above.

4.	If the internal rate of return is greater than the required rate of return

    a.	the present value of all the cash flows will be less than the initial outlay.
    b.	the payback will be less than the life of the investment.
    c.	the project should be accepted.
    d.	a and c.

5.	If the cash flow pattern for a project has two sign reversals, then there can be as many as ____ positive IRR's.

    a.	1
    b.	2
    c.	3
    d.	4

9-1B.(a)   IO   = ACF_t $[PVIF_{IRR\%,t\ yrs}]$

           \$10,000   =   \$19,926 $[PVIF_{IRR\%,8\ yrs}]$

           0.502   = $PVIF_{IRR\%,8\ yrs}$

           Thus, IRR =   9%

     (b)   \$10,000   =   \$20,122 $[PVIF_{IRR\%,12\ yrs}]$

           0.497   = $PVIF_{IRR\%,12\ yrs}$

           Thus, IRR =   6%

     (c)   \$10,000   =   \$121,000 $[PVIF_{IRR\%,22\ yrs}]$

           0.083   = $PVIF_{IRR\%,22\ yrs}$

           Thus, IRR =   12%

     (d)   \$10,000   =   \$19,254 $[PVIF_{IRR\%,5\ yrs}]$

           .519   = $PVIF_{IRR\%,5\ yrs}$

           Thus, IRR =   14%

9-5B. (a)   Payback Period = $160,000/$40,000 = 4 years

Discounted Payback Period Calculations:

Year	Undiscounted Cash Flows	PVIF$_{10\%,n}$	Discounted Cash Flows	Cumulative Discounted Cash Flows
0	-$160,000	1.000	-$160,000	-$160,000
1	40,000	.909	36,360	-123,640
2	40,000	.826	33,040	-90,600
3	40,000	.751	30,040	-60,560
4	40,000	.683	27,320	-33,240
5	40,000	.621	24,840	-8,400
6	40,000	.564	22,560	14,160

Discounted Payback Period = 5.0 + 8,400/22,560 = 5.37 years.

(b) $$NPV = \sum_{t=1}^{6} \frac{\$40,000}{(1+.10)^t} - \$160,000$$

$$= \$40,000 \,(4.355) - \$160,000$$

$$= \$174,200 - \$160,000 = \$14,200$$

(c) $$PI = \frac{\$174,200}{\$160,000}$$

$$= 1.0888$$

(d) $$\$160,000 = \$40,000 \,[PVIFA_{IRR\%,6\ yrs}]$$

$$4.000 = PVIFA_{IRR\%,6\ yrs}$$

$$IRR = \text{about } 13\% \ (12.978\%)$$

9-7B. Project A:

Payback Period = 2 years

Project B:

Payback Period = 2 years + \$1,000/\$3,000 = 2.33 years

Project C:

Payback Period = 3 years + \$1,000/\$2,000 = 3.5 years

9-9B. Project A:

$$\$75,000 = \frac{\$10,000}{(1 + IRR_A)^1} + \frac{\$10,000}{(1 + IRR_A)^2} + \frac{\$30,000}{(1 + IRR_A)^3}$$
$$+ \frac{\$25,000}{(1 + IRR_A)^4} + \frac{\$30,000}{(1 + IRR_A)^5}$$

Try 10%

$$\$75,000 = \$10,000(.909) + \$10,000(.826) + \$30,000(.751)$$
$$+ \$25,000(.683) + \$30,000(.621)$$

$$= \$9,090 + \$8,260 + \$22,530 + \$17,075 + \$18,630$$

$$= \$75,585$$

Try 11%

$75,000 $=$ $10,000(.901) + $10,000(.812) +$30,000(.731)
$\quad$ + $25,000(.659) + $30,000(.593)

$\quad$ $=$ $9,010 + $8,120 + $21,930+ $16,475 + $17,790

$\quad$ $=$ $73,325

Thus, IRR $=$ just over 10%

Project B:

$95,000 $=$ $25,000 [PVIFA$_{IRR\%,5\ yrs}$]

3.80 $=$ PVIFA$_{IRR\%,5\ yrs}$

Thus, IRR $=$ just below 10%

Project C:

$395,000 $=$ $150,000 [PVIFA$_{IRR\%,3\ yrs}$]

2.633 $=$ PVIFA$_{IRR\%,3\ yrs}$

Thus, IRR $=$ just below 7%

CHAPTER 10

Cash Flows and Other Topics
in Capital Budgeting

Orientation: Capital budgeting involves the decision-making process with respect to investment in fixed assets; specifically, it involves measuring the incremental cash flows associated with investment proposals and evaluating the attractiveness of these cash flows relative to the project's costs. This chapter focuses on the estimation of those cash flows based on various decision criteria, and how to adjust for the riskiness of a given project or combination of projects.

I.   What criteria should we use in the evaluation of alternative investment proposals?

    A.   Use cash flows rather than accounting profits because cash flows allow us to correctly analyze the time element of the flows.

    B.   Examine cash flows on an after-tax basis because they are the flows available to shareholders.

    C.   Include only the incremental cash flows resulting from the investment decision. Ignore all other flows.

    D.   In deciding which cash flows are relevant we want to:

        1.   Use cash flows rather than accounting profits as our measurement tool.

2. Think incrementally, looking at the company with and without the new project, only incremental after tax cash flows are relevant.

3. Beware of cash flows diverted from existing products, again, looking at the firm as a whole with the new product versus without the new product.

4. Bring in working capital needs. Take account of the fact that a new project may involve the additional investment in working capital.

5. Consider incremental expenses.

6. Do not include such costs as incremental cash flows.

7. Account for opportunity costs.

8. Decide if overhead costs are truly incremental cash flows.

9. Ignore interest payments and financing flows.

II. Measure cash flows. We are interested in measuring the incremental after-tax cash flows resulting from the investment proposal. In general, there will be three major sources of cash flows: initial outlays, differential cash flows over the project's life, and terminal cash flows.

    A. Initial outlays include whatever cash flows are necessary to get the project in running order, for example:

        1. The installed cost of the asset

        2. In the case of a replacement proposal, the selling price of the old machine plus (or minus) any tax gain (or loss) offsetting the initial outlay

3.   Any expense items (for example, training) necessary for the operation of the proposal

4.   Any other non-expense cash outlays required, such as increased working-capital needs

B.   Differential cash flows over the project's life include the incremental after-tax flows over the life of the project, for example:

1.   Added revenue (less added selling expenses) for the proposal

2.   Any labor and/or material savings incurred

3.   Increases in overhead incurred

4.   These values are measured on an after-tax basis, thus allowing for the tax savings (or loss) from incremental increase (or decrease) in depreciation to be included.

5.   A word of warning not to include financing charges (such as interest or preferred stock dividends), for they are implicitly taken care of in the discounting process.

C.   Terminal cash flows include any incremental cash flows that result at the termination of the project; for example:

1.   The project's salvage value plus (or minus) any taxable gains or losses associated with the project

2.   Any terminal cash flow needed, perhaps disposal of obsolete equipment

3.   Recovery of any non-expense cash outlays associated with the project, such as recovery of increased working-capital needs associated with the proposal

III. Mutually exclusive projects: Although the IRR and the present-value methods will, in general, give consistent accept-reject decisions, they may not rank projects identically. This becomes important in the case of mutually exclusive projects.

   A.   A project is mutually exclusive if acceptance of it precludes the acceptance of one or more projects. Then, in this case, the project's relative ranking becomes important.

   B.   Ranking conflicts come as a result of the different assumptions on the reinvestment rate on funds released from the proposals.

   C.   Thus, when conflicting ranking of mutually exclusive projects results from the different reinvestment assumptions, the decision boils down to which assumption is best.

   D.   In general, the net present value method is considered to be theoretically superior.

IV. Capital rationing is the situation in which a budget ceiling or constraint is placed upon the amount of funds that can be invested during a time period.

   A.   Theoretically, a firm should never reject a project that yields more than the required rate of return. Although there are circumstances that may create complicated situations in general, an investment policy limited by capital rationing is less than optimal.

Study Problems

1. The G. Wolfe Corporation is considering replacing one of its bottling machines with a new, more efficient one. The old machine presently has a book value of $75,000 and could be sold for $60,000 The old machine is being depreciated using a simplified straight line method down to zero over the next five years generating depreciation of $15,000 per year. The replacement machine would cost $250,000, and have an expected life of five years after which it could be sold for $20,000. Because of reductions in defects and materials savings, the new machine would produce cash benefits of $100,000 per year before depreciation and taxes. Assume simplified straight line depreciation, a 40 percent marginal tax rate, and a required rate of return of 18 percent, find:

    a. The payback period.
    b. The net present value.
    c. The profitability index.

SOLUTION

Initial Outlay

Outflows:	
Purchase Price	$250,000
Inflows:	
Tax Savings from sale of old machine below	
book value ($75,000 - $60,000) x .40	- 6,000
Salvage Value on Old Machine	-60,000
Net Initial Outlay	$184,000

Differential Annual Cash Flows (Years 1-4)

Savings:	Book Profit	Cash Flow
Cash Savings	$100,000	$100,000
Costs:		
Increased depreciation ($50,000 - $15,000)*	-35,000	
Net Savings Before Taxes	$ 65,000	$100,000
Taxes (40%)	-26,000	-26,000
		$ 74,000

*Note: Annual depreciation on the new machine was calculated by taking the purchase price ($250,000) and dividing by the expected life (5 years).

Terminal Cash Flow (Year 5)

Inflows:	
Differential Cash Flow Year 5	$ 74,000
Salvage Value	20,000
Outflows:	
Taxes due on sale of new machine ($20,000 - 0) x .40	-8,000
	$ 86,000

a. Payback Period $= \dfrac{\$184,000}{\$74,000} = 2.49$ years

b. Net Present Value $= \displaystyle\sum_{t=1}^{4} \dfrac{\$74,000}{(1+.18)^t} + \dfrac{\$86,000}{(1+.18)^5} - \$184,000$

$= \$74,000(2.690) + \$86,000(.437) - \$184,000$

$= \$201,750 + \$37,582 - \$184,000 = \$55,332$

c. The Profitability Index $= 1.3$

2. The Battling Bishops Corporation is considering two mutually exclusive pieces of machinery that perform the same task. The two alternatives available provide the following set of after-tax net cash flows:

Year	Equipment A	Equipment B
0	-$20,000	-$20,000
1	13,000	6,500
2	13,000	6,500
3	13,000	6,500
4		6,500
5		6,500
6		6,500
7		6,500
8		6,500
9		6,500

Equipment A has an expected life of three years, whereas equipment B has an expected life of nine years. Assume a required rate of return of 14 percent.

a. Calculate each project's payback period.

b. Calculate each project's net present value.

c. Calculate each project's internal rate of return.

d. Are these projects comparable?

e. Compare these projects using replacement chains and EAAs. Which project should be selected? Support your recommendation.

SOLUTION

(a)   Payback A = 1.5385 years
Payback B = 3.0769 years

(b) $$NPV_A = \sum_{t=1}^{3} \frac{\$13,000}{(1+0.14)^t} - \$20,000$$

$$= \$13,000 \, (2.322) - \$20,000$$

$$= \$30,186 - \$20,000$$

$$= \$10,186$$

$$NPV_B = \sum_{t=1}^{9} \frac{\$6,500}{(1+0.14)^t} - \$20,000$$

$$= \$6,500 \, (4.946) - \$20,000$$

$$= \$32,149 - \$20,000$$

$$= \$12,149$$

(c) $$\$20,000 = \$13,000 \, [PVIFA_{IRR_A\%,3 \text{ yrs}}]$$

Thus, IRR_A = over 40% (42.75%)

$$\$20,000 = \$6,500 \, [PVIFA_{IRR_B\%,9 \text{ yrs}}]$$

Thus, IRR_B = 29%

(d)   These projects are not comparable because future profitable investment proposals are affected by the decision currently being made. If project A is taken, at its termination the firm could replace the machine and receive additional benefits while acceptance of project B would exclude this possibility.

(e)   Using 3 replacement chains, project A's cash flows would become:

Year	Cash flow
0	-$20,000
1	13,000
2	13,000
3	- 7,000
4	13,000
5	13,000
6	- 7,000
7	13,000
8	13,000
9	13,000

$$NPV_A = \sum_{t=1}^{9} \frac{\$13,000}{(1+0.14)^t} - \$20,000 - \frac{\$20,000}{(1+0.14)^3} - \frac{\$20,000}{(1+0.14)^6}$$

$$= \$13,000(4.946) - \$20,000 - \$20,000\,(0.675) - \$20,000\,(0.456)$$

$$= \$64,298 - \$20,000 - \$13,500 - \$9,120$$

$$= \$21,678$$

The replacement chain analysis indicated that project A should be selected as the replacement chain associated with it has a larger NPV than project B.

Project A's EAA:

Step 1: Calculate the project's NPV (from part b):

$$NPV_A = \$10,186$$

Step 2: Calculate the EAA:

$$EAA_A = NPV / PVIFA_{14\%, 3\ yr.}$$

$$= \$10,186 / 2.322$$

$$= \$4,387$$

Project B's EAA:

Step 1: Calculate the project's NPV (from part b):

$$NPV_B = \$12,149$$

Step 2: Calculate the EAA:

$$EAA_B = NPV / PVIFA_{14\%, 9\ yr.}$$

$$= \$12,149 / 4.946$$

$$= \$2,256$$

Project B should be selected because it has a higher EAA.

Self-Tests

TRUE/FALSE

_____ 1. Cash flow, not income, is what is important in capital budgeting.

_____ 2. Capital rationing occurs because profitable projects must be rejected because of a lack of capital.

_____ 3. Capital rationing is not an optimal capital budgeting strategy.

_____ 4. If two projects are mutually exclusive, the one with the highest expected value should always be chosen, even if it is riskier.

_____ 5. One difference between the NPV and IRR approaches is the reinvestment rate assumption.

MULTIPLE CHOICE

1. Which of the following is important to capital budgeting decisions?

   a. Depreciation method.
   b. Salvage value.
   c. Timing of cash flows.
   d. Taxes.
   e. All of the above.

2. If the federal income tax rate were increased, the result would be to

   a. decrease the net present value.
   b. increase the net present value.
   c. increase the payback period.
   d. a and c.

10-3B. (a) Payback period $= \dfrac{\$47,600}{\$20,278} = 2.35$ years

(b) NPV $= \displaystyle\sum_{t=1}^{n} \dfrac{ACF_t}{(1+k)^t} - IO$

NPV $= \displaystyle\sum_{t=1}^{5} \dfrac{\$20,278}{(1+.17)^t} - \$47,600$

$= \$20,278\,(3.199) - \$47,600$

$= \$64,869.32 - \$47,600$

$= \$17,269.32$

(c) PI $= \dfrac{\displaystyle\sum_{t=1}^{n} \dfrac{ACF_t}{(1+k)^t}}{IO}$

$= \dfrac{\$64,869.32}{\$47,600}$

$= 1.36$

(d) IO $= \displaystyle\sum_{t=1}^{n} \dfrac{ACF_t}{(1+IRR)^t}$

$\$47,600 = \$20,278\,[PVIFA_{IRR\%,5\ yrs}]$

$$2.35 \quad = \quad \text{PVIFA}_{\text{IRR}\%,5 \text{ yrs}}$$

$$\text{IRR} \quad = \quad \text{Just over 32\%}$$

Yes, the NPV > 0, PI > 1.0, IRR > the required rate of return.

10-6B.
   (a)   Initial Outlay

       Outflows:

Purchase price	$ 100,000
Installation Fee	5,000
Training Session Fee	5,000
Increased Inventory	25,000
Net Initial Outlay	$135,000

   (b)   Differential annual cash flows (years 1-9)

Book Profit		Cash Flow
Savings:		
Reduction in labor costs	$25,000	$25,000
Costs:		
Increased Depreciation*	10,500	
Net savings before taxes	$14,500	$25,000
Taxes (.34)	4,930 →	4,930
Annual net cash flow after taxes		$20,700

*Annual Depreciation on the new machine is calculated by taking the purchase price ($100,000) and adding in costs necessary to get the new machine in operating order (the installation fee of $5,000) and dividing by the expected life.

(c)   Terminal Cash flow (year 10)

   Inflows:
Differential flow in year 10	$20,700
Recapture of working capital (inventory)	25,000
Total terminal cash flow	$45,700

(d)   NPV   = $20,700 (PVIFA$_{12\%,9 \text{ yr.}}$) + $45,700 (PVIF$_{12\%, 10 \text{ yr.}}$)
         - $135,000

         = $20,700 (5.382) + $45,700 (.322) - $135,000

         = $108,017 + $14,715 - $230,000

         =   - $107,268

10-7B.
   Initial Outlay
      Outflows:

Purchase price	$ 350,000

   Inflows:

Tax savings from sale of old machine below book value ($100,000-$60,000) (.34)	- 13,600
Salvage value of old machine	- 60,000
Net initial outlay	$ 276,400

   Differential annual cash flows (years 1-4):

	Book profit	Cash flow
Savings: cash savings	$ 100,000	$ 100,000
Costs: increased depreciation		
($70,000 - $20,000)*	- 50,000	
Net savings before taxes	$ 50,000	$ 100,000
Taxes (34%)	- 17,000	- 17,000
Annual net cash flow after taxes		$ 83,000

Terminal cash flow (year 5)

Inflows:

Differential cash flow year 5	$ 83,000
Salvage value	50,000

Outflows: Taxes due on sale of new machine

($50,000-$0) (.34)	- 17,000
Total terminal cash flow	$ 116,000

*Note: Annual depreciation on the new machine was calculated by taking the purchase price ($350,000), and dividing by the expected life (5 years).

(a) Payback period = 3.33

(b) NPV $= \sum_{t=1}^{4} \dfrac{\$83,000}{(1+.15)^t} + \dfrac{116,000}{(1+.15)^5} - \$276,400$

$= \$83,000\,(2.855) + \$116,000\,(0.497) - \$276,400$

$= \$236,965 + \$57,652 - \$276,400$

$= \$18,217$

(c) $\dfrac{\$294,617}{\$276,400}$ = 1.0659

(d) Try 17%

$276,400 = $83,000 (2.743) + $116,000 (.456)
            = $227,669 + $52,896
            = $280,565

Try 18%

$276,400 = $83,000 (2.690) + $116,000 (.437)
            = $223,270 + $50,692
            = $273,962

Thus, IRR = between 17-18%

10-9B.

Initial outlay
Outflows:

Purchase price	$ 100,000
Increased taxes, recapture of depreciation ($17,000-$12,500) (.34)	1,530
Total outflows	$ 101,530

Inflows:

Salvage value of old machine	- 17,000
Net initial outlay	$ 84,530

Differential annual cash flows (years 1-4)

	Book profit	Cash flow
Savings: cash savings	$ 30,000	$ 30,000
Costs: increased depreciation ($20,000-2,500)*	- 17,500	
Net savings before taxes	$12,500	$ 30,000
Taxes (.34)	- 4,250 →	- 4,250
Annual net cash flow after taxes		$ 25,750

Terminal cash flow (year 5)
 Inflows
  Differential cash flow year 5 $ 25,750
  Salvage value   35,000
 Outflows
  Taxes on sale of new machine ($35,000 x .34)   -11,900
   Total terminal cash flow $ 48,850

*Note: Annual Depreciation on the new machine is calculated by taking the purchase price ($100,000) and dividing by the expected life (5 years).

(a) Payback period = 3.28 years

(b) NPV $= \displaystyle\sum_{t=1}^{4} \frac{\$25,750}{(1+0.20)^t} + \frac{\$48,850}{(1+0.20)^5} - \$84,530$

    $=$ $\$25,750\,(2.589) + \$48,850\,(0.402) - \$84,530$

    $=$ $\$66,666.75 + \$19,637.70 - \$84,530$

    $=$ $\$1,774.45$

(c)   PI $= \dfrac{\$86,304.45}{\$84,530} = 1.021$

(d)   Try 20%

$84,530 =   \$25,750(2.589) + \$48,850\,(0.402)$

$=   \$66,666.75 + \$19,637.70$

$=   \$86,304.45$

Try 21%

$84,530 =   \$25,750\,(2.540) + \$48,850\,(0.386)$

$=   \$65,405 + \$18,856.10$

$=   \$84,261.10$

Thus, IRR is between 20 and 21 percent.

10-11B.
   (a)   Payback A   =   3.125 years
         Payback B   =   4.5 years

   B assumes even cash flow throughout year 5.

   (b) $NPV_A = \displaystyle\sum_{t=1}^{5} \dfrac{\$16,000}{(1+0.11)^t} - \$50,000$

         $=   \$16,000\,(3.696) - \$50,000$

         $=   \$59,136 - \$50,000$

         $=   \$9,136$

$$\text{NPV}_B = \frac{\$100,000}{(1 + 0.11)^5} - \$50,000$$

$$= \$100,000 \,(0.593) - \$50,000$$

$$= \$59,300 - \$50,000$$

$$= \$9,300$$

(c) $\$50,000 = \$16,000 \; [\text{PVIFA}_{\text{IRR}_A\%,5 \text{ yrs}}]$

     $3.125 = \text{PVIFA}_{\text{IRR}_A\%,5 \text{ yrs}}$

     Thus, $\text{IRR}_A = 18\%$

     $\$50,000 = \$100,000 \; [\text{PVIF}_{\text{IRR}_B\%,5 \text{ yrs}}]$

     $.50 = \text{PVIF}_{\text{IRR}_B\%,5 \text{ yrs}}$

Thus IRR_B is just under 15%.

(d)   The conflicting rankings are caused by the differing reinvestment assumptions made by the NPV and IRR decision criteria. The NPV criteria assume that cash flows over the life of the project can be reinvested at the required rate of return or cost of capital, while the IRR criterion implicitly assumes that the cash flows over the life of the project can be reinvested at the internal rate of return.

(e)   Project B should be taken because it has the largest NPV. The NPV criterion is preferred because it makes the most acceptable assumption for the wealth maximizing firm.

10-13B.

    (a) Project A's EAA:

    Step 1:   Calculate the project's NPV:

$$NPV_A = \$20{,}000 \ (PVIFA_{10\%, \ 7 \ yr.}) - \$40{,}000$$

$$= \$20{,}000 \ (4.868) - \$40{,}000$$

$$= \$97{,}360 - \$40{,}000$$

$$= \$57{,}360$$

    Step 2:   Calculate the EAA:

$$EAA_A = NPV \ / \ PVIFA_{10\%, \ 7 \ yr.}$$

$$= \$57{,}360 \ / \ 4.868$$

$$= \$11{,}783$$

Project B's EAA:

    Step 1:   Calculate the project's NPV:

$$NPV_B = \$25{,}000 \ (PVIFA_{10\%, \ 5 \ yr.}) - \$40{,}000$$

$$= \$25{,}000 \ (3.791) - \$40{,}000$$

$$= \$94{,}775 - \$40{,}000$$

$$= \$54{,}775$$

Step 2:   Calculate the EAA:

$$EAA_B = NPV / PVIFA_{10\%, 5\ yr.}$$

$$= \$54,775 / 3.791$$

$$= \$14,449$$

Project B should be selected because it has a higher EAA.

(b) $NPV_{\infty,A}$ = $11,783 / .10

$$= \$117,830$$

$NPV_{\infty,B}$ = $14,449 / .10

$$= \$144,490$$

CHAPTER 11

Capital Budgeting
and Risk Analysis

Orientation: The focus of this chapter will be on how to adjust for the riskiness of a given project or combination of projects.

I. Risk and the investment decision

    A. Up to this point we have treated the expected cash flows resulting from an investment proposal as being known with perfect certainty. We will now introduce risk.

    B. The riskiness of an investment project is defined as the variability of its cash flows from the expected cash flow.

II. What measure of risk is relevant in capital budgeting.

    A. In capital budgeting, a project's risk can be looked at on three levels.

        1. First, there is the project standing alone risk, which is a project's risk ignoring the fact that much of this risk will be diversified away as the project is combined with the firm's other projects and assets.

        2. Second, we have the project's contribution-to-firm risk, which is the amount of risk that the project contributes to the firm as a whole; this measure considers the fact that some of the project's risk will be diversified way as the project is combined with the firm's other projects and assets, but ignores the effects of diversification of the firm's shareholders.

3. Finally, there is systematic risk, which is the risk of the project from the viewpoint of a well-diversified shareholder; this measure considers the fact that some of a project's risk will be diversified away as the project is combined with the firm's other projects, and. in addition some of the remaining risk will be diversified away by shareholders as they combine this stock with other stocks in their portfolio.

B. Because of bankruptcy costs and the practical difficulties involved in measuring a project's level of systematic risk, we will give consideration to the project's contribution-to-firm risk and the project's systematic risk.

III. Methods for incorporating risk into capital budgeting

A. The certainty equivalent approach involves a direct attempt to allow the decision maker to incorporate his or her utility function into the analysis.

1. In effect, a riskless set of cash flows is substituted for the original set of cash flows between both of which the financial manager is indifferent.

2. To simplify calculations certainty equivalent coefficients (α_t's) are defined as the ratio of the certain outcome to the risky outcome between which the financial manager is indifferent.

3. Mathematically, certainty equivalent coefficients can be defined as follows:

$$\alpha_t = \frac{\text{certain cash flow}_t}{\text{risky cash flow}_t}$$

4. The appropriate certainty equivalent coefficient is multiplied by the original cash flow (which is the risky cash flow) with this product being equal to the equivalent certain cash flow.

11-2

5.	Once risk is taken out of the cash flows, those cash flows are discounted back to present at the risk-free rate of interest and the project's net present value or profitability index is determined.

6.	If the internal rate of return is calculated, it is then compared with the risk-free rate of interest rather than the firm's required rate of return.

7.	Mathematically, the certainty equivalent can be summarized as follows:

$$NPV = \sum_{t=1}^{n} \frac{\alpha_t ACF_t}{(1+i_F)^t} - IO$$

where α_τ	=	the certainty equivalent coefficient for time period t

ACF_t	=	the annual after-tax expected cash flow in time period t

IO	=	the initial cash outlay

n	=	the project's expected life

i_F	=	the risk-free interest rate

B.	The use of the risk-adjusted discount rate is based on the concept that investors demand higher returns for more risky projects.

1.	If the risk associated with the investment is greater than the risk involved in a typical endeavor, then the discount rate is adjusted upward to compensate for this risk.

2. The expected cash flows are then discounted back to present at the risk-adjusted discount rate. Then the normal capital budgeting criteria are applied, except in the case of the internal rate of return, in which case the hurdle rate to which the project's internal rate of return is compared now becomes the risk-adjusted discount rate.

3. Expressed mathematically the net present value using the risk-adjusted discount rate becomes

$$NPV = \sum_{t=1}^{n} \frac{ACF_t}{(1+i^*)^t} - IO$$

where ACF_t = the annual after-tax cash flow in time period t

IO = the initial outlay

i^* = the risk-adjusted discount rate

n = the project's expected life

IV. Methods for measuring a project's systematic risk

A. Theoretically, we know that systematic risk is the "priced" risk, and thus, the risk that affects the stock's market price and thus the appropriate risk with which to be concerned. However, if there are bankruptcy costs (which are assumed away by the CAPM), if there are undiversified shareholders who are concerned with more than just systematic risk, if there are factors that affect a security's price beyond what the CAPM suggests, or if we are unable to confidently measure the project's systematic risk, then the project's individual risk carries relevance. Moreover, in general, a project's individual risk is highly correlated with the project's systematic risk making it a reasonable proxy to use.

B.	In spite of problems in confidently measuring an individual firm's level of systematic risk, if the project appears to be a typical one for the firm, then using the CAPM to determine the appropriate risk return tradeoffs and then judging the project against them may be a warranted approach.

C.	If the project is not a typical project, we are without historical data and must either estimate the beta using accounting data or use the pure-play method for estimating beta.

1.	Using historical accounting data to substitute for historical price data in estimating systematic risk: To estimate a project's beta using accounting data we need only run a time series regression of the division's return on assets on the market index. The regression coefficient from this equation would be the project's accounting beta and serves as an approximation for the project's true beta.

2.	The pure play method for estimating a project's beta: The pure play method attempts to find a publicly traded firm in the same industry as the capital-budgeting project. Once the proxy or pure-play firm is identified, its systematic risk is determined and then used as a proxy for the project's systematic risk.

V.	Additional approaches for dealing with risk in capital budgeting

A.	A simulation imitates the performance of the project being evaluated by randomly selecting observations from each of the distributions that affect the outcome of the project, combining those observations to determine the final output of the final project, and continuing with this process until a representative record of the project's probable outcome is assembled.

1.	The firm's management then examines the resultant probability distribution, and if management considers enough of the distribution lies above the normal cutoff criterion, it will accept the project.

2. The use of a simulation approach to analyze investment proposals offers two major advantages:

    a. The financial managers are able to examine and base their decisions on the whole range of possible outcomes rather than just point estimates.

    b. They can undertake subsequent sensitivity analysis of the project.

B. A probability tree is a graphical exposition of the sequence of possible outcomes; it presents the decision maker with a schematic representation of the problem in which all possible outcomes are graphically displayed.

VI. Other sources and measures of risk

A. Many times, especially with the introduction of a new product, the cash flows experienced in early years affect the size of the cash flows experienced in later years. This is called time dependence of cash flows, and it has the effect of increasing the riskiness of the project over time.

Study Problems

1. A firm with a 15% required rate of return is considering a project with an expected life of 5 years. The initial outlay associated with this project involves a certain cash outflow of $100,000. The expected cash inflows and certainty equivalent coefficients, a_t are as follows:

Year	Expected Cash Flow	Certainty Equivalent Coefficient, a_t
1	$20,000	0.90
2	30,000	0.80
3	40,000	0.75
4	50,000	0.60
5	60,000	0.50

The risk-free rate of interest is 6%. What is the project's net present value?

SOLUTION

To determine the net present value of this project by using the certainty equivalent we must first remove the risk from the future cash flows. We do so by multiplying each expected cash flow by the corresponding certainty equivalent coefficient:

Year	Expected Cash Flow	Certainty Equivalent Coefficient, a_t	a_tX (Expected Cash Flow) = Equivalent Riskless Cash Flow
1	$20,000	0.90	$18,000
2	30,000	0.80	24,000
3	40,000	0.75	30,000
4	50,000	0.60	30,000
5	60,000	0.50	30,000

The equivalent riskless cash flows are then discounted back to the present at the riskless interest rate, not the firm's required rate of return:

Year	Equivalent Riskless Cash Flow	Present Value Factor at 6%	Present Value
1	$18,000	0.943	16,974
2	24,000	0.890	21,360
3	30,000	0.840	25,200
4	30,000	0 792	23,760
5	30,000	0.747	22,410

$$NPV = -\$100,000 + \$16,974 + \$21,360 + \$25,200 + \$23,760 + \$22,410$$

$$= \$9,704$$

Applying the normal capital budgeting decision criteria, we find that the project should be accepted because its net present value is greater than zero.

2. A firm is considering introducing a new product that has an expected life of 5 years. Since this product is much riskier than a typical project for this firm, the management feels that the normal required rate of return of 12% is not sufficient; instead, the minimally acceptable rate of return on this project should be 20%. The initial outlay would be $100,000 and the expected cash flows from this project are as given below:

Year	Expected Cash Flow
1	$40,000
2	40,000
3	40,000
4	40,000
5	40,000

Should this project be accepted?

SOLUTION

Discounting this annuity back to present at 20% yields a present value of the future cash flows of $119,640. Since the initial outlay on this project is $100,000, the net present value becomes $19,640. The project should be accepted.

Self-Tests

TRUE/FALSE

_____ 1. The certainty equivalent coefficient is the ratio of the risky outcome to the certain outcome between which the financial manager is indifferent.

_____ 2. The use of risk-adjusted discount rates is based on the concept that investors require a higher rate of return for more risky projects.

_____ 3. Probability trees allow the financial manager to see possible future events, their probabilities and their outcomes.

_____ 4. A diversification effect occurs only when cash flows from two different projects have zero correlation.

MULTIPLE CHOICE

1. Which of the following is not a method for adjusting for risk in capital budgeting?

   a. Certainty equivalent approach.
   b. Risk-adjusted discount rate.
   c. Skewed distributions.

2. An investment project will be more desirable:

    a. The smaller the standard deviation.
    b. The less positive its correlations with existing average cash flows.
    c. The larger the coefficient of variation of cash flow.
    d. a and b.

3. Probability tree analysis:

    a. Illustrates the impact of diversification.
    b. Fails to consider the probability distribution of cash flows.
    c. Is good only for single period investments since discounting is not possible.
    d. Graphically displays all possible outcomes of the investment.

SOLUTIONS TO SELECTED SET B PROBLEMS (See text for problems.)

11-3B.

Project A:

	(A)	(B)	(A x B)	Present Value	
	Expected		(Expected	Factor at	Present
Year	Cash Flow	α_t	Cash Flow) x (α_t)	5%	Value
0	-$1,000,000	1.00	-$1,000,000	1.000	-$1,000,000
1	600,000	.90	540,000	.952	514,080
2	750,000	.90	675,000	.907	612,225
3	600,000	.75	450,000	.864	388,800
4	550,000	.65	357,500	.823	294,222.50
				NPV$_A$ =	$ 809,327.50

Project B:

	(A)	(B)	(A x B)	Present Value	
	Expected		(Expected	Factor at	Present
Year	Cash Flow	α_t	Cash Flow) x (α_t)	5%	Value
0	-$1,000,000	1.00	-$1,000,000	1.000	-$1,000,000
1	600,000	.95	570,000	.952	542,640
2	650,000	.75	487,500	.907	442,162.50
3	700,000	.60	420,000	.864	362,880
4	750,000	.60	450,000	.823	370,350
				NPV_B =	$ 718,032.50

Thus, project A should be selected, as it has a higher NPV.

11-5B.

$$NPV_A = \sum_{t=1}^{N} \frac{ACF_t}{(1+i^*)^t} - IO$$

$$= \$30,000 (.885) + \$40,000(.783) + \$50,000(.693) + \$80,000(.613) + \$120,000(.543) - \$300,000$$

$$= \$26,550 + \$31,320 + \$34,650 + \$49,040 + \$65,160 - \$300,000$$

$$= - \$93,280$$

$$NPV_B = \sum_{t=1}^{N} \frac{ACF}{(1+i^*)^t} - IO$$

$$= \$130,000(3.127) - \$450,000$$

$$= \$406,510 - \$450,000$$

$$= -\$43,490$$

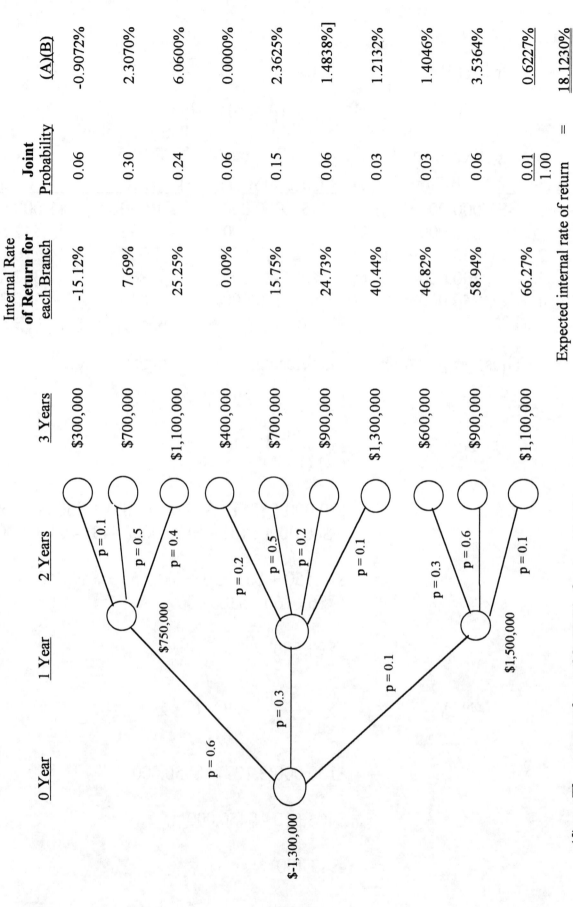

(d)   The range of possible IRR's from -15.12% to 66.27

CHAPTER 12

Cost of Capital

Orientation: In Chapter 6 and 7 we considered the valuation of debt and equity instruments. The concepts advanced there serve as a foundation for determining the required rate of return for the firm and for specific investment projects. The objective in this chapter is to determine the required rate of return to be used in evaluating investment projects.

I.   The concept of the cost of capital

    A.   Defining the cost of capital:

        1.   The rate that must be earned in order to satisfy the required rate of return of the firm's investors.

        2.   The rate of return on investments at which the price of a firm's common stock will remain unchanged.

    B.   Type of investors and the cost of capital.

        1.   Each type of capital used by the firm (debt, preferred stock, and common stock) should be incorporated into the cost of capital, with the relative importance of a particular source being based on the percentage of the financing provided by each source of capital.

        2.   Using the cost a single source of capital as the hurdle rate is tempting to management, particularly when an investment is financed entirely by debt. However, doing so is a mistake in logic and can cause problems.

II.   Factors determining the cost of capital

   A.   General economic conditions. These include the demand for and supply of capital within the economy, and the level of expected inflation. These are reflected in the riskless rate of return.

   B.   Market conditions. The security may not be readily marketable when the investor wants to sell; or even if a continuous demand for the security does exist, the price may vary significantly.

   C.   A firm's operating and financing decisions. Risk also results from the decisions made within the company. This risk is generally divided into two classes:

      1.   Business risk is the variability in returns on assets and is affected by the company's investment decisions.

      2.   Financial risk is the increased variability in returns to the common stockholders as a result of using debt and preferred stock.

   D.   In summary, as the level of risk rises a larger risk premium must be earned to satisfy a firm's investors.

III.   Computing the weighted cost of capital. A firm's weighted cost of capital is a function of (1) the individual costs of capital and (2) the capital structure mix.

   A.   Determining individual costs of capital.

      1.   The <u>before-tax cost of debt</u> is found by trial-and-error by solving for k_d in

$$NP_0 = \sum_{t=1}^{n} \frac{\$I_t}{(1+k_d)^t} + \frac{\$M}{(1+k_d)^N}$$

         where NP_0 =   the market price of the debt, less flotation costs,

$$\$I_t \quad = \quad \text{the annual dollar interest paid to the investor each year,}$$

$$\$M \quad = \quad \text{the maturity value of the debt}$$

$$k_d \quad = \quad \text{before-tax cost of the debt (before-tax required rate of return on debt)}$$

$$N \quad = \quad \text{the number of years to maturity.}$$

The <u>after-tax cost of debt</u> equals:

$$k_d(1 - T)$$

2. Cost of preferred stock (required rate of return on preferred stock), k_{ps}, equals the dividend yield based upon the net price (market price less flotation costs) or

$$k_{ps} \quad \frac{\text{dividend}}{\text{net price}} = \frac{D}{NP_0}$$

3. Cost of Common Stock. There are three measurement techniques to obtain the required rate of return on common stock.

    a. dividend-growth model
    b. capital asset pricing model
    c. risk-premium approach

4. Dividend growth model

    a. Cost of internally generated common equity, k_{cs}

    $$k_{cs} = \frac{\text{dividend in year 1}}{\text{market price}} + \left(\begin{array}{c} \text{annual growth} \\ \text{in dividends} \end{array} \right)$$

    $$k_{cs} = \frac{D_1}{P_0} + g$$

b. Cost of new common stock, k_{nc}

$$k_{ncs} = \frac{D_1}{NP_o} + g$$

where NP_o = the market price of the common stock less flotation costs incurred in issuing new shares.

5. Capital asset pricing model

$$k_{cs} = k_{rf} + b(k_m - k_{rf})$$

where k_{cs} = the cost of common stock
k_{rf} = the risk-free rate
b = beta, measure of the stock's systematic risk
k_m = the expected rate of return on the market

6. Risk-Premium Approach

$$k_{cs} = k_d + RP_c$$

where k_{cs} = cost of common stock
k_d = cost of debt
RP_c = risk-premium of common stock

7. It is important to notice that the major difference between the equations presented here and the equations from Chapter 7 is that the <u>firm</u> must recognize the flotation costs incurred in issuing the security.

B. Selection of weights. The individual costs of capital will be different for each source of capital in the firm's capital structure. To use the cost of capital in investment analyses, we must compute a weighted or overall cost of capital.

1. It will be assumed that the company's current financial mix resulting from the financing of previous investments is relatively stable and that these weights will closely approximate future financing patterns.

2. In computing weights we can either use the current market values of the firm's securities or the book values as shown in the balance sheet. Since we will be issuing new securities at their <u>current</u> market value, and not at book (historical) values we should use the market value of the securities in calculating our weights.

IV. PepsiCo approach to weighted average cost of capital

A. PepsiCo calculates the divisional cost of capital for its snack, beverage and restaurant organizations by first finding peer-group firms for each division and using their average betas, after adjusting for differences in financial leverage, to compute the division's cost of equity. They also use accounting betas in estimating the cost of equity. They then compute the cost of debt for each division. Finally, they calculate a weighted cost of capita for each division.

B. PepsiCo's WACC basic computation

$$k_o = k_{cs}\left(\frac{E}{D+E}\right) + k_d[1-T]\left(\frac{D}{D+E}\right)$$

where:

k_o =   the weighted average cost of capital

k_{cs} =   the cost of equity capital

k_d =   the before-tax cost of debt capital

T   =   the marginal tax rate

E/(D+E)   =   percentage of financing from equity

$$D/(D+E) \quad = \quad \text{percentage of financing from debt}$$

C.   Calculating the Cost of Equity

Based on capital assets pricing model:

$$k_{cs} \quad = \quad k_{rf} + b(k_m - k_{rf})$$

where k_{cs} = the cost of common stock
k_{rf} = the risk-free rate
b = beta, measure of the stock's systematic risk
k_m = the expected rate of return on the market

Beta's for each division are estimated by calculating an average un-levered beta from a group of divisional peers.

The average beta for each division's peer group is unlevered and then re-levered using that division's target debt-to-equity ratio.

D.   Calculating the Cost of Debt

The after-tax cost of debt is equal to:

$$k_d (1 - T)$$

where:

k_d = before-tax cost of debt

T = marginal tax rate

Study Problems

1. A $1,000 par-value bond will sell in the market for $1,072 and carries a coupon interest rate of 9 percent. Issuance costs will be 7.5 percent. The number of years to maturity is 15 and the firm's tax rate is 46 percent. What is the after-tax cost for this security?

    SOLUTION

    The problem can be stated mathematically as follows:

    $$\$1,072(1 - 0.075) \text{ or } \$991.60 = \sum_{t=1}^{15} \frac{\$90}{(1+k_d)^t} + \frac{\$1,000}{(1+k_d)^t}$$

    Using a financial calculator, we find that k_d is just over nine percent.

    $$k_d = .0911 = 9.11\%$$

    $$\frac{\text{After-tax}}{\text{Cost of debt}} = 9.11\%(1 - 0.46) = 4.92\%$$

2. The current market price of ABC Company's common stock is $32.50. The firm expects to pay a dividend of $1.90, and the growth rate is projected to be 7 percent annually. The company is in a 40 percent tax bracket. Flotation costs would be 6 percent if new stock were issued. What is the cost of (a) internal and (b) external common equity?

    SOLUTION

    Let k_c = cost of internal common
    $\quad k_{nc}$ = cost of external (new) common
    $\quad D_1$ = next dividend to be paid
    $\quad P_o$ = market price
    $\quad g$ = growth rate
    $\quad NP_o$ = market price less flotation costs

12-7

(a) $\quad k_{cs} \quad = \quad \dfrac{D_1}{P_0} + g$

$\quad k_{cs} \quad = \quad \dfrac{\$1.90}{\$32.50} + 0.07 = 12.85\%$

(b) $\quad K_{nc} \quad = \quad \dfrac{D_1}{NP_0} + g$

$\quad K_{nc} \quad = \quad \dfrac{\$1.90}{\$32.50(1 - 0.06)} + 0.07 = 13.22\%$

3.   Pharr, Inc.'s preferred stock pays a 16 percent dividend. The stock is selling for $62.75, and its par value is $40. Issuance costs are 5 percent and the firm's tax rate is 46 percent. What is the cost of this source of financing?

SOLUTION

$k_{ps} \quad = \quad \dfrac{D}{NP_0}$

$k_{ps} \quad = \quad \dfrac{\$40(0.16)}{\$62.75(1 - 0.05)} = \dfrac{\$6.40}{\$59.61} = 10.74\%$

4.   The current capital structure of Smithhart, Inc. is as follows:

Bonds (7%, $1,000 par, 15 years)		$ 750,000
Preferred stock ($100 par, 7.25% dividend)		1,000,000
Common stock:		
Par value ($2.50 par)	$500,000	
Retained earnings	350,000	850,000
Total		$2,600,000

The market price is $975 for the bonds, $60 for the preferred stock, and $21 for common stocks. Flotation costs are 9 percent for bonds and 5 percent for preferred stock. The firm's tax rate is 46 percent. Common stock will pay a $2.80 dividend which is not expected to grow. What is the weighted cost of capital using only internal common equity?

12-8

SOLUTION

Source of Financing	Market Value	Weight
Bonds	$731,250[1]	13.22%
Preferred stock	600,000[2]	10.85%
Common stock	4,200,000[3]	75.93%
	$5,531,250	100.00%

[1] 750 bonds at $975 value each
[2] 10, 000 shares at $60 value each
[3] 200, 000 shares at $21 value each

Cost of debt

$$\$975(1 - 0.09) \text{ or } \$887.25 = \sum_{t=1}^{15} \frac{\$70}{(1+k_d)}t + \frac{\$1,000}{(1 + k_d)}15$$

Using a financial calculator, k_d equals 8.35%

$$\frac{\text{After-tax}}{\text{cost of debt}} = 8.35\% \ (1 - 0.46)$$

$$\frac{\text{After-tax}}{\text{cost of debt}} = 4.51\%$$

Cost of preferred stock

$$k_{ps} = \frac{\$7.25}{\$60 \ (1 - 0.05)} = 12.72\%$$

Cost of internal common equity

$$k_{cs} = \frac{\$2.80}{\$21} + 0 = 13.33\%$$

Weighted Cost of Capital

Source of Financing	Cost	Weight	Weighted Costs
Bonds	4.51%	.1322	0.596%
Preferred stock	12.72	.1085	1.381
Common stock	13.33	.7593	10.124
		1.0000	12.101%

Self-Tests

TRUE-FALSE

_____ 1. If a firm earns more than its cost of capital on its investments then the price of the firm's common stock should rise.

_____ 2. The level of expected inflation is reflected in the risk premium.

_____ 3. The cost of capital is an appropriate investment criterion only for investments of similar risk to its existing investments.

_____ 4. Financial risk is the risk that the price of the security may vary significantly.

_____ 5. Only those projects exceeding the cost of capital should be accepted.

_____ 6. The cost of preferred stock must be adjusted for taxes.

_____ 7. In computing a weighted cost of capital, we generally assume that the company's current capital structure will not change.

_____ 8. New common stock would be issued only if retained earnings does not provide sufficient equity capital for the amount of investments under consideration.

_____ 9. The capital asset pricing model (CAPM) is based on estimates of three values: the risk free rate, the firm's beta coefficient, and the market risk premium.

_____ 10. Beta measures the volatility of the project returns relative to the investor's widely diversified portfolio.

MULTIPLE CHOICE

1.   What is/are the reason(s) for computing a firm's cost of capital?

      a.   To determine the firm's future financing needs.
      b.   To assure the investors that their required rate of return is being met.
      c.   To use the cost of capital as an investment criterion.
      d.   b and c.
      e.   a and c.
      f.   a, b, and c.

2.   The cost of capital can be defined as:

      a.   The rate that must be earned in order to satisfy the required rate of return of the firm's investors.
      b.   The rate of return on investments at which the price of the firm's common stock remains unchanged.
      c.   The rate of return on investments which will increase the price of the firm's common stock.
      d.   a and b.
      e.   a and c.

3.   All of the following variables are needed in the computation of the cost of debt except:

      a.   Market price of debt.
      b.   Issuance cost.
      c.   Tax rate for the firm.
      d.   Growth rate.
      e.   Maturity date.

4.   Adjustment for taxes is required for the _____.

      a.   cost of preferred stock.
      b.   cost of debt.
      c.   cost of common equity.
      d.   All of the above.
      e.   a. and c. only

5.	Which of the following is a limitation of the capital asset pricing model?

    a.	The assumption of no bankruptcy risk.
    b.	The requirement that the existing financial mix remains constant
    c.	The standardization of the risk premium relative to the riskiness of the firm's average project.
    d.	none of the above.
    e.	Both b. and c.

6.	An investment with a beta of 0.80 means that the returns of the investment:

    a.	Are more volatile than the market returns.
    b.	Are less volatile than the market returns.
    c.	Have no correlation with the market returns.
    d.	Are perfectly correlated with the market returns.
    e.	None of the above.

CHAPTER 13

Analysis and Impact of Leverage

Orientation: This chapter focuses on useful aids to the financial manager in his or her determination of the firm's proper financial structure. It includes the definitions of the different kinds of risk, a review of breakeven analysis, the concepts of operating leverage, financial leverage, the combination of both leverages, and their effect on EPS (earnings per share).

I.   Business risk and financial risk

   A.   Risk has been defined as the likely variability associated with expected revenue streams.

      1.   Focusing on the financial decision, the variations in the income stream can be attributed to:

         a.   The firm's exposure to business risk.

         b.   The firm's decision to incur financial risk.

   B.   Business risk can be defined as the variability of the firm's expected earnings before interest and taxes (EBIT).

      1.   Business risk is measured by the firm's corresponding expected coefficient of variation (i.e., the larger the ratio, the more risk a firm is exposed to).

      2.   Dispersion in operating income does not cause business risk. It is the result of several influences, for example, the company's cost structure, product demand characteristics, and intra-industry competition. These influences are a direct result of the firm's investment decision.

C.   Financial risk is a direct result of the firm's financing decision. When the firm is selecting different financial alternatives, financial risk refers to the additional variability in earnings available to the firm's common shareholders and the additional chance of insolvency borne by the common shareholder caused by the use of financial leverage.

   1.   Financial leverage is the financing of a portion of the firm's assets with securities bearing a fixed (limited) rate of return in hopes of increasing the ultimate return to the common shareholders.

   2.   Financial risk is to a large extent passed on to the common shareholders who must bear almost all of the potential inconsistencies of returns to the firm after the deduction of fixed payments.

II.   Breakeven analysis

   A.   The objective of breakeven analysis is to determine the breakeven quantity of output by studying the relationships among the firm's cost structure, volume of output, and operating profit.

   1.   The breakeven quantity of output is the quantity of output (in units) that results in an EBIT level equal to zero.

   B.   Use of the model enables the financial officer to:

   1.   Determine the quantity of output that must be sold to cover all operating costs.

   2.   Calculate the EBIT that will be achieved at various output levels.

   C.   Some actual and potential applications of breakeven analysis include:

   1.   Capital expenditure analysis as a complementary technique to discounted cash flow evaluation models.

2. Pricing policy.

3. Labor contract negotiations.

4. Evaluation of cost structure.

5. The making of financial decisions.

D. Essential elements of the breakeven model are:

1. Fixed costs are costs that do not vary in total amount as the sales volume or the quantity of output changes over some relevant range of output. For example, administrative salaries are considered fixed because these salaries are generally the same month after month. Other examples are:

   a. Depreciation.

   b. Insurance premiums.

   c. Property taxes.

   d. Rent.

   The total fixed cost is unchanged regardless of the quantity of product output or sales, although, over some relevant range, these costs may be higher or lower (i.e., in the long run).

2. Variable costs are costs that tend to vary in total as output changes. Variable costs are fixed per unit of output. For example, direct materials are considered a variable cost because they vary with the amount of products produced. Other variable costs are:

   a. Direct labor.

   b. Energy cost associated with the production area.

   c. Packaging.

   d. Freight-out.

   e. Sales commissions.

3.	To implement the behavior of the breakeven model, it is necessary for the financial manager to:

a.	Identify the most relevant output range for his or her planning purposes.

b.	Approximate all costs in the semifixed, semivariable range and allocate them to the fixed and variable cost categories.

4.	Total revenue and volume of output

a.	Total revenue from sales is equal to the price per unit multiplied by the quantity sold.

b.	The volume of output is the firm's level from operations and is expressed as sales dollars or a unit quantity.

E.	Finding the breakeven point

1.	The breakeven model is just a simple adaptation of the firm's income statement expressed in the following format:

sales - (total variable costs + total fixed costs) = profit

a.	Trial and error

(1)	Select an arbitrary output level.

(2)	Calculate the corresponding EBIT amount.

(3)	When EBIT equals zero, the breakeven point has been found.

b.	Contribution margin analysis

(1)	The difference between the unit selling price and the unit variable cost equals the contribution margin.

13-4

(2) Then, the fixed cost divided by the contribution margin equals the breakeven quantity in units.

c. Algebraic analysis

(1) Q_B = the breakeven level of units sold,
   P = the unit sales price,
   F = the total fixed cost for the period,
   V = unit variable cost.

(2) Then,

$$Q_B = \frac{F}{P - V}$$

F. The breakeven point in sales dollars:

1. Computing a breakeven point in terms of sales dollars rather than units of output is convenient, especially if the firm deals with more than one product. Also, if the analyst cannot get unit cost data, he or she can compute a general breakeven point in sales dollars by using the firm's annual report.

2. Since variable cost per unit and the selling price per unit are assumed constant, the ratio of total sales to total variable costs (VC/S) is a constant for any level of sales. So, if the breakeven level of sales is denoted S*, the corresponding equation is:

$$S^* = \frac{F}{1 - \frac{VC}{S}}$$

G. Limitations of breakeven analysis:

1. The cost-volume-profit relationship is assumed to be linear.

2. The total revenue curve is presumed to increase linearly with the volume of output.

3. A constant production and sales mix is assumed.

4. The breakeven computation is a static form of analysis.

13-5

III. Operating Leverage

   A. Operating leverage is the responsiveness of a firm's EBIT to fluctuations in sales. Operating leverage results when fixed operating costs are present in the firm's cost structure. It should be noted here that fixed operating costs do <u>not</u> include interest charges incurred from the firm's use of debt financing.

   B. The responsiveness of a firm's EBIT to fluctuating sales levels can be measured as follows:

$$\begin{pmatrix} \text{degree of operating} \\ \text{leverage from the} \\ \text{base sales level} \end{pmatrix} = DOL_S = \frac{\% \text{ change in EBIT}}{\% \text{ change in sales}}$$

   for example, if DOL_S equals five times, a 10% rise in sales over the coming period will result in a 50% rise in EBIT. (This means of measure also holds true for the negative direction.)

   C. If unit costs are available, the DOL_S can be measured by the following formula:

$$DOL_S = \frac{Q(P - V)}{Q(P - V) - F}$$

   D. If an analytical income statement is the only thing available, the following formula can be used to produce the same results:

$$DOL_S = \frac{\text{revenue before fixed costs}}{EBIT} = \frac{S - VC}{S - VC - F}$$

   E. It should be noted here that the three formulas stated above all produce the same results. But, more important is the understanding that in this example a 1% change in sales will result in a 5% change in EBIT.

F. Implications of operating leverage:

1. At each point above the breakeven level the degree of operating leverage decreases (i.e., the greater the sales level, the lower the DOL_S).

2. At the breakeven level of sales the degree of operating leverage is undefined.

3. Operating leverage is present anytime the percentage change in EBIT divided by the percentage change in sales is greater than one.

4. The degree of operating leverage can be attributed to the business risk that a firm faces.

IV. Financial leverage

A. Financial leverage, as defined earlier, is the practice of financing a portion of the firm's assets with securities bearing a fixed rate of return in hopes of increasing the ultimate return to the common stockholders. To see if financial leverage has been used to benefit the common shareholders, the discussion here will focus on the responsiveness of the company's earning per share (EPS) to changes in its EBIT. It should be noted here that not all analysts rely exclusively on this type of relationship. In fact, the weakness of such an approach will be examined in the following chapter.

B. The firm is using financial leverage and is exposing its owners to financial risk when:

$$\frac{\% \text{ change in EPS}}{\% \text{ change in EBIT}} \text{ is greater than } 1.00$$

C. A precise measure of the firm's use of financial leverage can be expressed in the following relationship:

$$\begin{pmatrix} \text{degree of financial} \\ \text{leverage from the} \\ \text{base EBIT level} \end{pmatrix} = DFL_{EBIT} = \frac{\% \text{ change in EPS}}{\% \text{ change in EBIT}}$$

1.   As was the case with operating leverage, the degree of financial leverage concept can be in the negative direction as well as in the positive direction.

2.   You should also note that the greater the degree of financial leverage, the greater the fluctuations (positive or negative) in EPS.

D.   An easier way of measuring the degree of financial leverage that produces the same results without computing percentage changes in EBIT and EPS is:

$$DFL_{EBIT} = \frac{EBIT}{EBIT - I}$$

where I is the sum of all fixed financing costs.

V.   Combining operating and financial leverage

A.   Since changes in sales revenues cause greater changes in EBIT, and if the firm chooses to use financial leverage, changes in EBIT turn into larger variations in both EPS and EAC (earnings available to common shareholders). Then, combining operating and financial leverage causes rather large variations in EPS.

B.   One way to measure the combined leverage can be expressed as:

$$\begin{pmatrix} \text{degree of combined} \\ \text{leverage from the} \\ \text{base sales level} \end{pmatrix} = DCL_S = \frac{\% \text{ change in EPS}}{\% \text{ change in sales}}$$

If the DCL is equal to 5.0 times, then it is important to understand that a 1% change in sales will result in a 5% change in EPS.

C.   The degree of combined leverage is actually the product of the two independent leverage measures. Thus, we have:

$$DCL_S = (DOL_S) \times (DFL_{EBIT})$$

D.   As you might have guessed, there is still another way to compute DCL_s. It is a more direct way in that no percentage fluctuations or separate leverage values have to be determined. You need only substitute the appropriate values into the following equation:

$$DCL_s = \frac{Q(P - V)}{Q(P - V) - F - I}$$

All variables have previously been defined.

E.   Implications of combining operating and financial leverage

     1.   The total risk exposure that the firm assumes can be managed by combining operating and financial leverage in different degrees.

     2.   Knowledge of the various leverage measures that have been examined here aids the financial officer in his or her determination of the proper level of overall risk that should be accepted.

Study Problems

1.   Columbia Products will earn $231,000 next year after taxes. Sales for Columbia will be $4,400,000. The firm operates in modern facilities near Columbia, South Carolina. The firm specializes in the production of furniture for lawyers' offices, accountants' offices, and college dormitories. The average unit sells for $220 and has an associated variable cost per unit of $165. Columbia experiences a 30 percent tax rate.

     (a)   What will fixed costs (in total) be next year for Columbia?

     (b)   Calculate Columbia's breakeven point both in units and dollars.

     (c)   Generate the analytical income statement at the breakeven level of sales dollars.

SOLUTION

(a)   All that we have to do here is use our knowledge of the breakeven model and the analytical income statement model (both are discussed in detail in Chapter 8 of your text). The calculations follow:

$$\{(P \cdot Q) - [V \cdot Q + (F)]\}\ (1\text{-}T) = \$231,000$$

$$[(\$4,400,000) - (\$3,300,000) - F]\ (.7) = \$231,000$$

$$(\$1,100,000 - F)\ (.7) = \$231,000$$

$$\$770,000 - .7F = \$231,000$$

$$.7F = \$539,000$$

$$F = \underline{\$770,000}$$

(b) $$Q_B = \frac{F}{P\text{-}V} = \frac{\$770,000}{\$55} = 14,000 \text{ units}$$

$$S^* = \frac{F}{1 - \dfrac{VC}{S}} = \frac{\$770,000}{1 - .75} = \frac{\$770,000}{.25}$$

$$= \$3,080,000$$

We have shown that the firm will break even (i.e., EBIT= 0) when it sells 14,000 units. With a selling price of $220 per unit the breakeven sales level is $3,080,000.

(c)   The analytical income statement at the breakeven level of sales would appear as follows:

Sales	$3,080,000
Variable costs	2,310,000
Revenue before	
fixed costs	$ 770,000
Fixed costs	770,000
EBIT	$ - 0 -

2.   Woody's Carry-Out Pizza expects to earn $16,000 next year before interest and taxes. Sales will be $130,000. The store is the only pizza parlor near the fraternity-row district of Gardiner University. The owner, Eric Nemeth, makes only one variety and size of pizza (the House Special) and it sells for $10. The variable cost per pizza is $6. Woody's Carry-Out Pizza experiences a 48% tax rate.

(a)   What are the pizza parlor's fixed costs expected to be next year?

(b)   Calculate the parlor's breakeven point in units and dollars.

SOLUTION

(a)   To compute fixed costs:

$$S - (VC + FC) = EBIT$$

$130,000/$10 = 13,000 units sold

$$\$130,000 - [(13,000)(\$6) + X] \quad = \quad \$16,000$$

$$\$130,000 \ - \ \$78,000 \ - \ X \quad = \quad \$16,000$$

$$X \quad = \quad \$36,000$$

(b)   First, the breakeven point in units:

$$Q_B \quad = \quad \frac{F}{P - V} = \frac{\$36,000}{\$10 - \$6} = 9,000 \text{ units}$$

Then, the breakeven point in dollars:

$$S^* \quad = \quad \frac{F}{1 - VC/S} = \frac{\$36,000}{1 - \frac{\$78,000}{\$130,000}} = \$90,000$$

3.   The ESM Corporation projects that next year its fixed costs will total
      $120,000. Its only product sells for $17 per unit, of which $9 is a variable
      cost. The management of ESM is considering the purchase of a new
      machine that will lower the variable cost per unit to $7. The new machine,
      however, will add to fixed costs through an increase in depreciation
      expense.

      (a)   How large can the addition to fixed costs be in order to keep the
            firm's breakeven point in units produced and sold unchanged?

SOLUTION

      (a)   Compute the present level of breakeven output:

            $$Q_B = \frac{F}{P - V}$$

            $$\frac{\$120,000}{17-9} = \frac{\$120,000}{8} = 15,000 \text{ units}$$

            Compute the new level of fixed costs at the breakeven output:

            F + (7) (15,000)   =   (17) (15,000)

            F + 105,000   =   255,000

            F   = $150,000

            Compute the addition to fixed costs:

            $150,000 - $120,000 = $30,000 addition

4.   The management of ESM Corporation decided not to purchase the new
      piece of equipment. Using the existing cost structure, calculate the degree
      of operating leverage at 35,000 units of output.

SOLUTION

$$\text{DOL at 35,000 units} = \frac{35,000(\$17 - \$9)}{35,000(\$17 - \$9) - \$120,000}$$

$$= \frac{\$280,000}{\$160,000} = 1.75 \text{ times}$$

This indicates, for example, that a 10% increase in sales for the ESM Corporation will result in a 17.5% increase in EBIT, provided the assumptions of cost-volume-profit analysis hold.

5. The Moose Hobby Company manufactures a full line of gold-plated model airplanes. The average selling price of a finished unit is $25. The associated variable cost is $15 per unit. Fixed costs for the company average $70,000 per year.

    (a) What would be the company's profit or loss at the following units of production sold? 5,000; 7,000; 9,000 units.

    (b) Find the degree of operating leverage for the production and sales given in part (a) above.

SOLUTION

(a) The company's profit or loss:

	@ 5,000 units	@ 7,000 units	@ 9,000 units
Sales (P X Q)	$125,000	$175,000	$225,000
- VC (VC/unit X Q)	75,000	105,000	135,000
- FC	70,000	70,000	70,000
Profit (loss)	($ 20,000)	-0-	$ 20,000

13-13

(b) The degree of operating leverage at the different levels of output

$$DOL_S = \frac{Q(P-V)}{Q(P-V) - F}$$

$$DOL_S \text{ at 5,000 units} = \frac{5,000(\$25-\$15)}{5,000(\$25-\$15) - \$70,000}$$

$$= \frac{\$50,000}{-20,000} = -2.5 \text{ times}$$

$$DOL_S \text{ at 7,000 units} = \frac{7,000(\$25-\$15)}{7,000(\$25-\$15) - \$70,000}$$

$$= \frac{\$50,000}{0} = \text{undefined}$$

$$DOL_S \text{ at 9,000 units} = \frac{9,000(\$25-\$15)}{9,000 (\$25-\$15) - \$70,000}$$

$$= \frac{\$90,000}{\$20,000} = 4.5 \text{ times}$$

6. An analytical income statement for the D. A. Bauer Corporation is shown below. It is based on an output level of 69,000 units.

Sales	$1,035,000
Variable costs	552,000
Revenue before fixed costs	$ 483,000
Fixed costs	183,000
EBIT	$ 300,000
Interest expense	80,000
Earnings before taxes	$ 220,000
Taxes	110,000
Net Income	$ 110,000

(a) Calculate the degree of operating leverage at this output level.

(b) Calculate the degree of financial leverage at this level of output.

(c) Determine the combined leverage effect at this output level.

SOLUTION

(a) DOL at 69,000 units $= \dfrac{69{,}000(\$15\text{-}\$8)}{69{,}000(\$15\text{-}\$8)\text{ - }\$183{,}000}$

$= 1.61$ times

(b) DFL at EBIT of \$300,000 $= \dfrac{\$300{,}000}{\$300{,}000\text{ - }\$80{,}000}$

$= 1.364$ times

(c) $\left(\begin{array}{c}\text{combined}\\\text{leverage effect}\end{array}\right) = \dfrac{69{,}000(\$15\text{-}\$8)}{69{,}000(\$15\text{-}\$8)\text{-}\$183{,}000\text{-}\$80{,}000}$

$= 2.195$ times

Notice that the combined leverage effect is the product of the degrees of operating and financial leverage. A 1% increase in sales for D. A. Bauer Corporation would be magnified into a 2.195% increase in net income because of the combined leverage effect.

7. You are supplied with the following analytical income statement for C. J. Omlette Shoppe. It reflects last year's operations.

Sales	$75,000
Variable costs	37,000
Revenue before fixed cost	$38,000
Fixed costs	19,000
EBIT	$19,000
Interest Expense	7,000
Earnings before taxes	$12,000
Taxes	6,000
Net Income	$ 6,000

(a) What is the degree of operating leverage at this level of output?

(b) What is the degree of financial leverage?

(c)   What is the degree of combined leverage?

(d)   If sales should increase by 30%, by what percent would earnings before interest and taxes increase?

(e)   What is C. J.'s breakeven point in sales dollars?

SOLUTION

(a)   The degree of operating leverage:

$$\text{DOL at \$75,000} = \frac{\text{Revenue before fixed costs}}{\text{EBIT}} = \frac{\text{S-VC}}{\text{S-VC-F}}$$

$$= \frac{\$38,000}{\$19,000} = 2 \text{ times}$$

(b)   The degree of financial leverage:

$$\text{DFL at \$19,000 EBIT} = \frac{\text{EBIT}}{\text{EBIT-I}} = \frac{\$19,000}{\$19,000-\$7,000}$$

$$= 1.58 \text{ times}$$

(c)   The degrees of combined leverage:

$$\text{DCL}_S = (\text{DOL}_S)(\text{DFL}_{EBIT}) = (2)(1.58) = 3.16 \text{ times}$$

(d)   An increase in sales of 30% would result in a 60% increase in EBIT.

(e)   Breakeven level in sales dollars:

$$S^* = \frac{F}{1 - VC/S} = \frac{\$19,000}{1 - \dfrac{\$37,000}{\$75,000}} = \$37,500$$

8. Delphi Parts produces three different lines of boating accessories for several Florida boat manufacturers. The product lines are numbered. Their sales mix and contribution margin ratios appear in the chart below.

PRODUCT LINE	% OF TOTAL SALES	CONTRIBUTION MARGIN RATIO
1	17	44%
2	53	30%
3	30	22%

Forecasted sales for the coming year are $1,200,000. The firm's fixed costs are $300,000.

(a) Prepare a table showing sales, total variable costs, and the total contribution margin (dollars) associated with each line.

(b) What is the aggregate contribution margin ratio indicative of this mix?

(c) What is the breakeven point in dollars for this particular sales mix?

SOLUTION

(a)
Product	1	2	3	Total
Sales	204,000	636,000	360,000	1,200,000
VC*	114,240	445,200	280,800	840,240
Contr. Margin	89,760	190,800	79,200	359,760

(b)
Contr. Margin Ratio	44%	30%	22%	30.0%

(c) $S^* = FC/(1 - VC/S) = 300,000/.300$

$S^* = \$1,000,000$

13-17

9. If Delphi (see problem 8) decides to change the sales mix for the next year to 40%, 33%, and 27% for products 1, 2, and 3, respectively, how will this affect their breakeven point in dollars? Which mix do you think they would prefer?

SOLUTION

Product Line	% of Total Sales	Contribution Margin Ratio
1	40	44%
2	33	30%
3	27	22%

Overall Contr. Ratio Margin $=$ .40(44) + .33(30) + .27(22)

$=$ 33.4%

S* $= 300,000/.334 = \$898,204$

This second mix would be preferred since the overall contribution margin ratio is higher and the breakeven point in dollars is now lower. The contribution to fixed costs is higher with the second mix.

Self-Test

TRUE-FALSE

_____ 1. Dispersion in operating income causes business risk.

_____ 2. Your firm adds to its facilities a completely automated product line. This will have no effect on the breakeven point (in units of output).

_____ 3. Variable costs are fixed per unit of output but vary in total as output changes.

_____ 4. Your firm expects a 7% increase in sales for the next year. The degree of operating leverage will decrease for your firm.

_____ 5. If the degree of operating leverage increases and if all else remains unchanged, the degree of combined leverage will decrease.

_____ 6. When the firm uses more financial leverage, its stockholders expect a greater return.

_____ 7. The breakeven model enables the financial officer to determine the quality of output that must be sold to cover all operating costs.

_____ 8. If EBIT were to remain constant while the firm incurred additional interest expense, the degree of financial leverage would increase.

_____ 9. If future sales are expected to increase, then decreasing the degree of operating leverage would be a wise decision.

_____ 10. Financial risk can be defined as the variability of the firm's expected earnings before interest and taxes (EBIT).

_____ 11. The incurrence of fixed operating costs in the firm's income stream is referred to as financial leverage.

_____ 12. Breakeven analysis is a long-run concept since all costs are variable in the long-run.

_____ 13. Operating leverage is the responsiveness of the firm's EBIT to fluctuations in profit.

_____ 14. Earnings per share is the most appropriate criterion for all financing decisions.

_____ 15. The decision to use financial leverage by the firm magnifies its variation in earnings per share, compared to the use of no financial leverage.

_____ 16. Variable costs are fixed per unit of output.

_____ 17. Fixed costs per unit vary with units of output.

_____ 18. Combining operating and financial leverage magnifies variations in earnings per share.

_____ 19. A firm faces a greater chance of insolvency with an increase in the use of financial leverage (other factors held constant).

_____ 20. The decision to use debt or preferred stock in the financial structure of a corporation means that those who own the common shares are exposed to financial risk.

_____ 21. The contribution margin is the difference between the unit selling price and the unit fixed cost.

_____ 22. Business risk provides a link between a firm's asset and financial structures.

_____ 23. Semi-variable costs may be fixed over a range of output then rise sharply as a higher output level is reached and remain fixed over this higher range of output.

_____ 24. Breakeven analysis must include allowance for all noncash expenses.

_____ 25. Financial Risk is a direct result of the firm's investment decision.

_____ 26. Financial Leverage is the financing of the firm's assets with securities bearing a fixed rate of return over a specific time period.

_____ 27. Firms can affect their total risk exposures by combining operating and financial leverage in different degrees.

_____ 28. The ratio of total variable costs to total sales is presumed constant in ordinary breakeven analysis.

MULTIPLE CHOICE

1. Which of the following is not a limitation of breakeven analysis?

    a. The price of the product is assumed to be constant.
    b. In multiple product firms, the product mix is assumed to be constant.
    c. It provides a method for analyzing operating leverage.
    d. Variable costs per unit are assumed to be constant.

2. Which of the following is not considered a fixed cost?

    a   Depreciation.
    b. Rent.
    c. Electricity.
    d. Administrative salaries.

3. At each point above the breakeven level the degree of operating leverage

    a. Increases; that is, the greater the sales level, the lower the DOL$_S$.
    b. Decreases; that is, the greater the sales level, the lower the DOL$_S$.
    c. Increases; that is, the greater the sales level, the greater the DOL$_S$.
    d. Decreases; that is, the greater the sales level, the greater the DOL$_S$.

4. The greater the degree of financial leverage, the greater the fluctuation in

    a. Variable costs.
    b. Administrative salaries.
    c. Earnings per share.
    d. None of the above.

5. At the breakeven level of sales the degree of operating leverage is

    a. Zero.
    b. Undefined.
    c. A positive number.
    d. Not enough information is given.

6. An operating leverage factor of 8.00 indicates that if sales increase by

    a. 1%, EBIT will increase by 1%.
    b. 1%, EBIT will increase by 8%.
    c. 8%, EBIT will fall by 1%.
    d. 8%, EBIT will rise by 8%.

7.	In the context of breakeven point in sales dollars, if the variable cost per unit rises and if all other variables remain constant, the breakeven level of sales will

	a.	Fall.
	b.	Rise.
	c.	Stay the same.
	d.	Either a or c.

8.	The combined effect of financial and operating leverage is

	a.	The sum of the degree of financial leverage and the degree of operating leverage.
	b.	The product of the two degrees.
	c.	The product of the degrees minus the sum of the degrees.
	d.	None of the above.

9.	The firm is exposing itself to financial risk when its % change in EPS ÷ % change in EBIT is:

	a.	Less than 1.
	b.	Greater than 1.
	c.	Equal to 1.
	d.	Between 0 and 1.

10.	Given that the degree of operating leverage is 10 and sales over the coming period are expected to increase by 5%, then the % change in EBIT would be:

	a.	2%.
	b.	5%.
	c.	2.5%.
	d.	none of the above.

11.	A firm that incurs a low level of fixed operating costs might prudently use:

	a.	A low degree of financial leverage.
	b.	A high degree of financial leverage.
	c.	A low degree of combined leverage.
	d.	None of the above.

12. As the firm's sales revenue increases over time,

    a.   It can lessen its business risks.
    b.   It can lessen its operating leverage.
    c.   Both a and b.
    d.   None of the above.

13. A combined leverage measure of 6.5 indicates that:

    a.   A 1% increase in sales would increase EPS by 6.5%.
    b.   A 1% increase in sales would increase EBIT by 6.5%.
    c.   A 1% increase in EPS would increase sales by 6.5%.
    d.   A 1% increase in EBIT would increase sales by 6.5%.

14. The practice of financing a portion of a firm's assets with securities bearing a fixed rate of return in hopes of increasing the ultimate return to shareholders refers to:

    a.   Operating leverage.
    b.   Financial leverage.
    c.   Breakeven sales level.

15. The selling price of a product is $25 and the unit variable cost is $17. If a firm's fixed costs are $20,000, what is the breakeven level in units:

    a.   800 units.
    b.   2,000 units.
    c.   2,500 units.
    d.   4,300 units.

16. Business risk is the residual effect of:

    a.   The company's cost structure.
    b.   Product demand characteristics.
    c.   Intra-industry competitive position.
    d.   All of the above.
    e.   None of the above.

17. The breakeven model assumes that if sales increase by 10% variable costs:

    a. Remain unchanged.
    b. Rise by 10%.
    c. Rise by 20%.
    d. The breakeven model makes no assumptions about variable costs and sales.

18. The breakeven level for the number of units sold is defined as:

    a. (Unit sales price minus unit variable cost) divided by total fixed costs.
    b. Unit sales minus (unit variable costs divided by total fixed costs).
    c. (Total fixed costs divided by unit sales price) minus unit variable costs.
    d. Trial and error analysis.
    e. All are acceptable techniques.

19. Breakeven analysis can be accomplished through each of the following techniques except:

    a. Contribution margin analysis.
    b. Algebraic analysis.
    c. Risk analysis.
    d. Trial and error analysis.
    e. All are acceptable techniques.

20. The degree of combined leverage can be defined as:

    a. The percentage change in EPS divided by the percentage change in sales.
    b. The degree of operating leverage divided by the degree of financial leverage.
    c. The percentage change in sales divided by the percentage change in EPS.
    d. The degree of financial leverage divided by the degree of operating leverage.

21.   As the quantity of product increases, the fixed cost per unit of output:

    a.   Increases.
    b.   Decreases.
    c.   Remains constant.
    d.   Increases to a certain level and then decreases.

22.   The degree of operating leverage can be attributed to _____ that a firm assumes.

    a.   The financial risk
    b.   The business risk
    c.   Both a. and b.
    d.   None of the above

23.   Breakeven Analysis and its assumptions can help the financial officer determine the:

    a.   Level of output that must be sold to recover all operating costs.
    b.   EBIT that will be achieved at various output levels.
    c.   Both of the above.
    d.   None of the above.

SOLUTIONS TO SELECTED SET B PROBLEMS (See text for problems.)

13-3B. (a) $Q_B = \dfrac{F}{P-V} = \dfrac{\$650,000}{\$175-\$115} = \dfrac{\$650,000}{\$60} = \underline{10,833 \text{ Units}}$

(b) $S_B = (10,833 \text{ units}) (\$175) = \underline{\$1,895,775}$

Alternatively,

$$S_B = \dfrac{F}{1 - \dfrac{VC}{S}} = \dfrac{\$650,000}{1 - \dfrac{\$115}{\$175}}$$

$$= \dfrac{\$650,000}{1-0.6571} = \dfrac{\$650,000}{.3429} = \underline{\$1,895,833}$$

Note: $1,895,833 differs from $1,895,775 only due to rounding.

(c)

	10,000 units	16,000 units	20,000 units
Sales	$1,750,000	$2,800,000	$3,500,000
Variable costs	1,150,000	1,840,000	2,300,000
Revenue before fixed costs	600,000	960,000	1,200,000
Fixed costs	650,000	650,000	650,000
EBIT	$ -50,000	$ 310,000	$ 550,000

(d)

10,000 units	16,000 units	20,000 units
$\dfrac{\$60,000}{-\$50,000}$	$\dfrac{\$960,000}{\$310,000}$	$\dfrac{\$1,200,000}{\$550,000}$
= -12 times	= 3.1 times	= 2.2 times

Notice that the degree of operating leverage decreases as the firm's sales level rises <u>above</u> the breakeven point.

13-7B.

(a) $\dfrac{\text{Revenue before Fixed costs}}{\text{EBIT}} = \dfrac{\$24,000,000}{\$14,000,000} = \underline{1.71 \text{ times}}$

(b) $\dfrac{\text{EBIT}}{\text{EBIT - I}} = \dfrac{\$14,000,000}{\$12,850,000} = \underline{1.09 \text{ times}}$

(c) $\text{DCL}_{\$40,000,000} = (1.71)\ (1.09) = \underline{1.86 \text{ times}}$

(d) $S^* = \dfrac{F}{1 - \dfrac{VC}{S}} = \dfrac{\$10,000,000}{1 - \dfrac{\$16\text{ m}}{\$40\text{m}}}$

$= \dfrac{\$10,000,000}{1 - 0.4} = \dfrac{\$10,000,000}{0.6} = \underline{\$16,666,667}$

(e) $(20\%)\ (1.86) = \underline{37.2\%}$

13-10B. (a)

	Farm City Seeds	Empire Sod	Golden Peaches
Sales	$1,800,000	$1,710,000	$1,400,000
Variable costs	1,410,000	1,305,000	950,000
Sales before fixed costs	$390,000	$ 405,000	$ 450,000
Fixed costs	30,000	110,000	33,000
EBIT	$ 360,000	$ 295,000	$ 417,000

(b) Farm City: $Q_B = \dfrac{F}{P-V} = \dfrac{\$30,000}{\$15.00-\$11.75} = \dfrac{\$30,000}{\$3.25} = \underline{9,231 \text{ units}}$

Empire Sod: $Q_B = \dfrac{\$110,000}{\$190-\$145} = \dfrac{\$110,000}{\$45} = \underline{2,444 \text{ units}}$

Golden Peaches: $Q_B = \dfrac{\$33,000}{\$28.00-\$19} = \dfrac{\$33,000}{\$9} = \underline{3,667 \text{ units}}$

(c)
Farm City

$\dfrac{\$390,000}{\$360,000} = 1.083 \text{ times}$

Empire

$\dfrac{\$405,000}{\$295,000} = 1.373 \text{ times}$

Golden

$\dfrac{\$450,000}{\$417,000} = 1.079 \text{ times}$

(d) Empire Sod, since its degree of operating leverage exceeds that of the other two companies.

13-13B.

(a) S (1 - 0.8) - $335,000 = $270,000

0.2S = $605,000

S = $3,025,000 = (P · Q)

Now, solve the above relationship for P:

175,000 (P) = $3,025,000

P = $17.29

13-27

(b)
Sales	$3,025,000
Less: Total variable costs	2,420,000
Revenue before fixed costs	$605,000
Less: Total fixed costs	335,000
EBIT	$ 270,000

13-17B.

(a) $Q_B = \dfrac{F}{P - V} = \dfrac{\$55,000}{\$28-\$17} = \dfrac{\$55,000}{\$11} = \underline{5,000 \text{ units}}$

(b) $S_B = \dfrac{F}{1 - \dfrac{VC}{S}} = \dfrac{\$55,000}{1 - \dfrac{\$17}{\$28}} = \dfrac{\$55,000}{1 - 0.607} = \dfrac{\$55,000}{.393} = \underline{\$140,000}$

(c)

	4,000 units	6,000 units	8,000 units
Sales	$112,000	$168,000	$224,000
Variable costs	68,000	102,000	136,000
Sales before fixed costs	$ 44,000	$ 66,000	$ 88,000
Fixed costs	55,000	55,000	55,000
EBIT	$-11,000	$ 11,000	$ 33,000

(d)

4000 units	6000 units	8000 units
$\dfrac{\$44,000}{-\$11,000} = 4X$	$\dfrac{\$66,000}{\$11,000} = 6X$	$\dfrac{\$88,000}{\$33,000} = 2.67X$

(e) The degree of operating leverage decreases as the firm's sales level rises above the breakeven point.

13-21B.   The task is to find the breakeven point in units for the firm. Several approaches are possible, but the one presented below makes intuitive sense to students.

Step (1)   Compute the operating profit margin:
(Margin) x (Turnover) = Return on Operating Assets
(M) x (6) = 0.16
M = 0.027

Step (2)   Compute the sales level associated with the given output
           level:

$$\frac{Sales}{\$3,250,000} = 6$$

Sales = $19,500,000

Step (3)   Compute EBIT:

(0.027) ($19,500,000) = EBIT = $520,000

Step (4)   Compute revenue before fixed costs.   Since the degree of
           operating leverage is 9 times, revenue before fixed costs
           (RBF) is 9 times EBIT as follows:
           RBF = (9) ($520,000) = $4,680,000

Step (5)   Compute total variable costs:
           Sales - Total variable costs = $4,680,000
           $19,500,000 - Total variable costs = $4,680,000
           Total variable costs = $14,820,000

Step (6)   Compute total fixed costs:
           RBF - Fixed costs = $520,000
           $4,680,000 - Fixed costs = $520,000
           Fixed costs = $4,160,000

Step (7)   Find the selling price per unit, and the variable cost per unit:

$$P = \frac{\$19,500,000}{1,700,000} = \$11.471$$

$$V = \frac{\$14,820,000}{1,700,000} = \$8.718$$

Step (8)   Compute the breakeven point:

$$Q_B = \frac{F}{P - V} = \frac{\$4,160,000}{(\$11.471) - (\$8.718)} = \frac{\$4,160,000}{\$2.753}$$

$$= \underline{1,511,079 \text{ units}}$$

13-25B.

	A	B	C	D	Total
Sales	$38,505	$61,995	$29,505	$19,995	$150,000
Variable costs*	23,103	42,157	23,604	7,998	96,862
Contribution margin	$15,402	$19,838	$ 5,901	$ 11,997	$ 53,138
Contribution margin ratio	40%	32%	20%	60%	35%

*Variable costs = (Sales) (1 - contribution margin ratio)

Breakeven point in sales dollars:

$$S^* = \frac{F}{1 - \frac{VC}{S}} = \frac{\$35,000}{1 - 0.65} = \frac{\$35,000}{0.35} = \underline{\$98,799}$$

CHAPTER 14

Planning the Firm's Financing Mix

Orientation: This chapter concentrates on the way the firm arranges its sources of funds. The cost of capital-capital structure argument is highlighted. A moderate view on the effect of financial leverage use on the composite cost of capital is adopted. Later, techniques useful to the financial officer faced with the determination of an appropriate financing mix are described.

I.   Introduction

    A.   A distinction can be made between the terms financial structure and capital structure.

        1.   Financial structure is the mix of all items that appear on the right-hand side of the firm's balance sheet.

        2.   Capital structure is the mix of the long-term, sources of funds used by the firm.

        3.   In this chapter we do not dwell on the question of dealing with an appropriate maturity composition of the firm's sources of funds. Our main focus is on capital structure management i.e., determining the proper proportions relative to the total in which the permanent forms of financing should be used.

    B.   The objective of capital structure management is to mix the permanent sources of funds in a manner that will maximize the company's common stock price. This will minimize the firm's composite cost of capital. This proper mix of funds sources is referred to as the optimal capital structure.

II.   A glance at capital structure theory

    A.   The cost of capital-capital structure argument may be characterized by this question:

        1.   Can the firm affect its overall cost of funds, either favorably or unfavorably, by varying the mixture of financing sources used?

    B.   The argument deals with the postulated effect of the use of financial leverage on the overall cost of capital of the company.

    C.   If the firm's cost of capital can be affected by the degree to which it uses financial leverage, then capital structure management is an important subset of business financial management.

    D.   The analytical discussion revolves around a simplified version of the basic dividend valuation model. Recall that the basic dividend valuation model can be expressed as:

$$P_0 = \sum_{t=1}^{\infty} \frac{D_t}{(1+K_c)^t}$$

    where P_0 =   the current price of the firm's common stock,

               D_t =   the cash dividend per share expected by investors during period

               K_c =   the cost of common equity capital.

        1.   If it is assumed that (1) cash dividends will not change over the infinite holding period and that (2) the firm retains none of its current earnings, then the cash dividend flowing to investors can be viewed as a level payment over an infinite holding period.

2. Under these conditions, the basic dividend valuation model reduces to the equation noted below, where E_t represents earnings per share during the time period t:

$$P_0 = \frac{D_t}{K_c} = \frac{E_t}{K_c}$$

3. The various capital structure theories discussed in Chapter 10 use the above equation in the context of a partial equilibrium analysis in order to assess the impact of leverage use on common stock price.

III. Capital structure theory: The independence hypothesis (Extreme position 1)

A. According to this position, made famous by Professors Franco Modigliani and Merton H. Miller, in a setting in which business income is not subject to taxation (and, thus, the deductibility of interest expense is irrelevant for valuation purposes) the firm's composite cost of capital, K_o, and common stock price, P_0, are both <u>independent</u> of the degree to which the firm chooses to use (or avoid) financial leverage.

B. This means that the total market value of the firm's outstanding securities (taken to be the market value of debt plus the market value of common stock) is <u>unaffected</u> by the manner in which the right-hand side of the balance sheet is arranged.

C. The independence hypothesis rests upon what is called the <u>net operating income</u> (NOI) approach to valuation. When corporate income is not taxed, this methodology arrives at the market value of the firm by capitalizing (discounting) the firm's expected net operating income stream. The division of that income stream to investors (either debt or equity) is a mere detail that does not affect enterprise value.

D.   In this framework, the use of a greater degree of financial leverage may result in greater earnings and dividends, but the firm's cost of common equity will rise at precisely the same rate as the earnings and dividends. This means that the firm's common stock price is unaffected by the use of financial leverage over all degrees of leverage use.

E.   This viewpoint is illustrated in Figures 14.1 and 14.2. Figure 14.1 shows that the weighted cost of capital, K_0, is independent of the degree of financial leverage used. The use of more debt would cause the cost of common equity to rise, resulting in exactly the same overall cost of capital that persisted before more debt was, in fact, used. Figure 14.2 shows that stock price, P_0, is not influenced by the degree of financial leverage used.

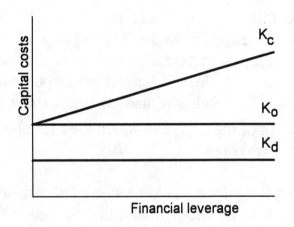

Figure 14.1
Capital Costs and Financial Leverage: No Taxes
The Independence Hypothesis (NOI Theory)

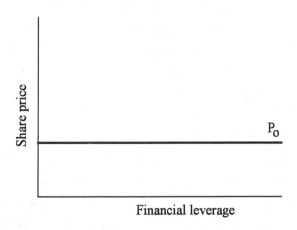

Figure 14.2
Stock Price and Financial Leverage: No Taxes
The Independence Hypothesis (NOI Theory)

IV.   Capital structure theory: The dependence hypothesis (Extreme position 2)

A.   This position is at the opposite pole from the previously outlined independence hypothesis. The dependence hypothesis suggests that both the weighted cost of capital, K_O and the firm's common stock price, P_0, are affected by the firm's use of financial leverage.

B.   At this extreme, no matter how modest or excessive the firm's use of debt financing, both its cost of debt capital, K_d, and cost of equity capital. K_c, will not be affected by capital structure adjustments.

C.   So, the cost of debt is less than the cost of common equity, which implies that greater financial leverage use will lower the firm's weighted cost of capital, K_O, indefinitely. Further, greater use of debt financing will have a favorable effect on the firm's stock price.

D.   The dependence hypothesis rests upon what is called the <u>net income</u> (NI) <u>approach to valuation</u>. Both the NOI model and the NI model are illustrated at the end of this <u>Study Guide</u> chapter in the first study problem. You should be familiar with their structure, assumptions, and implications.

E.   The dependence hypothesis viewpoint is shown in Figures 14.3 and 14.4. Notice in Figure 14.3 that the firm's cost of capital, K_O decreases as the debt-to-equity ratio increases. Figure 14.4 shows that according to this position, the common stock price rises with increased leverage use. The implication is that the firm should use as much financial leverage as is possible.

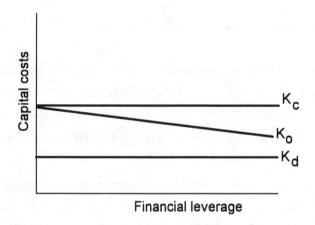

Figure 14.3
Capital Costs and Financial Leverage: No Taxes
The Dependence Hypothesis (NI Theory)

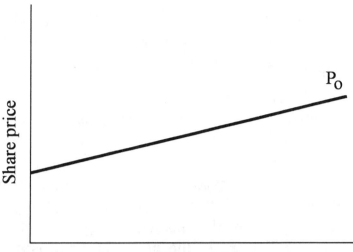

Figure 14.4
Stock Price and Financial Leverage: No Taxes
The Dependence Hypothesis (NI Theory)

V.   Capital structure theory: A moderate position

A.   The moderate position on capital structure importance admits to the facts that (1) interest expense is tax deductible in the world of corporate activity and (2) the probability of the firm's suffering bankruptcy costs is directly related to the company's use of financial leverage.

B.   When interest expense is tax deductible, the <u>sum</u> of the cash flows that the firm could pay to <u>all</u> contributors of corporate capital (debt investors and equity investors) is affected by its financing mix. This is <u>not</u> the case when an environment of no corporate taxation is presumed.

1.   The amount of the <u>tax shield on interest</u> may be calculated as:

Tax shield   = $r_d(M)(t)$

where r_d =   the interest rate paid on outstanding debt,

M   =   the principal amount of the debt,

t   =   the firm's tax rate.

2. The moderate position presents the view that the tax shield must have value in the marketplace. After all, the government's take is decreased and the investor's take is increased because of the deductibility of interest expense.

3. Therefore, according to this position, financial leverage affects firm value and it must also affect the cost of corporate capital.

C. To use too much financial leverage, however, would be imprudent. It seems reasonable to offer that the probability that the firm will be unable to meet the financial obligations contained in its debt contracts will increase the more the firm uses leverage-inducing instruments in its capital structure (debt). The likelihood of firm failure, then, carries with it certain costs (bankruptcy costs) that rise as leverage use increases. There will be some point at which the expected cost of default will be large enough to outweigh the tax shield advantage of debt financing. At that point the firm will turn to common equity financing.

D. Figure 14.5 depicts the moderate view on capital structure importance. This view of the cost of capital-capital structure argument produces a saucer-shaped or U-shaped average cost of capital curve. In Figure 14.5 the firm's optimal range of financial leverage use lies between points A and B. It would be imprudent for the firm to use additional financial leverage beyond point B because (1) the average cost of capital would be higher than it has to be and (2) the firm's common stock price would be lower than it has to be. Therefore, we can say that the degree of financial leverage use signified by point B represents the firm's <u>debt capacity</u>.

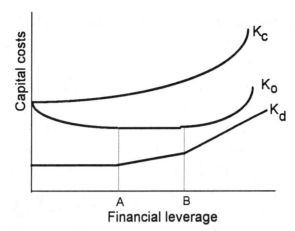

Figure 14.5
Capital Costs and Financial Leverage: The Moderate View Which Considers Taxes and Financial Distress

E. We conclude that the determination of the firm's financing mix <u>is</u> centrally important to both the financial manager and the firm's owners.

VI. Firm value, agency costs, the Static Trade-off theory, and the Pecking Order theory

A. To ensure that agent-managers act in the stockholders' best interest requires

1. Proper incentives to do so through compensation plans and perquisites

2. Decisions that are monitored through bonding, auditing financial statements, limiting decisions, and reviewing the perquisites

B. Agency problems stem from conflicts of interest, and capital-structure management encompasses a natural conflict between stockholders and bondholders.

1. To reduce the conflict of interest, creditors and stockholders may agree to include several protective covenants in the bond contract.

2. Monitoring costs should differ in direct proportion to low or high levels of leverage.

C. Static trade-off theory distinguished from pecking order theory.

1. Static trade-off theory provides for the identification of a precise optimum financing mix. This financing mix should logically determine the firm's *targeted* leverage ratio.

2. Static trade-off theory "prices" both expected financial distress costs and agency costs.

3. Pecking order theory suggests that firm's finance projects within a well-defined hierarchy that begins with internally generated funds and ends with new common equity (the least desired funds source).

4. Thus, pecking order theory provides no precisely defined target leverage ratio since typical leverage metrics just reflect the firm's cumulative external financing needs over time.

VII. Agency costs, free cash flow, and capital structure

A. Free cash flow as defined by Professor Michael C. Jensen is the "cash flow in excess of that required to fund all projects that have positive net present values when discounted at the relevant cost of capital."

B. Like the pecking order theory, the *free cash flow theory of capital structure* does not give a precise solution that determines the firm's optimal financing mix.

C. This free cash flow theory does provide a framework and rationale for justifying why shareholders and their boards of directors might use more debt (financial leverage) to control management behavior and decisions.

D. The upshot of all of these theories and perspectives is that the determination of the firm's financing mix is centrally important to the financial manager. The firm's stockholders are, indeed, affected by capital-structure decisions; these decisions affect the firm's stock price.

VIII. Basic tools of capital structure management

A. Recall that the use of financial leverage has two effects on the earnings stream flowing to the firm's common stockholders: (1) the added variability in the earnings per share (EPS) stream that accompanies the use of fixed-charge securities and (2) the level of EPS at a given earnings before interest and taxes level (EBIT) associated with a specific capital structure. The first effect is quantified by the degree of financial leverage measure discussed in Chapter 13. The second effect is analyzed by means of what is generally referred to as EBIT-EPS analysis.

B. The objective of EBIT-EPS analysis is to find the EBIT level that will equate EPS regardless of the financing plan chosen (from among two plans) by the financial manager.

1. A graphic analysis or an algebraic analysis can be used.

2. By allowing for sinking fund payments, the analysis can focus upon uncommitted earnings per share (UEPS).

3. Study problems 2 and 3 at the end of this chapter illustrate the nature of EBIT-EPS analysis.

4. EBIT-EPS analysis considers only the level of the earnings stream and ignores the variability (riskiness) in it. In other words, this tool of capital structure management disregards the implicit costs of debt financing. Therefore, it must be used with caution and in conjunction with other basic tools of capital structure management.

C. <u>Comparative</u> <u>leverage</u> <u>ratios</u> provide another tool of capital structure management. This involves the computation of various balance sheet leverage ratios and coverage ratios. Information for the latter comes essentially from the income statement. The ratios that would exist under alternative financing plans can then be computed and examined for their suitableness to management.

D. The use of <u>industry norms</u> in conjunction with comparative leverage ratios can aid the financial manager in arriving at an appropriate financing mix. Industry norms can be thought of as standards for comparison. We recognize that industry groupings contain firms whose basic business risk may differ widely. Nevertheless, corporate financial analysts, investment bankers, commercial loan officers, and bond rating agencies rely on industry classes in order to compute such "normal" ratios. Since so many observers are interested in industry standards, the financial officer must be too.

E. Finally, the financial officer can study the projected impact of capital structure decisions on corporate cash flows. This is often called <u>cash</u> <u>flow</u> <u>analysis</u> or the study of <u>company-wide</u> <u>cash</u> <u>flows</u>. This involves the preparation of a series of cash budgets under (1) different economic conditions and (2) different rent capital structures. The net cash flows under these different situations can be examined to determine if the financing requirements expose the firm to such a high degree of default risk that it is unbearable. According to this tool, the appropriate level of financial leverage use is reached when the chance of running out of cash is exactly equal to that which management will assume. An underlying assumption is that management's risk-bearing preferences are conditioned by the investing marketplace.

IX. How financial managers use this material

A. The opinions and practices of financial executives reinforce the major topics covered in this chapter. Most senior financial officers, for example, <u>do</u> believe there is an optimum capital structure for the corporation.

B. Target debt ratios are widely used by financial officers. Surveys indicate that the firm's actual target debt ratio is affected by several factors including (1) the firm's ability to adequately meet its financing charges, (2) maintaining a desired bond rating, (3) providing an adequate borrowing reserve, and (4) exploiting the perceived advantages of financial leverage. In practice the firm's own management group and staff of analysts seem to be the most important influence on actually setting the target debt ratio.

C. In this chapter we defined debt capacity as the maximum proportion of debt that the firm can include in its capital structure and still maintain its lowest composite cost of capital. Executives operationalize this concept in different ways. The most popular approach is to define the firm's debt capacity as a target percent of total capitalization (i.e., total long-term debt divided by the sum of all long-term debt, preferred equity, and common equity).

D. In the opinion of your authors, the single most important factor that should affect the firm's financing mix is the underlying nature of the business in which it operates. This means the firm's business risk must be carefully assessed. Recall that business risk was defined in Chapter 13. This means the firm's capital structure cannot be properly designed without a thorough understanding of its commercial (business) strategy.

Study Problems

1. The Columbia Camera Company has $10,000,000 of net operating earnings. In its capital structure, $14,500,000 worth of debt is outstanding, with an interest of 12 percent. The debt is selling in the marketplace at its book value. Parts (a) and (b) assume that there is no tax on corporate income.

    (a) According to the NOI valuation method, compute the total value of the firm and the implied equity capitalization rate. Assume an implied overall capitalization rate, k_O, of 20 percent.

(b) Compute the total value of the firm and the implied overall capitalization rate, k_O, according to the dependence hypothesis, (NI theory) capitalization model. Assume an equity-capitalization rate, k_c, of 25 percent.

(c) Now allow for the existence of a federal tax on corporate income at a 53 percent rate. Calculate the value of the firm's tax shield.

SOLUTION

(a)

O	Net operating earnings	$10,000,000
k_O	Overall capitalization rate	0.20
V	Total value of the firm	$50,000,000
B	Market value of debt	-14,500,000
S	Market value of stock	$35,500,000

$$k_c = \frac{O - I}{K} = \frac{\$10,000,000 - \$1,740,000}{\$35,500,000} = 23.27\%$$

where I = interest expense

(b)

O	=	$10,000,000
I	=	1,740,000
E	=	$8,260,000
k_c	=	0.25
S	=	$33,040,000
B	=	14,500,000
V	=	$47,540,000

$$k_O = \frac{O}{V} = \frac{\$10,000,000}{\$47,540,000} = 21.03\%$$

(c)

$$\begin{aligned} \text{Tax shield} &= r_d(M)(t) \\ &= (0.12)(14,500,000)(0.53) \\ &= \$922,200 \end{aligned}$$

2.   E. Wrok and Associates, Inc., are planning to open a small manufacturing corporation. The company will manufacture a full line of solar-energized home products. The investors of the company have proposed two financing plans. Plan I is an all common equity alternative. Under this plan 200,000 common shares will be sold to net the firm $20 per share. Financial leverage is stipulated in Plan II and 100,000 shares will be sold. A debt issue with a 30-year maturity period will be privately placed. The interest rate on the debt issue will be 18 percent while the principal borrowed will amount to $2,000,000. The corporate tax rate is 50 percent.

   (a)   Find the EBIT indifference level associated with the two financing proposals.

   (b)   Prepare an analytical income statement that proves EPS will be the same regardless of the plan chosen at the EBIT level found in part (a).

   (c)   If a detailed financial analysis projects that long-term EBIT will always be close to $100,000 annually, which plan would be chosen? Why?

SOLUTION

   (a)   In the following equation, E = EBIT.

$$\frac{(E - \$0)(1 - 0.5) - 0}{200,000} = \frac{(E - \$360,000)(1 - 0.5) - 0}{100,000}$$

$$\frac{0.5E}{200,000} = \frac{0.5E - \$180,000}{100,000}$$

$$\$50,000E = 100,000E - \$36,000,000,000$$

$$E = \underline{\$720,000}$$

(b)   Analytical Income Statement

	With C/S Financing	Financing With C/S and Debt
EBIT	$720,000	$720,000
Less: Interest Expense	0	360,000
Earnings before taxes	$720,000	$360,000
Less: Taxes @ 50%	360,000	180,000
Earnings available to common	$360,000	$180,000
C/S Outstanding	200,000	100,000
EPS	$1.80	$1.80

(c)   Plan II, because at any level above the indifference point, the more heavily levered financing plan will generate a higher EPS.

3.   Albina's Ice Cream Factory's capital structure for the past year of operations is shown below:

First Mortgage bonds at 15%	$ 4,000,000
Debentures at 17%	3,500,000
Common stock (1,500,000 shares)	10,500,000
Retained earnings	2,000,000
Total	$20,000,000

The federal income tax rate is 50%. Albina's Ice Cream Factory, home-based in San Antonio, wants to raise an additional $1,500,000 to open new facilities in Houston and Dallas. The firm can accomplish this via two alternatives. That is, it can sell a new issue of 20-year debentures with 18 percent interest; alternatively, 30,000 new shares of common stock can be sold to the public to net the ice cream factory $50 per share. A recent study performed by an outside consulting organization projected Albina's Ice Cream's long-term EBIT level at approximately $13,575,000.

(a)   Find the indifference level of EBIT (with regard to earnings per share) between the suggested financing plans.

14-16

(b) Which alternative do you recommend that Albina's Ice Cream Factory pursue?

SOLUTION

(a) In the following equations, E = EBIT

$$\frac{(E - \$1,195,000)\,(0.5)}{1,530,000} = \frac{(E - \$1,465,000)\,(0.5)}{1,500,000}$$

$$\frac{0.5E - \$597,500}{153} = \frac{0.5E - \$732,500}{150}$$

$$75E - \$89,625,000 = 76.5E - \$112,072,500$$

$$E = \underline{\$14,965,000} \text{ indifference level of EBIT}$$

(b) The consulting firm projected Albina's Ice Cream Factory's long-term EBIT at $13,575,000. Since this projected level of EBIT is less than the indifference level of $14,965,000, the earnings per share of the firm will be greater if the common stock is issued.

4. Carlton Sprinklers is considering a plan to increase its financial leverage. The plan being considered by management is to sell $5 million of bonds that would mature in 20 years. The interest rate on the bonds would be 12%. The bonds would have a sinking fund provision requiring that one-twentieth of the principal be retired each year. The management of Carlton feels that the upcoming year will be their toughest ever and could serve as a worst case scenario. Carlton usually carries an operating cash balance of $1 million. Cash collections for the coming year are expected to be $5 million. Miscellaneous cash receipts will be $300,000. Wages and salaries will be $1.2 million. Raw materials costs will be $1.5 million. The firm expects $750,000 in non-discretionary cash outflows and all taxes are included. The firm is in the 34% marginal tax bracket.

(a) At present, Carlton is unleveraged. What will be the total fixed financial charges that the firm must pay next year?

(b) If the bonds are issued, what is your forecast of the expected cash balance at the end of the next year?

(c)   Should Carlton's management consider issuing the bonds?

SOLUTION

(a)   FC   =   Interest + Sinking Fund
        FC   =   600,000 + 250,000
        FC   = $850,000

(b) CB_r = $CB_0 + NCF_r$ - FC
        CB_0 =   1,000,000;
        FC   =   850,000; and
        NCF_r =   5,300,000 - 3,450,000 = 1,850,000

    so CB_r =   1,000,000 + 1,850,000 - 850,000
                =   2,000,000

(c)   The above analysis suggests that Carlton could cover its cash obligations, if it issued the bonds.

Self-Test

TRUE-FALSE

____ 1.   Capital structure is the mix of all items that appear on the right-hand side of the firm's balance sheet.

____ 2.   The major influence on the maturity structure of the financing plan is the nature of the assets owned by the firm.

____ 3.   The optimal capital structure can be defined as the mix of permanent sources of funds that minimize the company's common stock price.

____ 4.   The EBIT-EPS analysis measures the variability (riskiness) of the earnings stream thereby recognizing the implicit costs of debt financing.

_____ 5. According to cash flow analysis, the appropriate level of financial leverage use is reached when the chance of running out of cash is exactly equal to that which management will assume.

_____ 6. In computing the firm's tax bill the interest expense is assumed not to be tax deductible.

_____ 7. Inputs to the coverage ratios generally come from the firm's balance sheet.

_____ 8. According to the moderate position of capital structure theory, financial leverage affects firm value but not the cost of corporate capital.

_____ 9. Above a critical level of EBIT the firm's earnings per share will be lower if greater degrees of financial leverage are employed.

_____ 10. Industry norms, used with other tools of capital structure management can be helpful in determining an appropriate financing mix.

_____ 11. If capital structures consist only of debt instruments and common equity and both K_c and K_d are the same, then a change in the capital structure would <u>not</u> affect the firm's stock price.

_____ 12. Whether or not corporate income is taxed, the sum of the cash flows made to all contributors of corporate financial capital is not affected by the firm's financing mix.

_____ 13. In practice, as more financial leverage is used, it will increase the firm's value indefinitely and lower its cost of capital continuously.

_____ 14. The EBIT-EPS analysis chart tells us that EPS will be greater than zero, if the EBIT level just covers the plan's financing cost.

_____ 15. At a point below the EBIT indifference level, the financing plan involving less leverage will generate a higher EPS.

_____ 16. Capital structure is equal to the financial structure less current liabilities.

_____ 17. According to NOI theory the real cost of debt includes the change in the cost of common equity brought about by the use of the debt.

_____ 18. NOI theory suggests that cost of capital and the stock price are independent of the degree to which the company chooses to leverage.

_____ 19. Debt capacity is the maximum proportion of debt that a company can include in its capital structure without affecting the cost of common equity.

_____ 20. A sinking fund is a real cash reserve used to buy back common equity in the event of a hostile takeover.

_____ 21. The net income approach to valuation implies that the fir should adopt an all-debt capital structure.

_____ 22. Agency costs refer to those expenses paid to lawyers. accountants, etc. during bankruptcy proceedings.

_____ 23. Financial managers must frequently use coverage ratios to operationalize debt capacity concepts.

_____ 24. External economic factors are an important influence on determining a firm's target debt-ratio, but firm-specific factors have to be considered as well.

_____ 25. The Independence Hypothesis differs from the Dependence Hypothesis in that the Dependence Hypothesis suggests that the total market value of a firm's outstanding securities is <u>unaffected</u> by the right hand side of the balance sheet--i.e., the firm's financing mix.

_____ 26. The purpose of EBIT-EPS analysis is to determine the level of operating income at which EBIT equals EPS for a single financing plan.

_____ 27. Most senior financial officers believe there is an <u>optimum capital structure</u> for the corporation.

MULTIPLE CHOICE

1.   According to the dependence hypothesis

   a.   Regardless of the amount of debt financing used by the firm, its cost of debt and equity capital are unaffected.
   b.   Greater use of debt financing results in a favorable effect on the firm's stock price.
   c   a and b.
   d.   None of the above.

2.   The firm's capital structure consists of

   a.   Long-term debt.
   b.   Common equity.
   c.   Preferred equity.
   d   Only b and c.
   e.   All of the above.

3.   A firm will turn to common equity financing when

   a.   The stock market is looking favorable.
   b.   The expected cost of default is greater than the tax advantage of debt financing.
   c.   It reaches optimal capital structure.
   d.   Only a and b.

4.   The objective of capital structure management is to

   a.   Minimize the composite cost of capital.
   b.   Determine the optimal capital structure.
   c.   Maximize the common stock price.
   d.   All of the above.

5. The implicit cost of debt is the change in the cost of common equity brought on by using _____.

    a. Operating leverage.
    b. Financial leverage.
    c. Stock options.
    d. All of the above.

6. Which of the following assumptions does capital structure theory not include?

    a. Corporate income is not subject to any tax.
    b. Transaction costs of selling securities are prevalent.
    c. The expected values of all investors' forecasts of the future levels of EBIT for each firm are identical.
    d. The capital structures consist only of stocks and bonds.

7. According to the independence hypothesis:

    a. The firm's cost of capital and stock price is unaffected by the degree of financial leverage.
    b. The firm's total market value is affected by the manner in which the right-hand side of the balance sheet is arranged.
    c. Both a and b.
    d. None of the above.

8. Which of the following is not a limitation of EBIT-EPS analysis?

    a. It disregards the explicit cost of debt financing.
    b. It ignores the level of the firm's earnings stream.
    c. Both a and b are limitations.
    d. None of the above.

9. Which of the following is not true about capital structure theory (moderate position)?

    a. Firm's bankruptcy cost is related to its use of financial leverage.
    b. The sum of the cash flows that the firm could pay to all contributors of corporate capital is not affected by its financing mix.
    c. Financial leverage affects the firm's value.
    d. a and c.

10. Which of the following is <u>not</u> a basic tool of capital structure management?

    a. EBIT-EPS analysis.
    b. Comparative leverage ratios.
    c. Use of industry norms.
    d. None of the above.

11. According to the NOI approach, a 10% increase in earnings and dividends per share caused by a financing mix change will:

    a. Cause the firm's cost of common equity to rise by 10%.
    b. Cause the cost of common equity to fall by some percentage less than 10%
    c. Cause the cost of common equity to rise by some percentage less than 10%.
    d. Cause no change in the cost of common equity.

12. The dependence hypothesis suggests that:

    a. The use of more debt will not change the cost of common equity.
    b. The use of more debt will decrease the overall cost of capital.
    c. Both a and b.
    d. Neither a or b.

13. Which of the following is/are a way of analyzing capital structure:

   a. EBIT-EPS analysis.
   b. Comparative leverage ratios.
   c. Analysis of cash flows.
   d. a and b.
   e. All of the above.

14. Which capital structure theory (theories) indicates that the firm <u>can</u> affect its overall cost of funding by varying the proportions of its financing sources?

      1. Net income theory
      2. Net operating income theory
      3. Moderate theory

   a. 1 and 2.
   b. 2 and 3.
   c. 1 and 3.
   d. None of the above.
   e. All of the above.

15. Within prudent limits, which factor influencing optimal capital structure can increase the firm's share price?

   a. Agency relationships.
   b. Bankruptcy costs.
   c. Debt tax shields.
   d. All of the above.

16. Uncommitted earnings per share (UEPS) differs from EPS in its recognition of:

   a. Sinking fund commitments.
   b. Taxes.
   c. Common stock dividends.
   d. None of the above.

17. The Optimal Capital Structure refers to a capital structure that:

    a.   Is comprised of 99.9 percent debt capital.
    b.   Will minimize the composite cost of a firm's capital for raising a given amount of funds.
    c.   Will minimize the firm's common stock price.
    d.   All of the above.

18. The Target Debt Ratio is affected by the firm's ability to:

    a.   Adequately meet is financing charges.
    b.   Maintain a desired bond rating.
    c.   Provide an adequate borrowing reserve.
    d.   Exploit the perceived advantages of financial leverage.
    e.   All of the above.

19. The most important factor that affects the firm's financing mix is:

    a.   The underlying nature of the business in which it operates.
    b.   The industry financing norms.
    c.   The firm's debt capacity.
    d.   None of the above.

SOLUTIONS TO SELECTED SET B PROBLEMS (See text for problems.)

14-3B.

    (a)

$$\frac{(EBIT - 0)\,(1 - 0.34)}{150,000\ (shares)} = \frac{(EBIT - \$220,000)\,(1 - 0.34)}{50,000\ (shares)}$$

$$\frac{0.66\ EBIT}{15} = \frac{0.66\ EBIT - \$145,200}{5}$$

$$EBIT = \underline{\$330,000}$$

    (b)   Since $450,000 exceeds the indifference level of $330,000 from part (a), the levered alternative (Plan B) will generate the higher EPS.

(c) Here we compute EPS for each financing plan, apply the relevant price/earnings ratios, and, thereby, forecast a common stock price for each plan. Thus, we have:

	Plan A	Plan B
EBIT	$450,000	$450,000
I	0	220,000
EBT	$450,000	$230,000
T (0.34)	153,000	78,200
NI	$297,000	$151,800
P	0	0
EAC	$297,000	$151,800
÷ No. of common shares	150,000	50,000
EPS	$ 1.98	$ 3.036
x P-E ratio	19	12.39
= Projected Stock Price	$37.62	$37.62

The added riskiness of Plan B, owing to the use of financial leverage, is reflected in the lower P-E ratio associated with Plan B (i.e., 12.39x versus 19x for Plan A). The rational investor will prefer Plan A (unlevered) as the same projected stock price ($37.62) can be obtained with a lower level of risk exposure.

14-6B.

(a) FC = Interest + Sinking Fund

$$FC = (\$11 \text{ million}) (.16) + \frac{(\$11 \text{ million})}{20 \text{ yr.}}$$

FC = $1,760,000 + \$550,000$ = $2,310,000$

(b) CB_r = $CB_0 + NCF_r - FC$

where: Cb_0 = $500,000

FC = $2,310,000

and, NCF_r = $3,800,000 - \$3,600,000 = \$200,000$

so, CB_r = $500,000 + $200,000 - $2,310,000

CB_r = $\underline{- \$1,610,000}$

(c)   We see that the company has a preference for a $500,000 cash balance. The combination of the recessionary period and the proposed issue of bonds would put the firm's recessionary cash balance (CB_r) at -$1,610,000.   The combination of this negative number and the statement that the firm likes a cash balance of $500,000 suggests strongly that the proposed bond issue be postponed.

14-10B.

(a)   FC   =   Interest + Sinking Fund

FC   = $600,000 + $300,000 = $\underline{\$900,000}$

(b) CB_r = $CB_o + NCF_r - FC$

where: Cb_o = $750,000

FC   = $900,000

and, NCF_r = $3,700,000 - $3,200,000 = $500,000

so, CB_r = $ 750,000 + $500,000 - $900,000

CB_r = $\underline{\$350,000}$

(c)   The firm ordinarily carries a $750,000 cash balance.   This analysis shows that during a tight economic period the firm's cash balance (CB_r) could fall to as low as $350,000. Management might well decide not to issue the proposed bonds.

14-13B.

(a)   ($22) (1,000,000 shares) = $\underline{\$22,000,000}$

(b) $K_c = \dfrac{D_t}{P_o} = \dfrac{E_t}{P_o} = \dfrac{\$4.75}{\$22} = \underline{21.59\%}$

In the all equity firm $K_c = K_o$, Thus, $K_o = \underline{21.59\%}$

(c) $K_c = \dfrac{\$4.882}{\$22.0} = \underline{22.19\%}$

        (1)

EBIT	$4,750,000
- I	90,000
EAC	$4,660,000
÷	954,545
= D_t	$4.882

        (2) $\dfrac{\$4.882 - \$4.750}{4.750} = 0.0278 \text{ or } \underline{2.78\%}$

        (3) $\dfrac{22.19\% - 21.59\%}{21.59\%} = 0.0278 \text{ or } \underline{2.78\%}$

        (4) $\dfrac{954,545}{1,000,000}(22.19) + \dfrac{45,455}{1,000,000}(9.00) = \underline{21.59\%}$

14-15B.

(a)   Plan B will always dominate Plan C, the preferred stock alternative, by 0.5 ($5,000)/10,000 shares or $0.25 a share. Thus, only alternatives A vs. B and A vs. C need be evaluated. Those calculations appear below.

Plan A vs. Plan B

$$\dfrac{(\text{EBIT} - \$0) (1 - 0.5) - 0}{15,000} = \dfrac{(\text{EBIT} - \$5,000) (1 - 0.5)}{10,000}$$

EBIT = $\underline{\$15,000}$

Plan A vs. Plan C

$$\frac{(EBIT - \$0)\ (1 - 0.5) - 0}{15,000} = \frac{(EBIT - 0)\ (1 - 0.5) - \$5,000}{10,000}$$

EBIT = $\underline{\$30,000}$

(b) Since long-term EBIT is forecast to be $36,000, the data favor use of financing alternative B, the bond plan. This is well above the A vs. B indifference level of $15,000.

CHAPTER 15

Dividend Policy and Internal Financing

Orientation: In determining the firm's dividend policy, two issues are important: the dividend payout ratio and the stability of the dividend payment over time. In this regard, the financial manager should consider the investment opportunities available to the firm and any preference that the company's investors have for dividend income or capital gains. Also, stock dividends, stock splits, or stock repurchases can be used to supplement or replace cash dividends.

I.   The trade offs in setting a firm's dividend policy

    A.   If a company pays a large dividend, it will thereby:

        1.   Have a low retention of profits within the firm.

        2.   Need to rely heavily on a new common stock issue for equity financing.

    B.   If a company pays a small dividend, it will thereby:

        1.   Have a high retention of profits within the firm.

        2.   Will not need to rely heavily on a new common stock issue for equity financing. The profits retained for reinvestment will provide the needed equity financing.

II. The importance of a firm's dividend policy depends on the impact of the dividend decision on the firm's stock price. That is, given a firm's capital budgeting and borrowing decisions, what is the impact of the firm's dividend policies on the stock price?

III. Three views about the importance of a firm's dividend policy.

    A.   View 1:   Dividends do not matter

        1.   Assume that the dividend decision does not change the firm's capital budgeting and financing decisions.

        2.   Assume perfect markets which means:

            a.   There are no brokerage commissions when investors buy and sell stocks.

            b.   New securities can be issued without incurring any flotation cost.

            c.   There is no income tax, personal or corporate.

            d.   Information is free and equally available to all investors.

            e.   There are no conflicts of interest between management and stockholders.

        3.   Under the foregoing assumptions, it may be shown that the market price of a corporation's common stock is unchanged under different dividend policies. If the firm increases the dividend to its stockholders, it has to offset this increase by issuing new common stock in order to finance the available investment opportunities. If on the other hand, the firm reduces its dividend payment, it has more funds available internally to finance future investment projects. In either policy the present value of the resulting cash flows to be accrued to the current investors is independent of the dividend policy. By varying the dividend policy, only the type of return is affected (capital gains versus dividend income), not the total return.

    B.   View 2:   High dividends increase stock value

        1.   Dividends are more predictable than capital gains because management can control dividends, while they cannot dictate the price of the stock. Thus, investors are less certain of receiving income from capital gains than from dividend income. The incremental risk associated with capital gains relative to dividend income should therefore cause us to use a

higher required rate in discounting a dollar of capital gains than the rate used for discounting a dollar of dividends. In so doing, we would give a higher value to the dividend income than we would the capital gains.

2.   Criticisms of view 2.

   a.   Since the dividend policy has no impact on the volatility of the company's overall cash flows, it has no impact on the riskiness of the firm.

   b.   Increasing a firm's dividend does not reduce the basic riskiness of the stock; rather, if dividend payment requires management to issue new stock, it only transfers risk and ownership from the current owners to new owners.

C.   View 3:   Low dividends increase value

Stocks that allow us to defer taxes (low dividends-high capital gains) will possibly sell at a premium relative to stocks that require us to pay taxes currently (high dividends-low capital gains). Only then will the two stocks provide comparable after-tax returns, which suggests that a policy to pay low dividends will result in a higher stock price. That is, high dividends hurt investors, while low dividends-high retention help the firm's investors.

D.   Additional thoughts about the importance of a firm's dividend policy.

   1.   Residual dividend theory: Because of flotation costs incurred in issuing new stock, firms must issue a larger amount of securities in order to receive the amount of capital required for investments. As a result, new equity capital will be more expensive than capital raised through retained earnings. Therefore, financing investments internally (and decreasing dividends) instead of issuing new stock may be favored. This is embodied in the residual dividend theory, where a dividend would be paid only when any internally generated funds remain after financing the equity portion of the firm's investments.

2.   The clientele effect: If investors do in fact have a preference between dividends and capital gains, we could expect them to seek out firms that have a dividend policy consistent with these preferences. They would in essence "sort themselves out" by buying stocks which satisfy their preferences for dividends and/or capital gains. In other words, there would be a "clientele effect," where firms draw a given clientele, given the stated dividend policy. However, unless there is a greater aggregate demand for a particular policy than is being satisfied in the market, dividend policy is still unimportant, in that one policy is as good as the other. The clientele effect only tells us to avoid making capricious changes in a company's dividend policy.

3.   Information effect.

    a.   We know from experience that a large, unexpected change in dividends can have significant impact on the stock price. Despite such "evidence," it is not unreasonable to hypothesize that dividend policy only appears to be important, because we are not looking at the real cause and effect. It may be that investors use a change in dividend policy as a signal about the firm's "true" financial condition, especially its earning power.

    b.   Some would argue that management frequently has inside information about the firm that it cannot make available to the investors. This difference in accessibility to information between management and investors, called information asymmetry, may result in a lower stock price than would be true if we had conditions of certainty. Dividends become a means in a risky marketplace to minimize any "drag" on the stock price that might come from differences in the level of information available to managers and investors.

4.   Agency costs: Conflicts between management and stockholders may exist, and the stock price of a company owned by investors who are separate from management may be less than the stock value of a closely-held firm. The difference in price is the cost of the conflict to the owners,

which has come to be called <u>agency</u> <u>costs</u>. A firm's dividend policy may be perceived by owners as a tool to minimize agency costs. Assuming the payment of a dividend requires management to issue stock to finance new investments, then new investors will be attracted to the company only if management provides convincing information that the capital will be used profitably. Thus, the payment of dividends indirectly results in a closer monitoring of management's investment activities. In this case, dividends may provide a meaningful contribution to the value of the firm.

5. Expectations theory: As the time approaches for management to announce the amount of the next dividend, investors form expectations as to how much the dividend will be. When the actual dividend decision is announced, the investor compares the actual decision with the expected decision. If the amount of the dividend is as expected, even if it represents an increase from prior years, the market price of the stock will remain unchanged. However, if the dividend is higher or lower than expected, the investors will reassess their perceptions about the firm and the value of the stock.

E. The empirical evidence about the importance of dividend policy

1. Statistical tests. To test the relationship between dividend payments and security prices, we could compare a firm's dividend yield (dividend/stock price) and the stock's total return, the question being, "Do stocks that pay high dividends provide higher or lower returns to the investors?" Such tests have been conducted using a variety of the most sophisticated statistical techniques available. Despite the use of these extremely powerful analytical tools involving intricate and complicated procedures, the results have been mixed. However, over long periods of time, the results have given a slight advantage to the low-dividend stocks; that is, stocks that pay lower dividends appear to have higher prices. The findings are far from conclusive, however, owing to the relatively large standard errors of the estimates.

2. Reasons for inconclusive results from the statistical tests.

   a. To be accurate, we would need to know the amount of dividends investors <u>expect</u> to receive. Since these expectations cannot be observed, we can only use historical data, which may or may not relate to expectations.

   b. Most empirical studies have assumed a linear relationship between dividend payments and stock prices. The actual relationship may be nonlinear, possibly even with discontinuities in the relationship.

3. Since our statistical prowess does not provide us with any conclusive evidence, researchers have surveyed financial managers about their perceptions of the relevance of dividend policy. In such surveys, the evidence favors the relevance of dividend policy, but not just overwhelming so. For the most part, managers are divided between believing that dividends are important and having no opinion in the matter.

F. Conclusions about the importance of dividend policy

   1. As a firm's investment opportunities increase, the dividend payout ratio should decrease.

   2. The firm's dividend policy appears to be important; however, appearances may be deceptive. The real issue may be the firm's <u>expected</u> earnings power and the riskiness of these earnings.

   3. If dividends influence stock price, it probably comes from the investor's desire to minimize and/or defer taxes and from the role of dividends in minimizing agency costs.

   4. If the expectations theory has merit, which we believe it does, it behooves management to avoid surprising the investors when it comes to the firm's dividend decision.

IV. Dividend policy decisions

A. Other practical considerations

1. Legal restrictions

a. A corporation may not pay a dividend

(1) If the firm's liabilities exceed its assets.
(2) If the amount of the dividend exceeds the accumulated profits (retained earnings).
(3) If the dividend is being paid from capital invested in the firm.

b. Debtholders and preferred stockholders may impose restrictive provisions on management, such as common dividends not being paid from earnings prior to the payment of interest or preferred dividends.

2. Liquidity position: The amount of a firm's retained earnings and its cash position are seldom the same. Thus, the company must have adequate _cash_ available as well as retained earnings to pay dividends.

3. Absence or lack of other sources of financing: All firms do not have equal access to the capital markets. Consequently, companies with limited financial resources may rely more heavily on internally generated funds.

4. Earnings predictability: A firm that has a stable earnings trend will generally pay a larger portion of its earnings in dividends. If earnings fluctuate significantly, a larger amount of the profits may be retained to ensure that enough money is available for investment projects when needed.

5. Ownership control: For many small firms, and certain large ones, maintaining the controlling vote is very important. These owners would prefer the use of debt and retained profits to finance new investments rather than issue new stock.

6. Inflation: Because of inflation, the cost of replacing equipment has increased substantially Depreciation funds tend to become insufficient. Hence, greater profit retention may be required.

B. Alternative dividend policies

1. Constant dividend payout ratio: The percentage of earnings paid out in dividends is held constant. Therefore, the dollar amount of the dividend fluctuates from year to year.

2. Stable dollar dividend per share: Relatively stable dollar dividend is maintained. The dividend per share is increased or decreased only after careful investigation by the management.

3. Small, regular dividend plus a year-end extra: Extra dividend is paid out in prosperous years. Management's objective is to avoid the connotation of a permanent dividend increase.

C. Bases for stable dividends

1. Investors may use the dividend policy as a surrogate for information that is not easily accessible. The dividend policy may be useful in assessing the company's long-term earnings prospects.

2. Many investors rely on dividends to satisfy personal income need. If dividends fluctuate from year to year, investors may have to sell or buy stock to satisfy their current needs, thereby incurring expensive transaction costs.

3. Legal listings stipulate that certain types of financial institutions may only invest in companies that have a consistent dividend payment.

4. Conclusion: An investor who prefers stable dividends will assign a lower required rate of return (a higher P/E ratio) for a stock paying a stable dividend. This results in a higher market price for the stock.

D. Dividend policy and corporate strategy: Things will change—even dividend policy.

    1. The recession of 1990 to 1991 induced a large number of American corporations to revisit their broadest corporate strategies, including adjusted dividend policies.

    2. One firm that altered its dividend policy in response to new strategies was the W.R. Grace & Co., headquartered in Boca Raton, Florida.

    3. Table 15-5 in the text reviews W.R. Grace's actual dividend policies over the 1992 to 1996 time frame. The firm's payout ratio and the absolute amount of the cash dividend paid per share declined in a significant fashion over this period.

V. Dividend payment procedures

A. Dividends are generally paid quarterly.

B. The declaration date is the date on which the firm's board of directors announces the forthcoming dividends.

C. The date of record designates when the stock transfer books are to be closed (who is entitled to the dividend).

D Brokerage firms terminate the right of ownership to the dividend four working days prior to the date of record. This date is called the ex-dividend date.

E. Dividend checks are mailed on the payment date.

VI. Stock dividends and stock splits

A. Both a stock dividend and a stock split involve issuing new shares of stock to current stockholders.

B. The investors' percentage ownership in the firm remains unchanged. The investor is neither better nor worse off than before the stock split/dividend.

C.   On an economic basis there is no difference between a stock dividend and a stock split.

D.   For accounting purposes the stock split has been defined as a stock dividend exceeding 25 percent.

E.   Accounting treatment

    1.   For a stock dividend, the dollar amount of the dividend is transferred from retained earnings to the capital accounts.

    2.   In the case of a split, the dollar amounts of the capital accounts do not change. Only the number of shares is increased while the par value of each share is decreased proportionately.

F.   Rationale for a stock dividend or split

    1.   The price of stock may not fall precisely in proportion to the share increase; thus, the stockholders' value is increased.

    2.   If a company is encountering cash problems, it can substitute a stock dividend for a cash dividend. Investors will probably look beyond the dividend to determine the underlying reasons for conserving cash.

VII.   Stock repurchases

A.   A number of benefits exists justifying stock repurchases instead of dividend payment. Included in these are:

    1.   To provide an internal investment opportunity.

    2.   To modify the firm's capital structure.

    3.   To impact earnings per share, thus increasing stock price.

B. Share repurchase as a dividend decision

    1. A firm may decide to repurchase its shares, increasing the earnings per share which should be reflected in a higher stock price.

    2. The investor's choice

        a. For tax purposes the investor may prefer the firm to repurchase stock in lieu of a dividend. Dividends are taxed as ordinary income, whereas any price appreciation resulting from the stock repurchase would be taxed as a capital gain.

        b. The investor may still prefer dividend payment because

            (1) Dividends are viewed more dependable than stock repurchases.
            (2) The price the firm must pay for its stock may be too high.
            (3) Riskiness of the firm's capital structure may increase, lowering the P/E ratio and thus the stock price.

C. Financing or investment decision

    1. A stock repurchase effectively increases the debt-equity ratio towards higher debt, thus repurchase is viewed as a financing decision.

    2. Buying its own stock at depressed prices, a firm may consider the repurchase as an investment decision. However, this action is not a true investment opportunity, as the extreme result would mean the company would consume itself.

D. The repurchase procedure

    1. A public announcement should be made detailing the amount, purpose and procedure for the stock repurchase.

    2. Open market purchase - at the current market price.

3. Tender offer - more formal and at a specified price.

4. Negotiated basis - repurchasing from specific large shareholders.

Study Problems

1. The Harvestor Corporation has the following capital structure:

Common Stock ($5 par; 300,000 shares)	$1,500,000
Paid in Capital	2,500,000
Retained Earnings	4,000,000
Total Net Worth	$8,000,000

(a) If the company issues a 20 percent stock dividend, how would the new capital structure appear? The market price per share for the stock is $10.

(b) How would the capital accounts appear after a two-for-one split?

SOLUTION

(a)

Decrease in retained earnings ($10 x 60,000 shares)	$600,000
Increase in par value of common stock ($5 x 60,000 shares)	300,000
Remainder to increase capital surplus	$300,000

The new capital structure after a 20 percent stock dividend:

Common Stock ($5 par; 360,000 shares)	$1,800,000
Paid in Capital	2,800,000
Retained Earnings	3,400,000
Total Net Worth	$8,000,000

(b)   The new capital structure after a two-for-one split:

Common Stock ($2.50 par; 600,000 shares)	$1,500,000
Capital Surplus	2,500,000
Retained Earnings	4,000,000
Total Net Worth	$8,000,000

2.   The Mansville Corporation's capital structure is as follows:

Common Stock ($4 par; 5,000,000 shares outstanding)	$20,000,000
Paid in Capital	1,000,000
Retained Earnings	9,000,000
Total Net Worth	$30,000,000

The firm's earnings after taxes are $2 million, of which the company paid out 25 percent in cash dividends. The price of the firm's common stock was $8.

(a)   If the firm declares a 20 percent stock dividend, how would the capital structure appear?

(b)   If a 20 percent stock dividend is assumed, what would be the earnings per share and dividends per share?

SOLUTION

(a)   Capital structure after a 20 percent stock dividend:

Increase in the shares outstanding:

20% x 5,000,000 shares = 1,000,000 shares

Increase in the par value:

$4 x 1,000,000 = $4,000,000

Increase in the capital surplus account:

($8 - $4) x 1,000,000 = $4,000,000

Result:

Common Stock (6,000,000 shares)	$24,000,000
Capital Surplus	5,000,000
Retained Earnings	1,000,000
Total Net Worth	$30,000,000

(b) Earnings per share after a 20 percent stock dividend:

$$\frac{\text{Earnings}}{\text{Number of Shares}} = \frac{\$2,000,000}{6,000,000} = \$0.33$$

Dividends per share after a 20 percent stock dividend:

$$\frac{\text{Dividends}}{\text{Number of Shares}} = \frac{\$500,000}{6,000,000} = \$0.083$$

3. Philips Limited treats dividends as a residual variable in its financial decisions (see residual dividend theory). Net income has been forecasted for the upcoming year to be $600,000, which may be used for reinvesting in the firm or for paying dividends. The firm has only equity in its capital structure and its cost of internally generated equity capital is 10 percent. If, however, new common stock were issued, flotation costs would raise this cost to 11 percent. If the firm considers the 10 percent cost of internal equity to be the opportunity cost of retained earnings,

(a) (1) How much in dividends should be paid if the company has $500,000 in projects with expected returns exceeding 10 percent?

(2) How much should the dividend be if $600,000 in investments are available having expected returns greater than 10 percent?

(b) How much should be paid in dividends if the firm has $1 million in projects whose expected returns exceed 11 percent?

(c) How would your answer change in part (b) if the firm's optimal debt-equity mix is 40 percent debt and 60 percent common and the cost of capital remains the same?

SOLUTION

(a) (1) According to the residual dividend theory, the firm should pay dividends only when it has exhausted its investments whose returns exceed the firm's cost of capital. Therefore, the firm should pay $100,000 in dividends ($600,000 income available for investing less $500,000 investments).

(2) The firm should use all of the $600,000 for investing in the projects and should not pay any dividends.

(b) If the firm has investment opportunities with returns exceeding the cost of capital, the firm should undertake these investments. In this example, the cost of capital increases (to 11 per cent) when new equity is issued. Since the returns on the available investment projects (totaling $1 million) exceed the cost of equity capital, the firm should use up its internally generated funds ($600,000) and raise the remaining $400,000 by issuing new common stock. Therefore, no dividends would be paid.

(c) We would need $400,000 in new debt, i.e., 40 percent of $1 million. The remaining $600,000 (which is 60 percent of the needed capital) will be supplied by internally generated funds. No dividend will be paid.

4. Beardsell Products and Voltas Products are identical firms in terms of (1) being in the same industry, (2) producing the same products, (3) being subject to the same risks, and (4) having equivalent earnings per share. Beardsell pays a constant cash dividend, whereas Voltas follows a constant percentage payout ratio of 50 percent. However, Voltas' common stock price has been lower than Beardsell's in spite of Voltas' dividend being substantially larger than Beardsell's in certain years. Given the data below:

	Beardsell Products			Voltas Products		
Year	EPS	Dividend	Market Price	EPS	Dividend	Market Price
1993	$2.50	$0.65	9	$2.50	$1.25	6 3/4
1994	-0.25	0.65	8 3/4	-0.25	0	6 1/2
1995	3.00	0.65	9 1/4	3.00	1.50	9
1996	2.00	0.65	9	2.00	1.00	10

(a) What might account for the differences in the market prices of the two companies?

(b) What might both companies do in order to enhance the market prices of their respective shares?

SOLUTION

(a) The dissimilarity between market prices might be a function of the different dividend policies, with a lower required rate of return, and, accordingly, a higher price being assigned to Beardsell as a result of the stable dividend stream.

(b) It appears that neither company would appear to be growth-oriented. If both firms are valued in terms of their dividend yield, which seems to be the case, higher dividend payouts might produce higher prices.

5. The Maple Syrup Company is considering two dividend policies for the years 1996 and 1997. The firm will be liquidated in 1997. One dividend plan would pay a dividend of $2.30 in 1996 and a liquidating dividend of $37.03 in 1997. The alternative plan would pay a dividend of $6.90 in 1996 and a final dividend of $31.74 in 1997. The required rate of return for the common stockholders is 15 percent. If perfect capital markets are assumed, what would be the effect of each dividend policy on the price of common stock?

SOLUTION

Under perfect market conditions, the effect of each dividend policy is determined by finding the present value of the dividend stream for each dividend plan.

Plan 1: Present value calculations

	1996	1997
Dividends	$2.30	$37.03

$$\text{Present Value} = \frac{\$2.30}{(1.15)} + \frac{\$37.03}{(1.15)^2} = \$30$$

Plan 2:

	1996	1997
Dividends	$6.90	$31.74

$$\text{Present Value} = \frac{\$6.90}{(1.15)} + \frac{\$31.74}{(1.15)^2} = \$30$$

We find that both plans have the same present value. The common stockholders should be indifferent about both plans.

6. Rexall Corporation is considering five investment opportunities. The required investment outlays and expected rates of return for these investments are shown below. The cost of capital for the firm is 13 percent. Investments are to be financed with 30 percent debt and 70 percent equity. Internally generated funds available for reinvestment equal $1 million.

(a) Which investments should be accepted?

(b) According to the residual dividend theory, what amount should be paid out in dividends?

Investment	Cost	Internal Rate of Return
A	$200,000	20%
B	300,000	15
C	900,000	14
D	100,000	10
E	400,000	7

SOLUTION

(a) Investments A, B, and C should be accepted because their expected returns exceed the firm's cost of capital.

(b) Dividends to be paid:

Total cost of three projects:

$200,000 + $300,000 + $900,000	=	$1,400,000
Equity financing: $1,400,000 x 70%	=	980,000
Debt financing: $1,400,000 - $980,000	=	420,000

Internally generated funds available:	$1,000,000
Less equity necessary for projects:	980,000
Funds available for dividend payment:	$ 20,000

7. International Computers Inc., a new firm, is financed only by common stock. The firm's life is limited to 2 years (1996 and 1997), at the end of which the firm will be liquidated. At the beginning of 1991 the firm's assets are $5 million and 200,000 shares are outstanding. Cash available for reinvestment or dividend payment for 1996 is $1 million. The expected return on investment is 15 percent. At the end of 1996 an additional investment of $500,000 will be required. This may be financed by retaining $500,000 of the 1996 profits or issuing new stock or a combination of both. In fact, management is considering one of two plans:

Plan A: The $500,000 investment would be financed entirely by internal financing with the investors receiving $500,000 in dividends.

Plan B: Investors would receive $600,000 in dividends, with the investment in 1996 being financed $400,000 internally and a $100,000 new stock issue.

The proposed dividend plans for 1996 are shown below:

	Plan A	Plan B
Internally generated cash flow	$1,000,000	$1,000,000
Dividend for 1996	500,000	600,000
Cash available for reinvestment	$ 500,000	$ 400,000
Amount of investment in 1996	500,000	500,000
External financing required	0	$ 100,000

Assume perfect markets, and demonstrate that under either dividend plan the market price of the firm's stock remains the same, i.e., the dividend policy of the firm is irrelevant from the investor's point of view.

SOLUTION

The solution to this problem is obtained by following two steps:

(1) Calculating the amount and timing of the dividend stream for the original investors, and

(2) Determining the present value of the dividend stream under each plan.

For Step 1:

Number of Original Shares Outstanding Equals 200,000

	Plan A	Plan B
Year: 1996		
Dividends	$ 500,000	$ 600,000
	($2.50 per share)	($3 per share)
Year: 1997		
Total Dividends		
A. Original Investment		
Old Investors	$5,000,000	$5,000,000
New Investors	0	100,000

B. Retained Earnings*	500,000	400,000
C. Profits for 1992**	825,000	825,000
Total Dividend to All Investors	$6,325,000	$6,325,000

Less Dividend to New Investors:

A. Original Investment	0	(100,000)
B. Profits for New Investors (15% of $100,000)	0	(15,000)
Dividends Available to Original Investors	$6,325,000	$6,210,000
Amount Per Share	$ 31.625	$ 31.05

*The portion of the 1996 profits that were reinvested in the firm at the conclusion of 1996.

**Profits for 1997 equal 15 percent of $5,500,000, the asset base in 1997.

For step 2, the present value of the dividend streams discounted at 15 percent must be determined:

Plan A: $\dfrac{\$2.50}{(1.15)^1} + \dfrac{\$31.625}{(1.15)^2} = \$26.09$

Plan B: $\dfrac{\$3.00}{(1.15)^1} + \dfrac{\$31.05}{(1.15)^1} = \$26.09$

We see that under both plans, the market price of International Computers is the same.

Self-Tests

TRUE-FALSE

_____ 1   If dividend policy is treated as a passive residual, dividends are paid only if the firm has any remaining capital after financing attractive investments.

_____ 2.   In practice, the firm should invest retained earnings as long as the required rate of return exceeds the expected rate of return from the investment.

_____ 3.   The greater the ability of a firm to borrow, the less is its ability to pay a cash dividend.

_____ 4.   If a firm has sporadic investment opportunities, it might be expected to pay out more dividends.

_____ 5.   A stock dividend results in a recapitalization of retained earnings.

_____ 6.   In a stock split, the only accounting change is the shifting of amounts from retained earnings to the common stock (par) account.

_____ 7.   The introduction of flotation costs to the "dividend irrelevance" concept favors the retention of earnings in the firm.

_____ 8.   The only wealth-creating activity under "perfect market" conditions for an all-equity firm is the management's investment decisions.

_____ 9.   Dividend income and capital gains from the sale of stock are taxed at the same personal income tax rate. Thus, there is no advantage to capital gains over dividend income for the investor.

_____ 10. An "expected" change in the dividend policy of a firm may not affect the price of the firm's stock when the change is actually announced.

_____ 11. A stock repurchase increases the debt-to-equity ratio.

_____ 12. Stock repurchases offer an attractive investment alternative any time prices are depressed.

_____ 13. The "bird-in-the-hand" theory assigns a higher value to capital gains than to dividend income.

_____ 14. A firm's dividend policy affects the variability of the firm's overall cash flows, even when we do not allow the dividend policy to impact investment decisions.

MULTIPLE CHOICE

1. Which of the following is not an assumption of the "dividend irrelevance" theory?

   a. No taxes.
   b. Efficient capital markets.
   c. No flotation costs.
   d. Costless information.

2. An argument for the relevance of dividends would be:

   a. Informational content.
   b. Resolution of uncertainty
   c. Preference for current income.
   d. All of the above.
   e. None of the above.

3. Possible advantages of a stock dividend is (are) that it:

   a. May help to conserve cash.
   b. Tends to increase the market price.
   c. Keeps the price of the stock within a desired trading range.
   d. All of the above.

4. When the assumption of no taxes is removed from the "dividend irrelevance" theory:

   a. There is a preference for the retention of earnings.
   b. There is a preference for paying out dividends.
   c. The preference depends on the individual investor's tax status, but generally there is a preference for retention of earnings.

5. The following factors may influence the dividend policy that a firm undertakes:

   a. The liquidity of the firm.
   b. Capital structure.
   c. Legal restrictions.
   d. a and c.
   e. a and b.

6. Advantages of a stock repurchase may be:

   a. A means to modify capital structure.
   b. To impact earnings per share.
   c. The elimination of a particular minority group.
   d. All of the above.

7. A firm may not legally pay dividends if:

   a. Its liabilities exceed its assets.
   b. The dividend is being paid from capital invested in the firm.
   c. Debtholders' contracts are not satisfied.
   d. All of the above.
   e. a and b.

8. For tax purposes, a corporation may exclude _____% of the dividend income received from another corporation.

   a. 0.
   b. 10.
   c. 50
   d. 70.
   e. 100.

9. When real-world considerations are taken into account, the amount of a firm's dividend payment depends on the following factors:

   a. Profitability of investment opportunities.
   b. Investor's preference for capital gains or dividend income.
   c. Debt-to-equity ratio.
   d. Trading range of the firm's stock.
   e. a and b.

10. Small-sized firms generally use retained earnings for investment purposes because:

    a. They do not have easy access to the capital markets.
    b. Ownership control is an important factor.
    c. Their earnings fluctuate widely.
    d. Inflation has greater impact on small companies.
    e. None of the above.
    f. a and b.

11. Which one of the following dividend policies is the most popular?

    a. Constant dividend payout ratio.
    b. Stable dividend (dollar) per share.
    c. Small, regular dividend plus a year-end extra.

12. The ex-dividend date is

    a. The same as the date of record.
    b. Four working days prior to date of record.
    c. Eight days prior to the payment date.
    d. Five days after the declaration date.
    e. None of the above.

13. Properly viewed, a stock repurchase should be used as:

    a. A dividend decision.
    b. An investment decision.
    c. A refinancing decision.
    d. Both a and c.
    e. All of the above.

15-2B.   Flotation Costs and Issue Size

Flotation costs   0.14
Stock price $76.00
Net to firm $6,100,000

Dollar issue size = $7,093,023 = $6,100,000/(1-.14)

Number of shares=   93,329   shares
                                        ($7,093,023 ÷ $76/share)

15-4B.   DCA - Stock Dividend

Before dividend
    Shares outstanding   2,500,000
    Net income $ 600,000
    Price/Earnings   10
    Stock dividend   18%
    Investor's shares   120
    Current price $ 2.40
    Value before dividend $ 288.00   = $2.40 x 120 shares

After dividend
    Shares outstanding   2,950,000 = 2,500,000 x (1+.18)
    New price $ 2.03 = P/E x EPS = 10 x
                                        ($600,000/2,950,000)

    Investor's shares   141.6 = 120 (1.18)
    Value after dividend $ 288.00 = 141.6 x $2.03

    Change $ 0.00 = $288(before)
                                        - $288 (after)

The value of the investors' holdings does not change because the price of the stock reacted fully to the increase in the shares outstanding.

15-5B.   Montford, Inc. - Dividends in Perfect Markets

Dividend Plans

Year	Plan A	Plan B
1997	$ 2.55	$ 4.35
1998	$ 2.55	$ 4.70
1999	$45.60	$40.62

Required rate of return   0.17

Value stock $32.51 = $2.55 ÷ (1 + .17)   +

$2.55 ÷ (1.17)^2 +

$45.60 ÷ (1.17)^3

Value stock B $32.51 = $4.35 ÷ (1.17)   +

$4.70 ÷ (1.17)^2 +

$40.62 ÷ (1.17)^3

a.   There is no effect on the value of the common stock.

b.   An investor's preference for current income, tax consequences, informational content, and transaction costs might change our conclusion.

15-8B.   Carlson Cargo, Inc. - Dividend Policies

Year	Profits After Taxes
1	$1,500,000
2	2,000,000
3	1,750,000
4	950,000
5	2,500,000
Total Profits After Taxes	$8,700,000

Shares Outstanding   1,000,000

a. <u>Constant</u> Payout Ratio of 40%

Year	Dividend	= Profits x Payout Ratio ÷ Shares
1	$0.60	= $1,500,000 (.4) ÷ 1,000,000
2	$0.80	= $2,000,000 (.4) ÷ 1,000,000
3	$0.70	= $1,750,000 (.4) ÷ 1,000,000
4	$0.38	= $ 950,000 (.4) ÷ 1,000,000
5	$1.00	= $2,500,000 (.4) ÷ 1,000,000

b. <u>Stable</u> target payout of 40%

$$\text{**Target dividend** } \$0.70 = \frac{\$8,700,000 \,(.4)}{1,000,000} \,/5 \text{ years}$$

c. Small regular dividend of $0.50 plus year-end extra

Base profits	1,500,000
% of extra profits	50.00%

Year	Dividend
1	0.50
2	0.75 = .50+($2,000,000-$1,500,000)(.5)/1,000,000
3	0.63 = .50+($1,750,000-$1,500,000)(.5)/1,000,000
4	0.50
5	1.00 = .50+($2,500,000-$1,500,000)(.5)/1,000,000

15-11B. Maness, Inc. - Residual Dividend Theory

Total financing needed	$ 1,500,000	
Retained earnings	$ 525,000	
Debt ratio	0.65	
Equity ratio	0.35	
Equity financing needed	$ 525,000	= $1,500,000 (0.35)
Dividends	$ 0	= $525,000 - $525,000

Thus, the firm would pay no dividend, but it would also not have to issue any stock.

15-12B.   Star Corporation - Stock Split

Market price	$ 90	
Split multiple	2	
Shares outstanding	90,000	

a.   You own   0.25 x 90,000 = 22,500 shares

Position before split $2,025,000 = 22,500 Shares x $90 per share

Price after split $ 45.00 = $90 ÷ 2
Your shares after split   45,000 = 22,500 x 2
Position after split $2,025,000 = 45,000 shares x $45 per share
Net gain $ 0

b.   Price fall   0.45
Price after split $ 49.50 = $90 (1 - .45)
Position after split $2,227,500 = 45,000 shares x $49.50 per share
Net gain $ 202,500 = $2,227,500 - $2,025,000

CHAPTER 16

Working-Capital Management and Short-Term Financing

<u>Orientation</u>: In this chapter we introduce working-capital management in terms of managing the firm's liquidity. Specifically, working capital is defined as the difference in current assets and current liabilities. The hedging principle is offered as one approach to addressing the firm's liquidity problems. It also deals with the sources of short-term financing that must be repaid within 1 year.

I. Managing current assets

    A. The firm's investment in current assets (like fixed assets) is determined by the marginal benefits derived from investing in them compared with their acquisition cost.

    B. However, the current-fixed asset mix of the firm's investment in assets is an important determinant of the firm's liquidity. That is, the greater the firm's investment in current assets, other things remaining the same, the greater the firm's liquidity. This is generally true since current assets are usually more easily converted into cash.

    C. The firm can invest in marketable securities to increase its liquidity. However, such a policy involves committing the firm's funds to a relatively low-yielding (in comparison to fixed assets) investment.

II. Managing the firm's use of current liabilities

    A. The greater the firm's use of current liabilities, other things being the same, the less will be the firm's liquidity.

B. There are a number of <u>advantages</u> associated with the use of current liabilities for financing the firm's asset investments.

　　1. <u>Flexibility</u>. Current liabilities can be used to match the timing of a firm's short-term financing needs exactly.

　　2. <u>Interest cost</u>. Historically, the interest cost on short-term debt has been lower than that on long-term debt.

C. Following are the <u>disadvantages</u> commonly associated with the use of short-term debt:

　　1. Short-term debt exposes the firm to an increased <u>risk of illiquidity</u> because short-term debt matures sooner and in greater frequency, by definition, than does long-term debt.

　　2. Since short-term debt agreements must be renegotiated from year to year, the <u>interest cost</u> of each year's financing <u>is uncertain</u>.

III. Determining the appropriate level of working capital

A. Pragmatically, it is impossible to derive the "optimal" level of working capital for the firm. Such a derivation would require estimation of the potential costs of illiquidity which cannot be precisely measured.

B. However, the "hedging principle" provides the basis for the firm's working-capital decisions.

　　1. The <u>hedging principle</u> or <u>rule of self- liquidating debt</u> involves the following: Those asset needs of the firm not financed by spontaneous sources (i.e., payables and accruals) should be financed in accordance with the following rule: Permanent asset investments are financed with permanent sources and temporary investments are financed with temporary sources of financing.

2. A <u>permanent</u> <u>investment</u> <u>in</u> <u>an</u> <u>asset</u> is one which the firm expects to hold for a period longer than 1 year. Such an investment may involve current or fixed assets.

3. <u>Temporary</u> <u>asset</u> <u>investments</u> comprise the firm's investment in current assets that will be liquidated and <u>not</u> replaced during the year.

4. <u>Spontaneous</u> <u>sources</u> <u>of</u> <u>financing</u> include all those sources which are available upon demand (e.g., trade credit--Accounts Payable) or which arise naturally as a part of doing business (e.g., wages payable, interest payable, taxes payable, etc.).

5. <u>Temporary</u> <u>sources</u> <u>of</u> <u>financing</u> include all forms of current or short-term financing not categorized as spontaneous. Examples include bank loans, commercial paper, and finance company loans.

6. <u>Permanent</u> <u>sources</u> <u>of</u> <u>financing</u> include all long-term sources such as debt having a maturity longer than 1 year, preferred stock, and common stock.

C. Although the hedging principle provides a useful guide to the firm's working-capital decisions, no firm will follow its tenets strictly. At times a firm may find itself overly reliant on temporary financing but at other times it may have excess cash as a result of excessive use of permanent financing.

IV. Selecting a source of short-term financing

A. In general, there are three basic factors that should be considered in selecting a source of short-term financing;

1. The effective cost of the credit source.

2. The availability of credit.

3. The effect of the use of a particular source of credit on the cost and availability of other sources.

B. The basic procedure used in estimating the cost of short-term credit utilizes the basic interest equation, i.e., interest = principal x rate x time.

C. The problem faced in assessing the cost of a source of short-term financing involves estimating the annual effective rate (RATE) where the interest amount, the principal sum, and the time for which financing will be needed is known. Thus, the basic interest equation is "rearranged" as follows:

$$RATE = \frac{interest}{principal} \times \frac{1}{time}$$

D. Compound interest was not considered in the simple RATE calculation. To consider compounding, the following relation is used:

$$APR = \left(1 + \frac{R}{M}\right)^M - 1$$

where APR is the annual percentage rate, R is the nominal rate of interest per year and M is the number of compounding periods within 1 year. The effect of compounding is thus to raise the effective cost of short-term credit.

V. Sources of short-term credit

A. The two basic sources of short-term credit are unsecured and secured credit.

1. Unsecured credit consists of all those sources which have as their security only the lender's faith in the ability of the borrower to repay the funds when due.

2. Secured funds include additional security in the form of assets that are pledged as collateral in the event the borrower defaults in payment of principal or interest.

16-4

B. There are three major sources of unsecured short-term credit: trade credit, unsecured bank loans, and commercial paper.

1. Trade credit provides one of the most flexible sources of financing available to the firm. To arrange for credit, the firm need only place an order with one of its suppliers. The supplier then checks the firm's credit and if the credit is good, the supplier sends the merchandise.

2. Commercial banks provide unsecured short-term credit in two basic forms: lines of credit and transaction loans (notes payable). Maturities of both types of loans are usually 1 year or less with rates of interest depending on the credit worthiness of the borrower and the level of interest rates in the economy as a whole.

3. A line of credit is generally an informal agreement or understanding between the borrower and the bank as to the maximum amount of credit that the bank will provide the borrower at any one time. There is no "legal" commitment on the part of the bank to provide the stated credit. There is another variant of this form of financing referred to as a revolving credit agreement whereby such a legal obligation is involved. The line of credit generally covers a period of 1 year corresponding to the borrower's "fiscal" year.

4. Transaction loans are another form of unsecured short-term bank credit; the transaction loan, in contrast to a line of credit, is made for a specific purpose.

5. Only the largest and most credit worthy companies are able to use commercial paper which consists of unsecured promissory notes in the money market.

    a. The maturities of commercial paper are generally 6 months or less with the interest rate slightly lower than the prime rate on commercial bank loans. The new issues of commercial paper are either directly placed or dealer placed.

b.   There are a number of advantages that accrue to the user of commercial paper: Interest rates are generally lower than rates on bank loans and comparable sources of short-term financing. No minimum balance requirements are associated with commercial paper. Commercial paper offers the firm with very large credit needs a single source for all its short-term financing needs. Since it is widely recognized that only the most credit worthy borrowers have access to the commercial paper market, its use signifies a firm's credit status.

c.   However, a very important "risk" is involved in using this source of short-term financing; the commercial paper market is highly impersonal and denies even the most credit worthy borrower any flexibility in terms of repayment.

B.   Secured sources of short-term credit have certain assets of the firm, such as accounts receivable or inventories pledged as collateral to secure a loan. Upon default of the loan agreement, the lender has first claim to the pledged assets.

1.   Generally, a firm's receivables are among its most liquid assets. Two secured loan arrangements are generally made with accounts receivable as collateral: (a) Under the arrangement of <u>pledged accounts receivable,</u> the amount of the loan is stated as a percent of the face value of the receivables pledged. (b) <u>Factoring accounts receivable</u> involves the outright sale of a firm's accounts receivables to a factor.

2.   Four secured loan arrangements are generally made with inventory as collateral: (a) Under the <u>floating lien agreement,</u> the borrower gives the lender a lien against all his or her inventories. (b) The <u>chattel mortgage agreement</u> involves having specific items of inventory identified in the security agreement. (c) The <u>field warehouse financing agreements</u> means that the

inventories used as collateral are physically separated from the firm's other inventories and are placed under the control of a third-party field warehousing firm. (d) Terminal warehouse agreements involve transporting the inventories pledged as collateral to a public warehouse which is physically removed from the borrower's premises.

Study Problems

1. In order to meet a temporary need for working capital during an upcoming seasonal peak in sales, Gregory Sales Co. needs $500,000. Gregory's bank has agreed to lend the funds for the necessary 3-month interval at a rate of 12% with a 20% compensating balance. Gregory Sales Co. normally maintains a demand deposit amount of $20,000. Estimate the annual (effective) cost of the loan to Gregory.

SOLUTION

To obtain the needed $500,000 and meet the compensating balance requirement, Gregory must borrow X dollars, where X is found as follows:

$$X - [0.20X - 20,000] = 500,000$$
$$0.80X = 480,000$$
$$X = \$600,000$$

Thus, Gregory borrows $600,000 for which it must maintain a compensating balance of 0.20 X 600,000 = $120,000, of which $20,000 will come from its normal demand deposit and $100,000 must be borrowed. This will leave the firm with the use of $500,000. The interest cost of the loan is computed as follows:

Interest = 0.12 x 600,000 ÷ 4 = $18,000

We divide by 4 since the loan is for only 3 months or one-fourth of a year. The effective annual cost of the loan is:

$$\text{Rate} = \frac{\$ \text{ loan cost}}{\$ \text{funds available}} \times \frac{\text{loan maturity as a}}{\text{fraction of 1 year}}$$

$$= \frac{18,000}{500,000} \times \frac{4}{1} = \underline{0.144 \text{ or } 14.4\%}$$

2.   A factor has agreed to buy Thomas Brothers' receivables ($250,000 per month) which have an average collection period of 90 days. The factor will advance up to 80% of the face value of the receivables for an annual charge of 10% of the funds advanced. The factor also charges a handling fee of 5% of the face value of all accounts purchased. What is the effective annual cost of the factoring arrangement to Thomas Brothers if the maximum advance is taken every month?

SOLUTION

With an average collection period of 90 days and monthly credit sales, Thomas Brothers could build up a loan advance over 3 months of 0.80 x 750,000 = $600,000. This loan would be constantly rolling over as accounts were being collected and as new credit sales were being made. The 90-day interest cost of the loan would be computed:

$$\text{Interest} = \$600,000 \text{ x } \frac{0.10}{4} = \$15,000$$

The factor's fee is calculated as follows:

$$\text{Fee} = 0.05 \text{ x } \$750,000 = \$37,500$$

Thus, the effective annual cost of the 90-day loan would be:

$$\text{Rate} = \frac{\$15,000 + \$37,500}{\$600,000} \div \frac{3}{12}$$

$$= \underline{0.35} \text{ or } \underline{35\%}$$

3.   For the past 7 years Warden Company has been factoring its accounts receivables. The factor's fee is 3% and the factor will lend up to 90% of the volume of receivables purchased for an additional 1% per month. The firm typically has sales of $200,000 per month; 75% are on credit. Warden Company will save credit department costs of $3,500, since it will no longer need to operate a credit department. In addition, there will no longer be bad-debt losses which previously were 1-1/4% per month.

The firm's bank has recently offered to lend the firm up to 90% of the face value of the receivables shown on the schedule of accounts. The bank would charge 9% per annum interest plus a 2% processing charge per dollar of receivables pledged. The firm extends terms of net 30, and all customers who plan to pay will do so by the thirtieth of the month. Should the firm discontinue its factoring arrangement in favor of the bank's offer if the firm borrows, on the average, $100,000 per month on its receivables?

SOLUTION

The cost of factoring is:	
Fee (0.03 x $200,000 x .75)	$4,500
Interest cost (0.01 x $100,000)	1,000
	$5,500
The cost of the bank loan is:	
Fee (0.02 x $100,000/.90)	$2,222
Interest (0.09 x $200,000 x 1/12)	1,500
	$3,722
Plus the costs that factoring eliminates:	
Credit department cost per month	$3,722
Bad-debt losses ($200,000 x .75 x	
0.0125)	1,875
Total cost	$9,097

No, in this case factoring is much cheaper.

4.   Calculate the effective cost of the following trade credit terms where payment is made on the net due date.

a.   2/10, net 30

b.   3/15, net 30

c.   3/15, net 45

d.   2/15, net 60

SOLUTION

(a) $\dfrac{0.02}{0.98} \times \dfrac{1}{20/360}$ = 0.36734 or 36.73%

(b) $\dfrac{0.03}{0.97} \times \dfrac{1}{15/360}$ = 0.74226 or 74.23%

(c) $\dfrac{0.03}{0.97} \times \dfrac{1}{30/360}$ = 0.37113 or 37.11%

(d) $\dfrac{0.02}{0.98} \times \dfrac{1}{45/360}$ = 0.16327 or 16.33%

5. Luft, Inc., recently acquired production rights to an innovative sailboard design but needs funds to pay for the first production run, which is expected to sell briskly. The firm plans to issue $450,000 in 180-day maturity notes. The paper will carry an 11 percent rate with discounted interest and will cost Luft $13,000 (paid in advance) to issue.

    a. What is the effective cost of credit to Luft?

    b. What other factors should the company consider in analyzing whether to issue the commercial paper?

SOLUTION

(a) RATE $= \dfrac{\text{interest}}{\text{principal}} \times \dfrac{1}{\text{time}}$

RATE $= \dfrac{\$24,750^* + 13,000}{\$450,000 - 13,000 - 24,750} \times \dfrac{1}{180/360}$

$=$ .1831 or 18.31%

*Interest = .11 x $450,000 x 1/2

(b)   The risk involved with the issue of commercial paper should be considered. This risk relates to the fact that the commercial paper market is highly impersonal and denies even the most creditworthy borrower any flexibility in terms of when repayment is made.

In addition, commercial paper is a viable source of credit to only the most credit worthy borrowers. Thus, it may simply not be available to the firm.

6.   DST, Inc., a producer of inflatable river rafts, needs $400,000 for the three-month summer season, ending September 30, 1999. The firm has explored two possible sources of credit.

a.   DST has arranged with its bank for a $400,000 loan secured by accounts receivable. The bank has agreed to advance DST 80 percent of the value of its pledged receivables at a rate of 11 percent plus a 1 percent fee based on all receivables pledged. DST's receivables average a total of $1 million year-round.

b.   An insurance company has agreed to lend the $400,000 at a rate of 9 percent per annum, using a loan secured by DST's inventory. A field warehouse agreement would be used, which would cost DST $2,000 a month.

Which source of credit should DST select? Explain.

SOLUTION

Pledged Receivables (A/R):

0.80 A/R   = $400,000 loan

A/R   = $400,000/.80 = $500,000

Fee   =   (0.01) ($500,000) = $5,000

Interest Cost = (0.11) ($400,000) x 1/4 = $11,000

$$\text{Effective Rate} = \left(\frac{\$11,000 + 5,000}{\$400,000}\right)\left(\frac{1}{90/360}\right)$$

$$= \quad .16 \text{ or } 16\%$$

Inventory Loan:

Warehousing cost $=$ $2,000 x 3 months $=$ $6,000

Interest cost $=$ 0.09 x $400,000 x 1/4 = $9,000

$$\text{Effective Rate} = \left(\frac{\$6,000 + 9,000}{\$400,000}\right)\left(\frac{1}{90/360}\right)$$

$$= \quad .15 \text{ or } 15\%$$

The inventory loan would be preferred since its cost is lowest under the conditions presented.

Self-Tests

TRUE-FALSE

_____ 1.   Working capital has traditionally been defined as the firm's total investment in assets.

_____ 2.   Generally, interest rates on short-term debt are higher than they are on long-term debt for a given borrower.

_____ 3.   The guiding principle for the firm's working capital policies is referred to as the "principle of self-liquidating debt" or the "hedging principle."

_____ 4.   The use of short-term sources of financing enhances the firm's liquidity and reduces the firm's rate of return on assets.

_____ 5. There are two basic problems encountered in attempting to manage the firm's use of short-term financing: determining how much financing is needed and what sources to select.

_____ 6. Investment decisions are undertaken in the expectation of receiving future benefits.

_____ 7. In order to reduce the risk of illiquidity, a firm should decrease its investment in cash and marketable securities.

_____ 8. Current liabilities provide a flexible source of financing.

_____ 9. The "hedging principle" is founded in valuation theory.

_____ 10. Spontaneous financing consists of trade credit and other accounts payable which arise "automatically" in the firm's day-to-day operations.

_____ 11. The amount of trade credit available to the firm varies inversely with the size of the cash discount.

_____ 12. Compensating balances are never required when a firm has a line of credit with a bank.

_____ 13. A transaction loan is generally used when the firm has a specific use for the borrowed funds.

_____ 14. An advantage of commercial paper to a creditworthy borrower is that repayment can be postponed if necessary.

_____ 15. Pledging involves selling accounts receivable to a factor.

_____ 16. The primary sources of collateral for secured short-term credit are accounts receivable and inventories.

_____ 17. Field warehouse financing agreements involve physically moving the pledged inventories to a public warehouse.

___ 18. Commercial paper and trade credit are both forms of secured credit.

___ 19. An advantage of trade credit is that the amount of credit extended expands and contracts with the needs of the firm.

MULTIPLE CHOICE

1. Which of the following is an advantage true with respect to the use of current liabilities?

   a. The use of current liabilities subjects the firm to greater risk of illiquidity.
   b. The firm's interest costs can vary from year to year.
   c. The firm's interest costs are generally lower than where long-term liabilities are used.
   d. All of the above.
   e. None of the above.

2. Spontaneous financing consists of:

   a. Accounts payable.
   b. Trade credit.
   c. Short-term notes payable.
   d. Common stock.
   e. a and b only.

3. Which of the following accounts would not be a prime consideration in working-capital management?

   a. Cash.
   b. Accounts payable.
   c. Bonds payable.
   d. Marketable securities.
   e. Accounts receivable.

4. The greatest margin of safety for a firm would be provided by:

    a. More current assets and less current liabilities.
    b. More current assets and more current liabilities.
    c. Less current assets and more current liabilities.
    d. Less current assets and less current liabilities.
    e. none of the above.

5. Which asset-liability combination would result in the firm having the greatest risk of technical insolvency?

    a. More current assets and less current liabilities.
    b. More current assets and more current liabilities.
    c. Less current assets and more current liabilities.
    d. Less current assets and less current liabilities.
    e. None of the above.

6. Which of the following illustrates the use of the hedging approach?

    a. Temporary assets financed with long-term liabilities.
    b. Permanent assets financed with long-term liabilities.
    c. Temporary assets financed with short-term liabilities.
    d. All of the above.
    e. b and c.

7. Which of the following is not a form of secured short-term credit?

    a. General lien.
    b. Chattel mortgages.
    c. Commercial paper.
    d. Terminal warehouse receipt.
    e. Factoring.

8. Under which of the following agreements does the borrower retain physical possession of the inventory used as collateral for a loan?

    a. Field warehouse financing.
    b. Chattel mortgage.
    c. Terminal warehouse.
    d. All of the above.
    e. None of the above.

9. An informal agreement between a bank and its customer with respect to the maximum amount of unsecured credit the bank will permit the firm to owe at any one time is

   a. Line of credit.
   b. Revolving credit agreement.
   c. Transaction loan.
   d. All of the above.
   e. None of the above.

10. When a firm needs short-term funds for only one purpose, it usually obtains a _____.

    a. Line of credit.
    b. Revolving credit agreement.
    c. Transaction loan.
    d. Compensating balance.
    e. None of the above.

11. If a firm borrows $1 million at 8% and is required to maintain $100,000 in a compensating balance, the effective annual interest cost is:

    a. 8%.
    b. 8.89%.
    c. 7.27%.
    d. 9.5%.
    e. None of the above.

CHAPTER 17

Cash and Marketable Securities Management

Orientation: This chapter initiates our study of cash management. Here, we focus on the cash flow process and the reasons why a firm holds cash balances. The objectives of a sound cash management system are identified. The concept of float is defined. Several techniques that firms can use to favorably affect their cash receipts and disbursement patterns are examined. Finally, the composition of the firm's marketable securities portfolio is discussed.

I.   Why a company holds cash

    A.   The firm's cash balance is constantly affected by a variety of influences. Sound cash management techniques are based on a thorough understanding of the cash flow process.

        1.   On an irregular basis cash holdings are increased from several external sources, such as from the sale of securities.

        2.   In a similar fashion, irregular cash outflows reduce the firm's cash balance. Typical examples include cash dividend payments and the interest requirements on debt agreements.

        3.   Other major sources of cash arising from internal operations occur on a rather regular basis. Accounts receivable collections are an example.

B. Three motives for holding cash balances have been identified by Keynes.[1]

   1. The <u>transactions motive</u> is the need for cash to meet payments that arise in the ordinary course of doing business. Holding cash to meet a payroll or to acquire raw materials characterizes this motive.

   2. The <u>precautionary motive</u> describes the investment in liquid assets that are used to satisfy possible but as yet indefinite needs for cash. Precautionary balances are a buffer against all kinds of things that might happen to drain the firm's cash resources.

   3. The <u>speculative motive</u> describes holding cash to take advantage of hoped-for, profit-making situations.

II. Variations in liquid asset holdings

   A. Considerable variation is present in the liquid asset holdings of major industry groups and individual firms.

      1. This is because (1) not all of the factors noted above affect every firm and (2) the executives in different firms who are ultimately responsible for cash management tasks have different risk-bearing preferences.

      2. Some industries invest very heavily in liquid assets. For example, the total liquid assets to total assets ratio of the contract construction industry greatly exceeds that of the utility industry.

   B. Because assets are acquired, wasted, and sold every day, the management of liquid assets must be viewed as a dynamic process. The cash flow process is complex. In order to cut through this complexity, it is necessary that the firm's cash management system operate within clearly defined objectives.

---

[1] John Maynard Keynes, <u>The General Theory of Employment Interest and Money</u> (New York: Harcourt Brace Jovanovich, Inc., 1936).

III. Cash management objectives and decisions

    A.   A properly designed cash management program forces the financial manager to come to grips with a risk-return trade-off.

        1.   He or she must strike an acceptable balance between holding too much cash and holding too little cash.

        2.   A large cash investment minimizes the chances of insolvency, but it penalizes company profitability.

        3.   A small cash investment frees excess (cash) balances for investment in longer-lived and more profitable assets, which increases the firm's profitability.

    B.   The firm's cash management system should strive to achieve two prime objectives:

        1.   Enough cash must be on hand to dispense effectively with the disbursal needs that arise in the course of doing business.

        2.   The firm's investment in idle cash balances must be reduced to a minimum.

    C.   In the attempt to meet the two objectives noted above, certain decisions dominate the cash management process. These decision areas can be reduced to the three following questions:

        1.   What can be done to speed up cash collections and slow down or better control cash outflows?

        2.   What should be the composition of the marketable securities portfolio?

        3.   How should the investment in liquid assets be split between actual cash holdings and marketable securities? This is covered in the Appendix to this chapter.

IV. Collection and disbursement procedures

   A. Cash acceleration and deceleration techniques revolve around the concept of <u>float</u>. Float can be broken down into four elements:

      1. <u>Mail float</u> refers to funds that are tied up as a result of the time that elapses from the moment a customer mails his or her remittance check until the firm begins to process the check.

      2. <u>Processing float</u> refers to funds that are tied up as a result of the firm's recording and processing remittance checks prior to their deposit in the bank.

      3. <u>Transit float</u> refers to funds that are tied up as a result of the time needed for a deposited check to clear through the commercial banking system and become "usable" funds to the firm.

      4. <u>Disbursing float</u> refers to funds that are technically usable to the firm until its <u>payment</u> check has cleared through the banking system and has been charged against its deposit account.

   B. Float reduction can result in considerable benefits in terms of (1) usable funds that are released for company use and (2) in the returns produced on these freed-up balances. A study problem at the end of this chapter illustrates the calculation of such savings.

   C. Several techniques are available to improve the management of the firm's cash inflows. These techniques may also provide for a reduction in float.

      1. The lock-box arrangement is a widely used commercial banking service for expediting cash gathering.

         a. The objective is to reduce <u>both</u> mail and processing float.

17-4

b. The procedure behind a lock-box system is very simple. The firm rents a local post office box and authorizes a local bank in which a deposit account is maintained to pick up remittances from the box.

 (1) Customers are instructed to mail their payments to the numbered post office box.

 (2) A deposit form is prepared by the bank for each batch of processed checks.

 (3) The bank may notify the firm daily as to the amount of funds deposited on the firm's behalf.

 (4) The firm that receives checks from all over the country establishes several lock boxes.

c. A lock-box arrangement provides for (1) increased working cash, (2) elimination of clerical functions, and (3) early knowledge of dishonored checks.

d. The firm must carefully evaluate whether this or any cash management service is worth the added costs. Usually, the bank levies a charge for each check processed through the system. The marginal income generated from released funds must exceed the added costs of the system to make it economically beneficial. A study problem at the end of this chapter illustrates this kind of calculation.

2. Pre-authorized checks (PACs) are another method for speeding up the conversion of receipts into working cash.

a. The objective of the PAC is to reduce mail and processing float.

b.   A PAC (1) is created with the individual's legal authorization, (2) resembles an ordinary check, and (3) does not contain the signature of the person on whose account it is being drawn.

c.   PAC systems are most useful to firms that (1) regularly receive a large volume of payments of a fixed amount (2) from the same customers. Insurance companies and savings and loan associations are prominent examples.

d.   The principle behind the PAC system is straight-forward. The firm simply obtains an authorization from its customers to draw checks (at specified times and for specified amounts) on their (the customers') demand deposit accounts.

e.   Figure 17.1 shows the operation of a PAC system.

f.   The benefits derived from a PAC system include (1) highly predictable cash flows, (2) reduced billing, postage, and clerical expenses, (3) customer preference, and (4) increased working cash stemming from reduced mail and processing float.

3.   Depository transfer checks are used in conjunction with concentration banking. A concentration bank is one in which the firm maintains a major disbursing account.

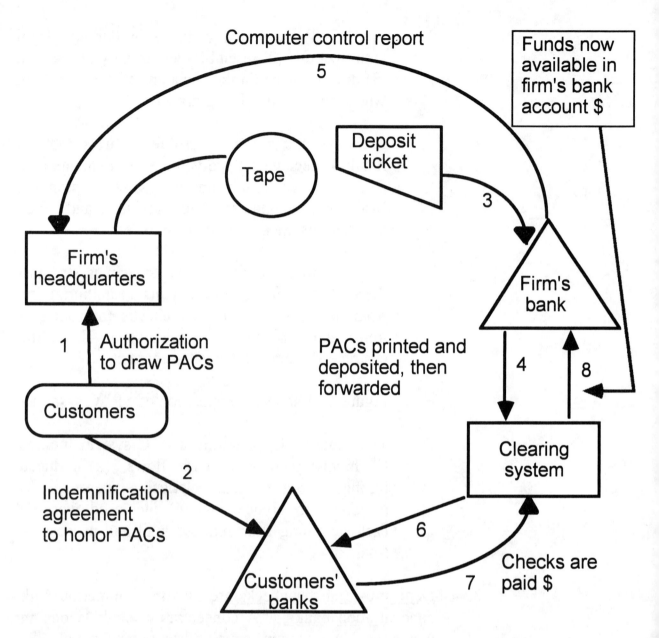

FIGURE 17.1
Pre-Authorized Check Systems (PAC)

a. The major objective of using depository transfer checks (DTCs) is to eliminate excess cash balances held by the firm in its several regional banks. A secondary objective is to reduce float.

b. The DTC provides a means for moving (transferring) funds from a local bank to a concentration bank.

(1) The DTC is an unsigned, non-negotiable instrument.

(2) The DTC is payable only to the bank of ultimate deposit.

(3) DTCs can operate through the use of the U.S. mail system or an automated system (ADTC).

c. With the conventional DTC, a company employee deposits the day's cash receipts in a local bank, fills out a DTC for the amount of the deposit, and mails the DTC to the concentration bank. When the DTC is received at the concentration bank, the transferred funds are credited to the firm's demand deposit account.

4. Wire transfers offer the fastest method for moving funds between commercial banks. Usable ("good") funds are transferred and thereby immediately become usable funds at the receiving bank. There is no transit float with wire transfers. Two major communication facilities are used to accommodate wire transfers: (1) bank wire, which is privately operated by about 250 major commercial banks in the United States, and (2) Federal Reserve wire system, which is accessible to members of the Federal Reserve system. The movement of small dollar amounts does not usually justify use of this system.

D. Techniques used by firms that hope to improve the management of their cash flow

1. Zero balance accounts (ZBAs) permit centralized control, but also allow the firm to maintain disbursing authority at the local level. The major objective is to achieve better control over cash payments. It might also increase disbursement float.

2. Payable-through drafts (PTDs) have the physical appearance of ordinary checks but they are drawn on and paid by the issuing firm instead of the bank.

   a. The objective of a PTD system is to provide for effective control of field authorized payments.

   b. Stop payment orders can be initiated on any drafts considered inappropriate.

   c. Legal payment of individual drafts takes place after review and approval of the drafts by the company. Disbursing float is usually not increased by the use of drafts.

3. Remote disbursing is intended to increase disbursing float.

   a. To implement, the firm opens and uses a DDA located in a city distant from its customers' banks.

   b. Since checks written on that account take longer to clear, the firm has use of its funds for a longer period of time.

   c. Alienation of important customers who must wait longer for usable funds is a major constraint.

V. Electronic funds transfer systems (EFT) reduce transit, mail, and processing float.

   A. Transactions are immediately reflected on the books and bank accounts of firms doing business.

   B. This ideal has not yet been reached.

   C. The purpose of the EFT is the elimination of the check as a method of transferring funds.

D.   Perspective on evaluating costs

VI.   Evaluating the costs of cash management services

    A.   Whether a cash management system will provide an economic benefit can be evaluated by:

    added costs = added benefits

    B.   If the benefits exceed the costs, the system is economically feasible.

    C.   On a per unit basis, this relationship can be expressed as follows:

$$P = (D)\,(S)\,(i)$$

    where P   =   increase in per-check processing cost, if new system is adopted
            D   =   days saved in the collection process
            S   =   average check size in dollars
            i   =   the daily, before-tax opportunity cost of carrying cash.

    D.   The sum of (D) x (S) x (i) must exceed P for the system to be beneficial to the firm.

    E.   Perspective on the marketable securities portfolio.

VII.   Composition of marketable securities portfolio

    A.   Five factors to consider when selecting a proper marketable securities mix

        1.   Financial risk

        2.   Interest rate risk

        3.   Liquidity

4. Taxability of interest income and capital gains

5. Yield criterion

B. Marketable security alternatives

1. A Treasury bill is a direct obligation of the U.S. government.

    a. May be purchased in denominations of $10,000, $15,000, $50,000, $100,000, $500,000, and $1,000,000

    b. Currently offered with maturities of 91, 182, and 365 days

    c. Since Treasury bills are sold on a discount basis, the investor does not receive an actual interest payment.

    d. The bills are considered risk-free and sell at lower yields than other marketable securities of like maturity.

    e. Income from Treasury bills is subject to the federal income tax and is taxed as ordinary income.

2. Federal agency securities represent debt obligations of federal government agencies.

3. Bankers' acceptances are drafts drawn on a specific bank by an exporter in order to obtain payment for goods shipped to a customer who maintains an account with that bank.

    a. Maturities run mostly from 30 to 180 days.

    b. Acceptances are sold on a discount basis.

c. Income generated is fully taxable at all levels.

d. Provide investors with a higher yield than do Treasury bills.

4. A negotiable certificate of deposit (CD) is a marketable receipt for funds that have been deposited in a bank for a fixed time period at a fixed interest rate.

   a. CDs are offered in denominations ranging from $25,000 to $10,000,000

   b. Maturities range from 1 to 18 months.

   c. Yields are higher than that of Treasury bills.

   d. Income received is taxed at all governmental levels.

5. Commercial paper refers to short-term, unsecured promissory notes .

   a. Paper ranges from $25,000 up to $1,000,000.

   b. The notes are sold on a discount basis with maturities ranging from 3 to 270 days.

   c. Paper has no <u>active</u> trading in a secondary market.

   d. Return received is taxable at all governmental levels.

6. Repurchase agreements involve the actual sale of securities by a borrower to the lender, with a commitment on the part of the borrower to repurchase the securities at the contract price plus a stated interest charge.

   a. These agreements are usually executed in sizes of $500,000 or more.

b.   There is no specified maturity date or time period.

c.   Yields are less than Treasury bills and are taxable at all governmental levels.

7.   Money market mutual funds usually invest in a diversified portfolio of short-term, high-grade debt instruments.

a.   Shares are sold to a large number of small investors.

b.   Funds offer a high degree of liquidity.

c.   Returns are taxable at all governmental levels.

8.   Money market deposit accounts

a.   Accounts offered by commercial banks and thrift institutions which compete with but differ from money market mutual funds.

b.   Transactions per month on each account are limited.

c.   Accounts are popular with individual investors.

Study Problems

1.   Buckeye equipment has $3,000,000 in excess cash that it might invest in marketable securities. In order to buy and sell the securities though, the company must pay a transactions fee of $67,500.

(a)   Would you recommend purchasing the securities if they yield 13 percent annually and are held for:

1.   one month?
2.   two months?

3. three months?
4. six months?
5. one year?

(b) What minimum required yield would the securities have to return for the firm to hold them for three months?

SOLUTION

(a) It is necessary to calculate the dollar value of the estimated return for each holding period and compare it with the transactions fee. This will allow you to determine if a gain can be made by investing in the securities. The calculations and recommendations are shown below:

				Recommendation
1.	$3,000,000(.13)(1/12)	=	$ 32,500 < $67,500	NO
2.	$3,000,000(.13)(2/12)	=	$ 65,000 < $67,500	NO
3.	$3,000,000(.13)(3/12)	=	$ 97,500 > $67,500	YES
4.	$3,000,000(.13)(6/12)	=	$195,000 > $67,500	YES
5.	$3,000,000(.13)(12/12)	=	$390,000 > $67,500	YES

(b) Now we find the break-even yield for a three-month holding period. Let (%) be the required yield. With $3,000,000 to invest for three months we have:

$3,000,000 (%) (3/12) = $ 67,500
$3,000,000 (%)   = $270,000
            (%)   = $270,000/$3,000,000=9%

2. Portland Energy Products is evaluating whether or not to use an additional lock box. If the lock box is used, check processing costs will rise by $.20 a check. The average check size that will be mailed to the lock-box location is $1,000. Funds that are freed by using the lock box will be invested in marketable securities to yield an annual before-tax return of 7%. The firm uses a 365 day year in its analysis procedures. What reduction in check-collection time is required to justify use of the lock box?

SOLUTION

Solve the following relationship for D:

$$P = (D)\ (S)\ (i)$$

$$\$.20 = (D)(\$1{,}000)\left(\frac{0.07}{365}\right)$$

$$\$.20 = (D)\ (\$.192)$$

$$\frac{\$.20}{\$.192} = D = \underline{1.0417\ days}$$

Thus, the lock box is justified if it can speed up collections by <u>more</u> than 1.0417 days.

3. Annual sales for Austin Drilling Supply will total $250,000,000 next year. What would be the annual value of 1-day's float reduction to this firm if it could invest the freed-up balances at 8% per year?

SOLUTION

Compute Austin's sales per day:

$$\frac{annual\ revenues}{days\ in\ years} = \frac{250{,}000{,}000}{365} = \$684{,}932$$

Compute the annual value of the 1-day float reduction:

$$(\$684{,}932)\ (0.08) = \underline{\$54{,}795}$$

4. The corporate treasurer of Buckeye Bottling is considering purchasing a municipal obligation with a 7% coupon and a $1,000 par value. Mr. Inside Info has telephoned the treasurer about another $1,000 par value offering which provides a 12% yield. This latter offering is, however, fully taxable. Buckeye is taxed at a 48% rate.

    (a) Should the treasurer take Mr. Info's advice and purchase the 12% security?

(b)   What is the equivalent before-tax yield on the municipal assuming Buckeye is in a 48% tax bracket?

SOLUTION

(a)   The after-tax yield to Buckeye on the 12% offering is (0.12) (1-0.48) = 6.24%. Since the yield on the municipal is already stated on an after-tax basis the treasurer should ignore Mr Info's advice and purchase the municipal offering.

(b)   The equivalent before-tax yield is:

$$r = \frac{0.07}{(1-0.48)} = \underline{13.46\%}$$

Thus, the taxable issue would have to yield in excess of 13.46% to be more attractive than the municipal to Buckeye.

5.   Tech Electronics, manufacturers of fine calculators, has recently purchased 10-year bonds at their par value of $1,000 per security. Texas Parts, a close competitor, has just purchased 5-year bonds at their $1,000 par value . Both securities have a coupon rate set at 8%, are compounded annually, and have a maturity value of $1,000. Suppose the prevailing interest rate 1 year from now rises to 10%. What would the decline in market price be for each bond in 1 year?

SOLUTION

One year from now the 5-year issue has 4 years remaining to maturity. The market price in 1 year can be found by computing P according to the following:

$$P = \sum_{T=1}^{4} \frac{\$80}{(1+0.10)^T} + \frac{\$1,000}{(1+0.10)^4} = \$936.60$$

where $80 = (0.08) ($1,000). Similarly, for the l0-year issue which now has 9 years to maturity,

$$P = \sum_{T=1}^{9} \frac{\$80}{(1+0.10)^T} + \frac{\$1,000}{(1+0.10)^9} = \$884.82$$

Thus the 10-year security declines in price $115.18 ($1,000 - $884.82), while the 5-year security declines in price by only $63.40 ($1,000-$936.60). This illustrates the concept of <u>interest rate risk</u>, discussed in the text in Chapter 15.

6. Gavin International expects to generate sales of $74,000,000 in the coming year. All sales are done on a credit basis, net 30 days. Gavin has estimated that it takes an average of 4 days for payments to reach their central office and an additional day to process the payments. What is the opportunity cost of the funds tied up in the mail and processing? Gavin uses a 360 day year in all calculations and can invest free funds at 7%.

    SOLUTION

    Daily collections = 74,000,000/360 = $ 205,555.56

    Opportunity Cost = (205,555.56) (5) (.07) = <u>$71,944</u>

7. The corporate treasurer of Chester Motors is considering the purchase of either an offering carrying a 7.6% coupon or a municipal obligation with a 5% coupon. Both bonds have a $1,000 par value. The company is currently in the 34% marginal tax bracket. Which security should the treasurer recommend?

    SOLUTION

    The after-tax yield to Chester Motors on the 7.6% offering is
    (1-.34) (.076) = 5%. The municipal's after-tax rate is the stated 5%. There is no difference in yield. If the risk is considered equal for each security then the treasurer would be indifferent between the two.

Self-Tests

TRUE-FALSE

_____ 1. Accounts receivable are usually referred to as "near-cash assets."

_____ 2. Holding cash to pay for next week's labor bill (payroll) is an example of the precautionary motive for holding cash.

_____ 3. Ready borrowing power enables the firm to reduce the cash balances actually held for precautionary purposes.

_____ 4. Technical insolvency means that the firm is able to meet its short-term obligations on time but that its long-term obligations are in jeopardy.

_____ 5. Cash flow forecasting is the initial step in any effective cash management program.

_____ 6. Wire transfers provide the fastest and least costly method of transferring funds among depository institutions.

_____ 7. A possible benefit stemming from the use of preauthorized checks is that cash flows can be more predictable.

_____ 8. The major objective of using payable-through drafts is to extend disbursing float.

_____ 9. The major reason for using lock boxes is to enjoy a reduction in transit float.

_____ 10. Zero balance accounts are used to accelerate cash receipts.

_____ 11. Although they have a lower yield, agency securities are more readily marketable by the purchasing corporation than are Treasury bills.

_____ 12. Bankers' acceptances generally mature from 9 to 12 months after "sight."

_____ 13. Commercial paper is backed by specific assets of the firm.

_____ 14. The most common denomination for the negotiable CD is $10,000.

_____ 15. The longer the term of maturity, the less sensitive the price of a security to changes in interest rates.

_____ 16. Long-term bonds may serve as a useful (comfortable) hedge against interest rate risk.

_____ 17. Because of their higher financial risk, agency securities always yield more than Treasury securities of a comparable maturity do.

_____ 18. The higher the marginal tax bracket the lower the after-tax rate of return on a taxable security.

_____ 19. Bankers' acceptances provide for a steady flow of interest payments to the investor in the form of coupon payments.

_____ 20. With respect to interest risk, Treasury securities are risk-free.

_____ 21. Money market deposit accounts (MMDAs) are more suited to individual investors than business firms as a tool of liquid asset management.

_____ 22. The lock-box system is the most widely used commercial banking service for expediting cash gathering.

_____ 23. A concentration bank is one where the firm generally maintains several minor disbursing accounts.

_____ 24. There is an inverse relationship between a financial instrument's chance of default and financial risk.

_____ 25. The contract price of the securities that make up the repurchase agreement is fixed for the duration of the transaction.

_____ 26. According to Keynes the demand for cash can be divided into three categories: transactions, precautionary, and speculative.

_____ 27. A PAC or Preauthorized Check does not ordinarily bear the name of the person on whose account the check was drawn.

_____ 28. To calculate the annual savings due to float reduction you would multiply the sales per day by the days of float reduction.

_____ 29. Payable-Through Drafts provide control over field payments.

_____ 30. A liquid asset is an asset that can be sold regardless of the time it takes to make the sale and the price concession suffered to make the sale.

_____ 31. Commercial paper is sometimes described as short term, corporate IOU's.

_____ 32. Increases in cash holdings from external sources of funds tend to be more regular than internal generation of cash.

_____ 33. The motives for holding cash apply equally to all firms. Variations in cash holdings from firm to firm result from differing management risk preferences.

_____ 34. The prime objectives of cash management are to reduce idle cash balances and to have sufficient cash on hand to meet disbursal needs.

_____ 35. Under the lock-box arrangement, a deposit form is prepared by the <u>depositor</u> for each batch of processed checks.

_____ 36. Most cash management techniques should be adopted regardless of their economic benefits, in order to financially aid commercial banks.

_____ 37. The use of payable-through drafts will usually increase disbursing float to the issuing firm.

_____ 38. Commercial paper refers to short-term, unsecured promissory notes sold by <u>government agencies</u> to raise cash.

MULTIPLE CHOICE

1.   Indicate the item that is not an advantage of the lock-box system.

      a.   The cost is minimal.
      b.   Speeds up the flow of cash to the firm.
      c.   Remittances are collected sooner.
      d.   All of the above are advantages.

2.   Which of the following is not a cash acceleration technique?

      a.   Lock boxes.
      b.   Automated depository transfer checks.
      c.   Preauthorized checks.
      d.   Payable-through drafts.
      e.   All of the above are cash acceleration techniques.

3.   Depository transfer checks mainly:

      a.   Reduce mail and processing float.
      b.   Extend disbursing float.
      c.   Provide a method of moving funds from local banks to concentration banks.
      d.   Centralize disbursing authority.

4.   Zero balance accounts:

      a.   Permit centralized control over disbursements.
      b.   Provide for effective control over field payments.
      c.   Are an integral part of the lock-box system.
      d.   Are the same thing as pre-authorized checks.

5.   A preauthorized check system:

      a.   Reduces mail float.
      b   Reduces processing float.
      c.   Extends disbursing float.
      d.   a and b.
      e.   b and c.

6. Generally, the least important component of a firm's preference for liquidity is:

   a. the transaction motive
   b. the precautionary motive.
   c. the speculative motive.
   d. all motives are of equal importance.

7. Which of the following is <u>not</u> an objective of the lockbox system?

   a. reduce mail float.
   b. reduce processing float.
   c. reduce transit float.
   d. reduce disbursing float.

8. The advantages of a preauthorized check system include:

   a. reduced expenses.
   b. highly predictable cash flows.
   c. increased working cash
   d customer preference.
   e. all of the above are benefits of a PAC.

9. The uncertainty of expected returns from a security attributable to possible changes in the financial capacity of the security issuer to make future payments to the security owner refers to:

   a. interest rate risk.
   b. liquidity.
   c. financial risk.
   d. taxability.
   e. yield.

10. Which short-term investment has, for all practical purposes, <u>no</u> active trading in a secondary market?

    a. treasury bills.
    b. federal agency securities.
    c. negotiable certificates of deposit.
    d. commercial paper.
    e. banker's acceptances.

11. Which of the following is a benefit of centralizing the firm's pool of cash:

    a.   Lower levels of excess cash.
    b.   Stricter control over available cash.
    c.   More efficient investments in near-cash assets.
    d.   a and b.
    e.   All of the above.

12. The fact that funds are available in the company's bank account until its payment check has cleared through the banking system refers to:

    a.   Mail float.
    b.   Processing float
    c.   Transit float.
    d.   Disbursing float.

13. Which is not an objective of zero balance accounts:

    a.   Achieve better control over cash payments.
    b.   Reduce excess cash balances held in regional banks for disbursing purposes.
    c.   Decrease disbursing float.

14. Firms use remote disbursements to:

    a.   Decrease mail float.
    b.   Increase disbursing float.
    c.   Decrease disbursing float.
    d.   Increase processing float.

15. Interest rate risk is of concern to a firm's financial officer because:

    a.   It is more difficult to issue securities when interest rates are low.
    b.   Changes in interest rates affect the expected return of financial instruments.
    c.   Federal government taxation increases as interest rates rise, reducing the cash available to the firm.
    d.   Inflationary periods may reduce the real earnings of the firm.

16. Which of the following does not describe U.S. Treasury bills?

    a. Maturities include 3-month, 6-month and 1 year securities.
    b. Discount instrument.
    c. Issued only in bearer form.
    d. Income subject to federal, state and local income tax.
    e. All of the above describe U.S. Treasury bills.

17. Which security (assuming identical maturities) would be expected to have the highest yield based on recent experience?

    a. Banker's acceptances.
    b. Agencies.
    c. CDs.
    d. Commercial paper.
    e. Treasury bills.

18. Which of the following is not a motive for holding cash balances?

    a. transactions motive.
    b. speculative motive.
    c. convenience motive.
    d. precautionary motive.

19. A concentration bank is:

    a. a bank that has the most deposit accounts.
    b. a bank that concentrates its service in one geographic area.
    c. a bank that concentrates on one type of service.
    d. a bank in which the firm maintains a major disbursing account.

20. Wire transfers can be used to:

    a. move steel wire between two utility companies.
    b. move funds between two industrial companies.
    c. move funds between commercial banks.
    d. move funds between investment banks.
    e. b, c, and d above.
    f. none of the above.

Appendix 17A

CASH MANAGEMENT MODELS:
THE SPLIT BETWEEN CASH AND NEAR CASH

I.   Dividing liquid assets between cash and marketable securities.

   A.   When the need for cash is certain, the financial manager may utilize the economic order quantity formula (inventory model).

      1.   Objective: The purpose of this analysis is to balance the lost income that the firm suffers from holding cash rather than marketable securities against the transactions costs involved in converting securities into cash.

      2.   Strategy: The inventory model minimizes the total cost of maintaining the cash balance whenever the costs include:

         a.   The carrying cost of holding cash.

         b.   The fixed cost of converting marketable securities into cash.

      3.   Assumptions:

         a.   Cash payments over the planning period are:

            (1)   A regular or constant amount

            (2)   Continuous

            (3)   Certain

         b.   No unanticipated cash receipts will be received during the planning period.

         c.   The interest rate on investments remains constant over the analysis period.

d. Transfers between cash and the securities portfolio may take place at any time at a cost that is fixed, regardless of the amount to be transferred.

4. Computation

    a. Notation:

        C = the amount per order of marketable securities to be converted into cash.

        i = the interest rate per period available on investments in marketable securities.

        b = the fixed cost per order of converting marketable securities into cash.

        T = the total cash requirements over the planning period.

        TC = the total costs associated with maintenance of a particular cash average.

    b. Computation of costs:

        T/C = the number of transfers during the period.

        $C/2$ = the average cash balance.

    Thus the total costs (TC) of having cash on hand can be expressed as:

$$TC = i\left(\frac{C}{2}\right) + b\left(\frac{T}{C}\right)$$

total interest income forgone   total ordering costs

c.   Minimization of total costs: The optimal cash conversion size, C*, can be found by using the following equation:

$$C* = \sqrt{\frac{2bT}{i}}$$

5.   Example: Management estimates the total cash needs for the next 2 months to be $15,000. The cost of transferring marketable securities into cash is $30 for each trade, and the annual yield on securities is 12% (2% for 2 months). Find the optimal cash order size.

$$C* = \sqrt{\frac{2bT}{i}} = \sqrt{\frac{2(30)\,(15{,}000)}{0.2}} = \$6{,}708.20$$

Further, the optimal average cash balance is $3,354.10 ($6,708.20/2).

6.   Implications of the inventory model for cash management:

a.   Notice that the optimal case order size, C*, varies directly with the square root of the ordering costs, bT, and inversely with the yield, i, obtained on marketable securities.

b.   Also notice that as T increases, C* does not rise proportionately. This implies the existence of economies of scale in cash management.

c.   When the total cost of ordering and holding cash is minimized, the cash conversion cost and the interest income forgone are exactly equal.

d.   The strict assumptions of the inventory model for cash management will not be completely satisfied in actual business practice.

B.   When cash balances fluctuate randomly, the financial manager may use a stochastic (probabilistic) control-limit model to facilitate the decision process.

  1.   Objective: The control-limit model seeks to minimize the total costs of managing the firm's cash balance.

  2.   Strategy: Through the use of control theory, the model determines upper and lower limits beyond (out of) which the cash balance is not permitted to reach (or wander).

    a.   When the cash balance reaches the upper control limit (UL), a conversion of cash into marketable securities takes place. The amount converted is equal to UL-RP dollars, where RP is some calculated cash return point.

    b.   When the cash balance reaches the lower control limit (LL), a conversion of marketable securities into cash is initiated by the financial officer. The amount converted is equal to RP-LL dollars.

  3.   Assumptions:

    a.   The firm's cash balance changes in an irregular, unpredictable manner over time.
    b.   The probability (chance) of a cash balance change being either positive or negative is 0.5 (i.e., equally likely).

  4.   Computation of UL and RP:

    a.   Notation:

        b   =   the fixed cost per order of converting marketable securities into cash.

        i   =   the daily interest rate available on investments in marketable securities into cash.

$$\sigma^2 = \text{the variance of daily changes in the firm's expected cash balances.}$$

b. The optimal cash return point, RP, can be determined by using the following equation:

$$RP = \sqrt[3]{\frac{3b\sigma^2}{4i}} + LL$$

c. The upper control limit (UL) can be calculated:

$$UL = 3\,RP - 2\,LL$$

d. The lower control limit (LL) is determined by management.

5. Example: Assume that the annual yield available on marketable securities is 11%. During a 365-day year, it becomes $0.11/365 = 0.0003$ per day. Also assume that the fixed cost of transacting a marketable securities trade (b) is $40. In addition, the firm has observed a variance of $490,000 in past daily cash balance changes. Management has decided that $2,000 is an appropriate lower control limit.

a. The optimal cash return point becomes

$$RP = \sqrt[3]{\frac{3(40)\,(490,000)}{4(0.0003)}} = \$3,659 + \$2,000$$

$$= \$5,659$$

b. The upper cash balance limit is

$$UL = 3\,(\$5,659) - 2\,(\$2,000) = \$12,977$$

c. Once the cash balance reaches the upper limit of $12,977, the financial manager would buy $7,318 (UL-RP) of marketable securities. Should the cash balance drop to the lower limit of $2,000, the financial manager would sell $3,659 (RP-LL) of marketable securities.

6. Implications of the control-limit model for cash management:

a. The optimal cash return level, RP, will vary, directly with the cube root of both the transfer cost, b, and the volatility of daily cash balance changes, σ^2,

b. The larger the transfer cost or cash balance volatility, the greater the absolute dollar spread between the upper control limit and the cash return point.

c. The optimal cash return point varies inversely with the cube root of the lost interest rate.

d. Like the inventory model, the control-limit model implies the existence of economies of scale in cash management.

C. Compensating balances.

1. The bank requires that the firm maintain deposits of a given minimum amount in its demand deposit account.

2. These balances are normally required of corporate customers in three situations:

a. Whenever the firm has a loan commitment at the bank which is not entirely used, a compensating balance is required.

b.   If the firm has a loan outstanding at the bank, a compensating balance is required.

c.   Instead of paying directly for certain banking services (e.g., check clearing), a firm will be asked to maintain such a balance. The current trend, however, is toward unit pricing for these services.

3.   Compensating balance policies vary among commercial banks and are influenced by general economic and financial market conditions. Several guidelines may, however, be offered.

a.   For the case of the unused portion of a loan commitment, the bank might require that the compensating balance range from 5% to 10% of the commitment.

b.   If a loan is outstanding with the bank, the requirement may be 10% to 20% of the unpaid balance.

c.   In order to compensate for various bank services, the firm may be asked to maintain a balance based on either an absolute amount or an average amount.

4.   When determining the optimal split between cash and marketable securities the financial officer must explicitly consider the compensating balance requirement.

a.   One approach is to ignore the requirement when performing the necessary calculations and then select the maximum of that suggested by the model or the bank's compensating balance requirement.

b.   A second approach is to include the compensating balance requirement in the requisite calculations.

(1) The requirement could be treated as a safety stock in the inventory model.

(2) The requirement could be considered the lower control limit in the control-limit model.

Study Problems

1. Using the inventory model, determine: (a) the optimal cash conversion size; (b) the optimal level of cash the firm should hold; and (c) the total cost of having the optimal amount of cash on hand during the next 6 months. The financial officer has developed the following information:

(1) The firm needs $5,000 in cash for transactions purposes during the next 6 months.

(2) The cost of transferring marketable securities into cash is $60 per order.

(3) The interest rate on marketable securities is 10% for the next year (5% for 6 months).

SOLUTION

(a) $$C^* = \sqrt{\frac{2(60)\,(5,000)}{0.05}} = \underline{\$3,464}$$

(b) Optimal level of cash is

$$\frac{C^*}{2} = \frac{\$3,464}{2} = \underline{\$1,732}$$

(c) $$TC = 0.05(\$1,732) + \$60\left(\frac{\$5,000}{\$3,464}\right) = \underline{\$173.20}$$

2. Using the inventory model, determine the optimal level of cash the firm should hold if:

   (a) The available annual yield on marketable securities is 6%.

   (b) The cost of converting from cash to marketable securities is $50 per transaction.

   (c) The firm's transaction needs will total $1,000 over the next year.

SOLUTION

$$\text{transaction balance} \quad = \quad C^* = \sqrt{\frac{2(50)\,(1,000)}{0.06}} = \underline{\$1,291}$$

$$\begin{array}{l} \text{optimal level} \\ \text{of cash} \end{array} \quad = \quad \text{transaction balance} \div 2 = \frac{C^*}{2} = \frac{\$1,291}{2}$$

$$= \quad \underline{\$645.50}$$

3. Wolfpack Industries is considering taking out a loan at the Piedmont National Bank. The firm is evaluating the option of a 10 % one-year loan for $1,000, with interest and principal due at the end of the year. The alternative is a 9%, 1-year loan for $1,000 with the same repayment terms as the other loan, but a 13% compensating balance is required. Which loan do you recommend that Wolfpack take?

SOLUTION

The cost of the 10% loan is actually 10%. The cost of the 9% loan is

$$\frac{\$\text{interest}}{\text{funds available}} = \frac{\$90}{\$1,000 - \$130} = \frac{\$90}{\$870} = 10.34\%$$

Wolfpack should take the straight 10% loan option.

4. The cash balances of South Tampa Cigars fluctuate randomly, with a standard deviation of daily cash flows of $500. The current annual rate of interest on securities is 9%, with fixed conversion costs of $150. Also, management desires to have <u>at least</u> $3,000 in cash on hand at any point in time. The firm uses a 365-day year in its analysis procedures.

    (a) Find the upper and lower control limits.

    (b) In what lot sizes will marketable securities be purchased and sold?

SOLUTION

    (a) The lower control limit (LL) is simply <u>$3,000</u>,

$$RP = \sqrt[3]{\frac{3(150)\,(500)^2}{4(0.000247)}} = \$4,847 + \$3,000 = \$7,847$$

where $i = \dfrac{0.09}{365} = 0.000247$ and the optimal upper limit

(UL) is

$$UL = 3RP\text{-}2LL = \$23,541\text{-}\$6,000 = \underline{\$17,541},$$

    (b) Marketable securities will be purchased in lot sizes equal to

$$UL - RP = \$17,541 - \$7,847 = \underline{\$9,694},$$

Securities will be sold in lot sizes equal to

$$RP - LL = \$7,847 - \$3,000 = \underline{\$4,847}.$$

SOLUTIONS TO SELECTED SET B PROBLEMS (See text for problems.)

17-3B.

(a)

					Recommendation
1.	$700,000 (.115) (1/12)	=	$6,708	< $25,000	No
2.	$700,000 (.115) (2/12)	=	$13,417	< $25,000	No
3.	$700,000 (.115) (3/12)	=	$20,125	< $25,000	No
4.	$700,000 (.115) (6/12)	=	$40,250	> $25,000	Yes
5.	$700,000 (.115) (12/12)	=	$80,500	> $25,000	Yes

(b)

Let (%) be the required yield. With $700,000 to invest for two months and a two-month holding period, we have:

$700,000 (%) (2/12) = $ 25,000
$700,000 (%) = $150,000
(%) = $150,000/$700,000 = 21.43%

The break-even yield, therefore, is 21.43%.

17-6B. Annual collections = $10,000,000 (5 regions) = $50,000,000

Daily collections = $50,000,000/365 = $136,986

The value of the 3.0 days' float reduction is found by presuming the freed balances will be added to the marketable securities portfolio and will earn 11.0% (see text of problem). The gross annual savings from the system are:

($136,986) (3.0 days) (.11) = $45,205

The annual cost of operating the lock-box system is:

($600 per month) (5 regions) (12 months) = $36,000

The net annual savings are:

$$\begin{array}{r} \$45,205 \\ - \ \underline{36,000} \\ \underline{\$9,205} \quad \text{Savings} \end{array}$$

The data indicate that Regency Components should adopt the lock-box system.

17-10B.

(a)   First, it is necessary to compute Colorado Comm's average remittance check size and the daily opportunity cost of carrying cash. The average check size is:

$$\frac{\$10,000,000}{7,000} = \$1,429 \text{ per check.}$$

The daily opportunity cost of carrying cash is:

$$\frac{0.07}{365} = 0.0001918 \text{ per day}$$

Second, the days saved in the collection process can be evaluated according to the general format of

Added Costs = Added Benefits
or
P = (D) (S) (i)
0.30 = (D) ($1,429) (0.0001918)
<u>1.0946 days</u> = D

Therefore, Colorado Comm will experience a financial gain if it adopts the lock-box system and by doing so, will speed up its collections by <u>more</u> than 1.0946 days.

(b)   In this situation the daily opportunity cost of carrying cash is:

$$\frac{0.045}{365} = 0.0001233 \text{ per day}$$

For Colorado Comm to break even should it choose to install the lock-box system, the cash collections must be accelerated by 1.7027 days as follows:

$$\$0.30 = (D)\ (\$1,429)\ (0.0001233)$$
$$\underline{1.7027 \text{ days}} = D$$

(c)   The break-even cash acceleration period of 1.7027 days is greater than the 1.0946 days found in part (a). This is due to the lower yield available on near-cash assets (or 4.5 percent annually versus 7.0 percent). Since the alternative rate of return on the freed-up balances is lower in the second situation, more funds must be invested to cover the costs of operating the lock-box system. The greater cash acceleration period generates this increased level of required funds.

17-14B.

Annual collections = (\$5,000,000) (10) = \$50,000,000
Daily collections = \$50,000,000/365 = \$136,986
The opportunity cost of the mail and processing float is:

(\$136,986) (4.0) (0.09) = $\underline{\$49,315}$

17-18B.

(a)   The after-tax yield to Ward Grocers on the BBB-rated bond is (0.08) (1-0.46) = .0432 = 4.32%. Since the yield on the tax-exempt issue is already stated on an after-tax basis, we can conclude the 5 1/2 percent return on the municipal is preferable.

(b) $r = \dfrac{r^*}{(1-T)}$

$$r = \frac{0.055}{(1-0.46)} = \frac{0.055}{0.54} = \underline{10.185\%}$$

CHAPTER 18

Accounts Receivable, Inventory, and Total Quality Management

Orientation: The investment of funds in accounts receivable inventory involves a trade off between profitability and risk. For accounts receivable this trade off occurs as less creditworthy customers with a higher probability of bad debts are taken on to increase sales. With respect to inventory management, a larger investment in inventory leads to more efficient production and speedier delivery, hence, increased sales. However, additional financing to support the increase in inventory and increased handling and carrying costs is required. In addition, the concept of total quality management and single-sourcing have had a major impact on inventory purchasing.

I.   Accounts receivable

      A.   Typically, accounts receivable accounts for just over 20 percent of a firm's assets.

      B.   The size of the investment in accounts receivable varies from industry to industry and is affected by several factors including the percentage of credit sales to total sales, the level of sales, and the credit and collection policies, more specifically the terms of sale, the quality of customer, and collection efforts.

      C.   Although all these factors affect the size of the investment, only the credit and collection policies are decision variables under the control of the financial manager.

D. The terms of sale are generally stated in the form a/b net c, indicating that the customer can deduct a percentage if the account is paid within b days; otherwise, the account must be paid within c days.

E. If the customer decides to forego the discount and not pay until the final payment date, the annualized opportunity cost of passing up this a% discount and withholding payment until the cth day is determined as follows:

$$\text{annualized opportunity cost of foregoing the discount} = \frac{a}{1-a} \times \frac{360}{c-b}$$

Example: Given the trade credit terms of 3/20 net 60, what is the annualized opportunity cost of passing up the 3-percent discount and withholding payment until the 60th day?

Solution: Substituting in the values from the example, we get

$$27.8\% = \frac{0.03}{1-0.03} \times \frac{360}{60-20}$$

F. A second decision variable in determining the size of the investment in accounts receivable in addition to the trade credit terms is the type of customer.

   1. The costs associated with extending credit to lower-quality customers include:

      a. Increased costs of credit investigation
      b. Increased probability of customer default
      c. Increased collection costs

G. Analyzing the credit application is a major part of accounts receivable management.

1. Several avenues are open to the firm in considering the credit rating of an applicant. Among these are financial statements, independent credit ratings and reports, bank checking, information from other companies, and past experiences.

2. One commonly used method for credit evaluation is called credit scoring and involves the numerical evaluation of each applicant in which an applicant receives a score based upon the answers to a simple set of questions. The score is then evaluated relative to a predetermined standard, its level relative to that standard determining whether or not credit scoring should be extended to the applicant. The major advantage of credit scoring is that it is inexpensive and easy to perform.

3. Once the decision to extend credit has been made and if the decision is yes, a maximum credit line is established as a ceiling on the amount of credit to be extended.

H. The third and final decision variable in determining the size of the investment in accounts receivable is the firm's collection policies.

1. Collection policy is a combination of letter sending, telephone calls, personal visits, and legal actions.

2. The greater the amount spent on collecting, the lower the volume of bad debts.

a. The relationship is not linear, however, and beyond a point is not helpful.

b. If sales are independent of collection efforts, then methods of collection should be evaluated with respect to the reduction in bad debts against the cost of lowering those bad debts.

I. Credit should be extended to the point that marginal profitability on additional sales equals the required rate of return on the additional investment in receivables necessary to generate those sales.

II. Inventory

  A. Typically, inventory accounts for about four to five percent of a firm's assets.

  B. The purpose of carrying inventories is to uncouple the operations of the firm, that is, to make each function of the business independent of each other function.

  C. As such, the decision with respect to the size of the investment in inventory involves a basic trade off between risk and return.

  D. The risk comes from the possibility of running out of inventory if too little inventory is held, while the return aspect of this trade off results because increased inventory investment costs money.

  E. There are several general types of inventory.

    1. Raw materials inventory consists of the basic materials that have been purchased from other firms to be used in the firm's productions operations. This type of inventory uncouples the production function from the purchasing function.

    2. Work in process inventory consists of partially finished goods that require additional work before they become finished goods. This type of inventory uncouples the various production operations.

    3. Finished goods inventory consists of goods on which the production has been completed but the goods are not yet sold. This type of inventory uncouples the production and sales function.

4.   Stock of cash inventory, already discussed in some detail in preceding chapters, serves to make the payment of bills independent of the collection of accounts due.

F.   In order to effectively manage the investment in inventory, two problems must be dealt with: the order quantity problem and the order point problem.

G.   The order quantity problem involves the determination of the optimal order size for an inventory item given its expected usage, carrying, and ordering costs .

H.   The economic order quantity (EOQ) model attempts to determine the order size that will minimize total inventory costs. The EOQ is given as

$$Q^* = \sqrt{\frac{2SO}{C}}$$

where C   =   carrying costs per unit
      O   =   ordering costs per order
      S   =   total demand in units over the planning period
      Q* =   the optimal order quantity in units

I.   The order point problem attempts to answer the following question: How low should inventory be depleted before it is reordered?

J.   In answering this question two factors become important:

1.   What is the usual procurement or delivery time and how much stock is needed to accommodate this time period?

2.   How much safety stock does the management desire?

K.   Modification for safety stocks is necessary since the usage rate of inventory is seldom stable over a given timetable.

L.   This safety stock is used to safeguard the firm against changes in order time and receipt of shipped goods.

M.   The greater the uncertainty associated with forecasted demand or order time, the larger the safety stock.

1.   The costs associated with running out of inventory will also determine the safety stock levels.

2.   A point is reached where it is too costly to carry a larger safety stock given the associated risk.

N.   Inflation can also have an impact on the level of inventory carried.

1.   Goods may be purchased in large quantities in anticipation of price rises.

2.   The cost of carrying goods may increase causing a decline in Q^*, the optional order quantity.

O.   The just-in-time inventory control system is more than just an inventory control system; it is a production and management system.

1.   Under this system inventory is cut down to a minimum and the time and physical distance between the various production operations is also minimized.

2.   Actually the just-in-time inventory control system is just a new approach to the EOQ model which tries to produce the lowest average level of inventory possible.

3.   Average inventory is reduced by locating inventory supplies in convenient locations and setting up restocking strategies that cut time and thereby reducing the needed level of safety stock.

III. TQM and Inventory Purchasing management.

   A.   The concept of total quality management has led to strong customer-supplier relationships in an effort to increase quality.

   B.   In many cases firms that only a few years ago placed an upper limit of 15 or 20 percent on the purchases of any part from a single supplier now rely on a single supplier using the **single-sourcing** relationship.

   C.   Single sourcing ties the interests of the supplier to the firm to which it supplies and allows the supplier to provide input on production techniques that might improve quality.

   D.   Financially, the TQM view argues that higher quality will result in increased sales and market share and as a result the traditional economic analysis of inventory management is flawed.

Study Problems

1.   The Swank Furniture Company is trying to determine the optimal order quantity for sofas. Annual sales for sofas are 800 and the retail price is $300 per sofa. The cost of carrying sofas is $50 per sofa per year. It costs $35 to prepare and receive an order. The inventory planning period is one year.

   a.   Determine the EOQ (assuming a one-year planning period).

   b.   If the annual sales are 1200, what is the EOQ? If the annual sales are 300, what is the EOQ?

SOLUTION

   a.   EOQ $= \sqrt{\dfrac{2(800)(35)}{50}} = \sqrt{1120} = 33.47 = 33$ sofas

b. $\text{EOQ} = \sqrt{\dfrac{2(1200)(35)}{50}} = \sqrt{1680} = 40.99 = 41 \text{ sofas}$

$\sqrt{\dfrac{2(300)(35)}{50}} = \sqrt{420} = 20.49 = 20 \text{ sofas}$

2. The Celeccorp makers of Sum'a'dis is considering relaxing its current credit policy. Currently the firm has annual sales (all credit) of $15 million and an average collection period of 50 days. The firm's pre-tax required rate of return on new investment in receivables and inventory is 20 percent. Variable costs account for 70 percent of the selling price on their product, Sum'a'dis. Thus, the contribution margin is 30 percent. Given the following information should Celeccorp adopt the proposed policy (assume a 360 day year) ?

	Present Policy	Proposed Policy
Annual Sales (all credit)	15,000,000	18,000,000
Average Collection Period		
Original Sales	50 days	70 days
New Sales		70 days
Average Inventory	1,200,000	1,300,000
Bad Debt Losses in Percent		
New Sales		7%

SOLUTION

Step 1:   Estimate the Change in Profits. This is equal to the increased sales times the profit contribution on those sales less any additional bad debts incurred.

$=$ (new sales x contribution margin)
      - (new sales x % bad debt losses on new sales)

$=$ ($3,000,000 x .30) - ($3,000,000 x .07)

$=$ $900,000 - $210,000

$=$ $690,000

Step 2:   Estimate the Cost of Additional Investment in Accounts Receivable and Inventory. This involves first calculating the change in the investment in accounts receivable; the new and original levels of investment in accounts receivable are calculated by multiplying the daily sales level times the average collection period. The additional investment in inventory is added to this, and the sum is then multiplied by the pre-tax required rate of return.

= (additional A/R + additional Inv.) x (pre-tax required rate of return)

First, calculate the additional investment in accounts receivable.

= [($18,000,000/360) x 70] - [($15,000,000/360) x 50]

= $3,500,000 - $2,083,333

= $1,416,667

Second, sum additional investment in accounts receivable and inventory ($1,300,000 - $1,200,000 = $100,000) and multiply this times the pre-tax required rate of return.

= ($1,416,667 + $100,000)

= $1,516,667 x .20

= $303,333

Step 3:   Estimated the Change in the Cost of the Cash Discount (if a Change in the Cash Discount is Enacted). Here, no change is enacted.

18-9

Step 4: Compare the Incremental Revenues with the Incremental Costs.

$$= \text{Step 1} - (\text{Step 2} + \text{Step 3})$$

$$= \$690,000 - \$303,333$$

$$= \$386,667$$

3. What is the effective annualized cost of foregoing a trade discount with terms 4/40 net 60?

SOLUTION

$$\text{The annualized opportunity cost of foregoing the trade discount} = \frac{a}{1-a} \times \frac{360}{c-b}$$

where the terms of sale are stated in the form a/b net c, indicating that they can deduct a% if the account is paid within b days; otherwise, the account must be paid within c days.

Thus,

$$\text{annualized opportunity cost of foregoing the trade discount} = \frac{a}{1-a} \times \frac{360}{c-b}$$

$$= \frac{.04}{1-.04} \times \frac{360}{60-40}$$

$$= 0.75$$

$$= 75\%$$

Self-Tests

TRUE-FALSE

_____ 1. The objective in credit policy management is to minimize losses.

_____ 2. An increase in the time period over which credit must be repaid will increase demand.

_____ 3. Receivables arise from credit sales.

_____ 4. To speed up the turnover of receivables, a firm may either shorten the discount term or increase the discount offered.

_____ 5. The expression "5/10, net 30" means that the customers receive a 10% discount if they pay within 5 days; otherwise, they must pay within 30 days.

_____ 6. There is no one level of inventory that is efficient for all firms.

_____ 7. In determining the level of safety stock it is important to evaluate the tradeoff between the cost of carrying the additional inventory with the risk of running out of inventory.

_____ 8. Lead time in determining the reorder point refers to the time between the receipt of a customer's order and the shipment of that order.

_____ 9. Large safety stocks tend to reduce the possibility of stockouts.

_____ 10. The EOQ provides for an optimal safety stock determination.

MULTIPLE CHOICE

1.   The major objective of a credit policy is to:

    a.   Maximize sales.
    b.   Minimize losses.
    c.   Maximize profits.
    d.   None of the above.

2.   Which of the following is not part of the firm's credit and collection policy decisions?

    a.   The credit period.
    b.   The cash discount given.
    c.   The dividend decision.
    d.   The level of collection expenditures.
    e.   The quality of account accepted.

3.   Which of the following would be a source of credit information?

    a.   Firm's financial statement.
    b.   Credit ratings from Dun & Bradstreet
    c.   A credit check through a bank.
    d.   The company's past experience.
    e.   All of the above.

4.   Which of the following is a cost associated with relaxed credit standards?

    a.   Enlarged credit department.
    b.   Increased probability of bad debt.
    c.   Additional investment in receivables.
    d.   All of the above.
    e.   None of the above.

5. All of the following are relationships that exist for safety stock except:

   a. The greater the risk of running out of stock, the larger the safety stock.
   b. The larger the opportunity cost of the funds invested in inventory, the smaller the safety stock.
   c. The greater the uncertainty associated with future forecasts of use, the larger the safety stock.
   d. The higher the profit margin per unit, the lower the safety stock necessary.

6. In the basic model the optimal inventory level is the point at which

   a. total depreciation is minimized.
   b. total cost is minimized.
   c. total revenue is maximized.
   d. carrying costs are minimized.
   e. ordinary costs are minimized.

7. Determine the effective annualized cost of forgoing the trade discount on terms 2/10 net 45 (round to nearest .01%).

   a. 21.0%
   b. 16.3%
   c. 16.0%
   d. 20.6%

8. The Janjigian Company uses approximately 4,000 oxygen tanks in its manufacturing process each year. The carrying cost of the oxygen tanks inventory is $.60 per tank and the ordering cost per order is $20. What is Janjigian's economic ordering quantity of tanks (round to the nearest unit)?

   a. 15
   b. 365
   c. 417
   d. 516

18-1B.
$$\frac{a}{1-a} \times \frac{360}{c-b}$$

where a = amount of the discount
b = the discount period
c = the net period

$$\frac{0.02}{1 - 0.02} \times \frac{360}{60 - 10} = 14.69\%$$

18-5B.

(a)
$$\frac{Sales - cost\ of\ goods\ sold}{Sales} = Gross\ Profit\ Margin$$

$$\frac{\$550,000 - Cost\ of\ goods\ sold}{\$550,000} = 0.10$$

Cost of goods sold   = $495,000

$$\frac{Cost\ of\ goods\ sold}{Average\ inventory} = Inventory\ turnover\ ratio$$

$$\frac{\$495,000}{Average\ inventory} = 5$$

Average inventory   = $99,000

(b) Inventory turnover ratio $= \dfrac{360}{\text{Average Collection Period}}$

Inventory turnover $= \dfrac{360}{35}$

Inventory turnover ratio $= 10.285$ times

$\dfrac{\text{Cost of goods sold}}{\text{Average inventory}} = 10.285$ times

$\dfrac{\$480,000}{\text{Average inventory}} = 10.285$ times

Average inventory $= \$46,669.90$

(c) $\dfrac{\text{Cost of goods sold}}{\text{Average inventory}} = $ Inventory turnover ratio

$\dfrac{\$1,250,000}{\text{Average inventory}} = 6$

Average inventory $= \$208,333$

(d) (1 - Gross profit margin) (Sales) $= \$21,250,000$ cost of goods
                                                    $(0.85)(\$25,000,000)$

Inventory turnover ratio $= \dfrac{360}{50}$ $= 7.2$ times

$\dfrac{\$21,250,000}{\text{Average inventory}}$ $= 7.2$ times

Average inventory $= \$ 2,951,389$

18-15

18-7B.   Step 1:   Estimate the Change in Profit.

= ($1,000,000 x .20) - ($1,000,000 x .08)

= $200,000 - $80,000

= $120,000

Step 2:   Estimate the cost of additional investment in account receivable and inventory.

Estimate the additional investment in accounts receivable:

= ($18,000,000 / 360 x 50) - ($17,000,000 / 360 x 30)

= $2,500,000 - $1,416,667

= $1,083,333

Additional accounts receivable and inventory times the required rate of return:

= ($1,083,333 + $60,000) .15

= $171,500

Step 3:   Estimate the change in the cost of the cash discount

= $0 (no change)

Step 4: Compare the incremental revenues with the incremental costs.

$$= \text{Step } 1 - (\text{Step } 2 + \text{Step } 3)$$

$$= \$120,000 - \$171,500$$

$$= -\$51,500$$

The change should not be made.

18-9B.

(a) $$Q^* = \sqrt{\frac{2SO}{C}}$$

$$= \sqrt{\frac{2(21,000)55}{0.20}}$$

$$= 3398.5 \text{ boxes}$$

(b) It assumes among other things that the rolls are not perishable. Other assumptions include:
(1) constant or uniform demand
(2) constant unit price
(3) constant carrying costs
(4) constant ordering costs
(5) instantaneous delivery
(6) independent orders

18-11B.

(a) $Q^* = \sqrt{\dfrac{2SO}{C}}$

$ = \sqrt{\dfrac{2(600,000)90}{.45}}$

$ = $ 15,492 units or 15,400 units

(b) $\dfrac{600,000}{15,400} = $ 38.96 orders per year (or about 39 orders)

(c) Inventory order point = delivery time stock + safety stock

$\phantom{(c) \quad \text{Inventory order point} \ } = \dfrac{1}{50}$ x 600,000 + 15,000

$\phantom{(c) \quad \text{Inventory order point} \ } = $ 12,000 + 15,000

$\phantom{(c) \quad \text{Inventory order point} \ } = $ 27,000 units

(d) Average inventory $= \dfrac{EOQ}{2} + $ safety time stock

$\phantom{(d) \quad \text{Average inventory} \ } = \dfrac{15,400}{2} + $ 15,000

$\phantom{(d) \quad \text{Average inventory} \ } = $ 7,700 + 15,000

$\phantom{(d) \quad \text{Average inventory} \ } = $ 22,700 units

CHAPTER 19

Term Loans and Leases

Orientation: The first section of this chapter provides an overview of the major sources of intermediate term financing or term loans and their characteristics. The second section of the chapter provides an overview of lease financing, including a discussion of leasing arrangements, the accounting treatment of financial leases, the lease versus purchase decision, and the potential economic benefits from leasing.

I.   Term loans

    A.   In general, term loans have maturities from 1 to 10 years and are repaid in periodic installments over the life of the loan. Term loans are usually secured by a chattel mortgage on equipment or a mortgage on real property. The principal suppliers of term credit include commercial banks, insurance companies, and to a lesser extent pension funds.

    B.   The common attributes of term loans include the following:

        1.   The maturities of term loans are usually as follows:

            a.   Commercial banks: 1 to 5 years.

            b.   Insurance companies: 5 to 15 years.

            c.   Pension funds: 5 to 15 years.

        2.   The collateral backing term loans is usually as follows:

            a.   Shorter maturity loans are usually secured with a chattel mortgage on machinery and equipment or securities such as stocks and bonds.

b.　Longer maturity loans are frequently secured by mortgages on real estate.

3.　In addition to collateral, the lender on a term loan agreement will very often place <u>restrictive</u> <u>covenants</u> which are designed to maintain the borrower's financial condition on a par with that which existed at the time the loan was made.

a.　<u>Working</u> <u>capital</u> <u>restrictions</u> involve maintaining a minimum, current ratio that reflects the norm for the borrower's industry, as well as the lender's desires.

b.　<u>Additional</u> <u>borrowing</u> <u>restrictions</u> prevent the borrower from increasing the amount of debt financing outstanding without the lender's approval.

c.　A third covenant that is very popular requires that the borrower supply <u>periodic</u> <u>financial</u> <u>statements</u> to the lender.

d.　Term loan agreements often include a provision that requires that the lender approve major personnel changes and insure the lives of "key" personnel with the lender as the beneficiary.

4.　Term loans are generally repaid in periodic installments in accordance with <u>repayment</u> <u>schedules</u> established by the lender. Each installment includes both an interest and a principal component.

II.　Leasing

A.　There are three major lease agreements: direct leasing, sale and leaseback, and leveraged leasing.

1.　In a <u>direct</u> <u>lease</u> the firm acquires the services of an asset it did not previously own. Direct leasing is available through a number of financial institutions, including manufacturers, banks, finance companies, independent leasing companies, and special-purpose leasing companies. Basically, direct leasing involves the purchase of the asset by the lessor from a vendor and leasing the asset to the lessee.

2.	A <u>sale</u> <u>and</u> <u>leaseback</u> arrangement occurs when a firm sells buildings or equipment that it already owns to a financial institution and simultaneously enters into an agreement to lease the property back for a specified period under specific terms. The lessee firm receives cash in the amount of the sales price of the asset sold and the use of the asset over the term of the lease. In return, the firm must make periodic rental payments throughout the term of lease to the lessor.

3.	In a <u>leveraged</u> <u>lease</u> a third participant is added who finances the acquisition of the asset to be leased for the lessor. From the lessee's standpoint, this lease is no different from the two lease arrangements discussed above. But with a leveraged lease, specific consideration is given to the financing arrangement used by the lessor in acquiring the asset to be leased.

B.	The accounting profession through <u>Financial</u> <u>Accounting</u> <u>Statement</u> <u>No.</u> 13 requires the capitalization or any lease that meets one or more of the following criteria:

1.	The lease transfers ownership of the property to the lessee by the end of the lease term.

2.	The lease contains a bargain repurchase option.

3.	The lease term is equal to 75% or more of the estimated economic life of the leased property.

4.	The present value of the minimum lease payments equals 90% of the excess of the fair value of the property over any related investment tax credit retained by the lessor.

C.	The <u>lease</u> <u>versus</u> <u>purchase</u> decision requires a standard capital budgeting type of analysis, as well as an analysis of two alternative "packages" of financing. Two models are used to evaluate the lease versus purchase decision.

1.	The first model computes the net present value of the purchase option which can be defined as follows:

$$NPV \ (P) \quad = \quad \sum_{t=1}^{n} \frac{ACF_t}{(1+K)^t} - IO$$

where ACF_t = the annual after-tax cash flow resulting from the purchase in period t,

K = the firm's cost of capital applicable to the project being analyzed and the particular mix of financing used to acquire the project,

IO = the initial cash outlay required to purchase the asset in period zero (now),

n = the productive life of the project.

2. In the second model a net advantage to lease (NAL) over purchase equation is used which indicates the more favorable (least expensive) method of financing. The equation used to arrive at NAL is as follows:

$$NAL \quad = \quad \sum_{t=1}^{n} \frac{O_t(1-T) - R_t(1-T) - TI_t - TD_t}{(1+r_b)^t}$$

$$- \frac{V_n}{(1+K_s)^n} + IO$$

where O_t = any operating cash flows incurred in period t which are incurred only where the asset is purchased. Most often this consists of maintenance expenses and insurance that would be paid by the lessor.

R_t = the annual rental for period t.

T	=	the marginal tax rate on corporate income.
I_t	=	the tax deductible interest expense foregone in period t if the lease option is adopted. This level of interest expense was set equal to that which would have been paid on a loan equal to the full purchase price of the asset.
D_t	=	depreciation expense in period t for the asset.
V_n	=	the after-tax salvage value of the asset expected in year n.
K_s	=	the discount rate used to find the present value of V_n. This rate should reflect the risk inherent in the estimated V_n. For simplicity, the after-tax cost of capital is often used as a proxy for this rate.
IO	=	the purchase price of the asset which is not paid by the firm in the event the asset is leased.
r_b	=	the after-tax rate of interest on borrowed funds. This rate is used to discount the relatively certain after-tax cash flow savings accruing through leasing the asset.

If NAL were positive, there would be a positive cost advantage to lease financing. If NAL were negative, then purchasing the asset and financing with a debt plus equity package would be the preferred alternative. However, we would lease or purchase the asset in accordance with the value of NAL in only two circumstances:

a. If NPV (P) were positive, then the asset should be acquired through the preferred financing method as indicated by NAL.

b. If NPV (P) were negative, then the asset's services should be acquired via the lease alternative only if NAL is positive and greater in absolute value than NPV(P). That is, the asset should be leased only if the cost advantage of leasing (NAL) is great enough to offset the negative NPV(P). In effect, if a positive NAL were to more than offset a negative NPV(P), then the net present value through lease would be positive.

D. Over the years a number of potential benefits have been offered for lease financing. Some of the more frequently cited advantages are enumerated and commented upon here.

1. Flexibility and convenience. It is often argued that lease financing is more convenient than other forms of financing because smaller amounts of funds can be raised at lower cost. In addition, it is often argued that lease payment schedules can be made to coincide with cash flows generated by the asset. These may or may not be real advantages. It depends on the actual circumstances faced by the lessee firm.

2. Lack of restrictions. It has been argued that leases require fewer restrictions on the lessee than do debt agreements.

3. Avoiding the risk of obsolescence. This argument is generally conceded to be fallacious because the lessor includes his or her estimated cost of obsolescence in the lease patents.

4. Conservation of working capital. Here it is argued that leasing involves no down payment. However, the borrower might obtain the same effect by borrowing the down payment.

5. 100% financing. The lease involves 100% financing but purchasing the asset would surely involve some equity. As we noted above, the down payment could be borrowed to produce 100% financing via a loan. In addition, it is not clear that 100% lease financing is desirable because it represents 100% non-owner financing. Finally the lease agreement does not entitle the lessee to the asset's salvage value. Thus, the lease provides 100% financing for the "use value" of the asset but not its "salvage value."

6.   Tax savings. The difference in tax shelters between leasing and other forms of financing can only be evaluated by using a net advantage of lease model as we discussed earlier.

7.   Ease of obtaining credit. Lease financing may be more or less difficult to obtain than other forms of financing. This advantage (or disadvantage) can only be evaluated on a case-by-case basis.

Study Problem

1.   Palmer Industries, which has a 50% tax rate, wants to acquire a $200,000 piece of equipment. The equipment would be depreciated over a 5-year life on a straight-line basis. At the end of the 5-year period the equipment is expected to have a zero salvage value. Palmer has two alternatives available to it with regard to how the equipment is to be financed. It can borrow the $200,000 at 10% interest and repay the loan in 5 equal annual installments or lease the equipment for 5 annual rental payments of $55,000 each (payable at the beginning of the year). Palmer usually finances its assets by using 40% debt and 60% equity. Maintenance services are estimated to be $4,000 under the leasing contract and net cash flows from the equipment are estimated to be $100,000 per year before depreciation and taxes.

Required :

(a)   Compute the annual installments, principal, interest, and remaining balance for a loan equal to the full purchase price of the asset (i.e., $200,000).

(b)   Assuming Palmer's after-tax cost of capital is 12%, compute the net present value of the purchase alternative.

(c)   Provided that Palmer has a target debt ratio of 100% for projects like this, compute the net advantage to leasing (NAL) the equipment.

(d)   Which method of financing should be used by Palmer? Why?

SOLUTION:

Problem Inputs:

Operating Costs	$4,000.00
Salvage Value	$0.00
Lease Term	5
K_{wacc}	12%
$K_{salvage}$	12%
Borrowing Rate	10%
Tax Rate	50%
Initial Outlay	$200,000.00
Lease Payment	$55,000.00
Annual Cash Revenues	$100,000.00
Depr. Factors	0.2
	0.2
	0.2
	0.2
	0.2

Calculation of Loan Payment Components

Loan Pymts	Interest	Principle	Remaining Balance
			$200,000.00
$52,759.50	$20,000.00	$32,759.50	167,240.50
52,759.50	16,724.05	36,035.45	131,205.06
52,759.50	13,120.51	39,638.99	91,566.07
52,759.50	9,156.61	43,602.89	47,963.18
52,759.50	4,796.32	47,963.18	0.00

Calculation of the NPV(Purchase):

Year	Revenues	Depreciation	Net Income	NCF	Discount Factors (12%)	Present Value
0						
1	$100,000.00	$40,000.00	$30,000.00	$70,000.00	0.893	62,500.00
2	100,000.00	40,000.00	30,000.00	70,000.00	0.797	55,803.57
3	100,000.00	40,000.00	30,000.00	70,000.00	0.712	49,824.27
4	100,000.00	40,000.00	30,000.00	70,000.00	0.636	44,486.27
5	100,000.00	40,000.00	30,000.00	70,000.00	0.567	39,719.88
				PV of Salvage Value		0.00
				NPV(P) = 52,334.33		$52,334.33

Evaluation of the Lease Option:

Year	O(1-T)	-	L(1-T)	-	Dt*	-	It*T	Cash Flow	Present Value
0			-$55,000.00		-$20,000.00			-$55,000.00	-$55,000.00
1	$2,000.00		-27,500.00		-20,000.00		-10,000.00	-55,500.00	-52,857.14
2	2,000.00		-27,500.00		-20,000.00		-8,362.03	-53,862.03	-48,854.44
3	2,000.00		-27,500.00		-20,000.00		-6,560.25	-52,060.25	-44,971.60
4	2,000.00		-27,500.00		-20,000.00		-4,578.30	-50,078.30	-41,199.54
5	2,000.00		-27,500.00		-20,000.00		-2,398.16	7,101.84	5,564.48

Present Value of Annual CFs	-237,318.26
Less: PV of Salvage Value	0.00
Plus: Initial Outlay	200,000.00
Net Advantage of Leasing =	($37,318.26)

Since NPV(Purchase) is positive the equipment should be acquired. However, since the NAL is negative the equipment should not be leased.

Self-Tests

TRUE-FALSE

_____ 1. One of the primary economic reasons for borrowing is the inability of a firm to utilize all of the tax benefits associated with the leasing of an asset.

_____ 2. A lease payment is generally deductible as an expense for federal income tax purposes.

_____ 3. If leases are capitalized on the balance sheet, it permits easier analysis of the contractual obligations of the firm.

_____ 4. Over the years the accounting treatment of leases has changed toward greater disclosure.

_____ 5. Under a sale and leaseback arrangement, a company acquires the use of an asset that it did not own previously.

_____ 6. The distinguishing feature between a financial lease and an operating lease is cancelability.

_____ 7. A chattel mortgage is a lien on real property.

_____ 8. Insurance company term loans are generally have similar terms to bank term loans.

_____ 9. The working capital requirement is probably the most commonly used and most comprehensive provision in a term loan agreement.

_____ 10. The interest rate on a term loan is generally higher than the rate on a short-term loan to the same borrower.

MULTIPLE CHOICE

1. Which of the following distinguishes a bank term loan from trade credit?

    a. A final maturity of one year or more.
    b. Credit is extended under an informal loan agreement.
    c. Credit is extended under a formal loan agreement.
    d. a and b only.
    e. a and c only.

2. Rarely will a bank make a term loan that has a final maturity of more than:

    a. 5 years.
    b. 10 years.
    c. 20 years.
    d. 25 years.
    e. All of the above.

3. The interest rate on a term loan is not set by:

    a. Periodic negotiations between the borrower and the lender over the term of the loan.
    b. A fixed rate effective over the life of the loan.
    c. A variable rate that is adjusted in keeping with changes in the prime rate.
    d. All of the above.
    e. None of the above.

4. Which of the following is a source of equipment financing?

    a. Commercial bank.
    b. Finance company.
    c. Seller of the equipment.
    d. All of the above.
    e. None of the above.

CHAPTER 20

The Use of Futures, Options, and Currency Swaps to Reduce Risk

Orientation: The purpose of this chapter is to look at futures, options, and swaps and explain how they are used by financial managers to control risk.

I.   Futures and options can be used by the financial manager to reduce the risks associated with interest and exchange rate and commodity price fluctuations.

      A.   A futures contract is a contract to buy or sell a stated commodity (such as soybeans or corn) or a financial claim (such as U.S. Treasury bonds) at a specified price at some future specified time.

            1.   A futures contract is a specialized form of a forward contract distinguished by: (1) an organized exchange, (2) a standardized contract with limited price changes and margin requirements, (3) a formal clearinghouse and (4) daily resettlement of contracts.

                  a.   An organized exchange provides a central trading place and encourages confidence in the futures market by allowing for effective regulation of trading.

                  b.   Standardized contracts lead to greater liquidity in the secondary market for that contract, which in turn draws more traders into the market.

c. The futures clearinghouse serves to guarantee that all trades will be honored. This is done by having the clearinghouse interpose itself as the buyer to every seller and the seller to every buyer.

d. Under the daily resettlement process maintenance margins must be maintained.

2. For the financial manager financial futures provide an excellent way of controlling risk in interest rates, foreign exchange rates, and stock fluctuations.

B. There are two basic types of options: puts and calls. A call option gives its owner the right to purchase a given number of shares of stock or some other asset at a specified price over a specified time period. A put gives its owner the right to sell a given number of shares of common stock or some other asset at a specified price over a given time period.

1. The popularity of options can be explained by their leverage, financial insurance, and investment alternative expansion features.

a. The leverage feature allows the financial manager the chance for unlimited capital gains with a very small investment.

b. When a put with an exercise price equal to the current stock price is purchased, it insures the holder against any declines in the stock price over the life of the put. This is the financial insurance feature of options and can be used by portfolio managers to reduce risk exposure in portfolios.

c. From the point of view of the investor, the use of puts, calls, and combinations of them can materially increase the set of possible investment alternatives available.

2.   Recently, four new variations of the traditional option have appeared: the stock index option, the interest rate option, the foreign exchange option and the Treasury bond futures option.

   a.   Stock index options are merely options with the underlying asset being the value or price of an index of stocks -- for example, the S&P 100.

   b.   Interest rate and foreign exchange options are also merely options with the underlying asset being the Treasury bonds or a specific foreign currency.

   c.   Options on Treasury bond futures are different from other bond options in that they involve the acquisition of a futures position rather than the delivery of actual bonds. The buyer of an option on a futures contract achieves immunization against any unfavorable price movements, whereas the buyer of a futures contract achieves immunization against any price movements regardless of whether they are favorable or unfavorable.

II.   Currency Swaps are another technique for controlling exchange rate risk available to the financial manager. Whereas options and futures contracts generally have a fairly short duration, a currency swap provides the financial manager with the ability to hedge away exchange rate risk over longer periods. It is for that reason that currency swaps have gained in popularity.

   A.   A *currency swap* is simply an exchange of debt obligations in different currencies. Interest rate swaps are used to provide long-term exchange rate risk hedging. Actually, a currency swap can be quite simple, with two firms agreeing to pay each other's debt obligation.

   B.   The nice thing about a currency swap is that it allows the firm to engage in long-term exchange rate risk hedging since the debt obligation covers a relatively long time period.

C. One of the more popular is the interest rate currency swap where the principle is not included in the swap. That is, only interest payment obligations in different currencies are swapped.

D. The key to controlling risk is to get an accurate estimate on the net exposure level the firm is subjected to. Then, the firm must decide whether it fells it is prudent to subject itself to the risk associated with possible exchange rate fluctuations.

Self-Tests

TRUE-FALSE

____ 1. A futures contract requires its holder to buy or sell the asset regardless of what happens to its value during the interim.

____ 2. An option contract requires its holder to buy or sell the asset regardless of what happens to its value during the interim.

____ 3. A naked option is illegal in most states.

____ 4. The futures clearinghouse is a division of the futures exchange that guarantees the fulfillment of obligations by acting as one side of every transaction.

____ 5. Daily resettlement is the practice required by the futures exchange of realizing trading gains or losses on a daily basis through additions or subtractions from the margin account.

____ 6. An out-of-the-money option is a call option whose exercise prices are below the market price of the underlying stock or a put whose exercise price is above the market price of the underlying stock.

___ 7.   For a call option, the intrinsic value is the stock price minus the exercise price.

___ 8.   The call option time value is equal to the call premium minus the call intrinsic value.

___ 9.   A covered call price is one that can be exercised any time before the expiration date.

MULTIPLE CHOICE

1.   The term option premium refers to:

    a.   The amount the option price exceeds the exercise price.
    b.   The amount the exercise price exceeds the option price.
    c.   The price of the option.
    d.   None of the above.

2.   The intrinsic value of a call option refers to:

    a.   The call premium less the amount by which the stock price exceeds the exercise price.
    b.   The exercise price less the stock price.
    c.   The stock price less the exercise price.
    d.   None of the above.

3.   The money that futures traders must place with their brokers in order to trade futures contracts are called _____ deposits.

    a.   security
    b.   minimum
    c.   marking to market money
    d.   margin
    e.   parity funds

4.   Trading on the futures exchanges actually occurs in an area called a _____.

   a.   floor
   b.   booth
   c.   pit
   d.   stand
   e.   local

5.   The futures exchange required that all offers to buy or sell a futures contract must be made to all other traders in the pit by _____.

   a.   open-outcry
   b.   computer listing
   c.   a message system called "contango"
   d.   telex
   e.   telephone

6.   If the writer of a call option does not own the underlying stock then that trader is said to have written a _____ option.

   a.   naked
   b.   pure
   c.   covered
   d.   spot
   e.   short

7.   If two options are identical other than the expiration date, then the option with more time to sell for _____ than the option that expires at the earlier date.

   a.   less than
   b.   more than
   c.   equal to or less than
   d.   equal to or more than
   e.   cannot be determined

8. The options market is referred to a zero-sum game because:

    a.   the Options Clearing House guarantees that trades will be honored.
    b.   options can expire out-of-the-money.
    c.   what one trader makes, another trader must lose.
    d.   the intrinsic value of an option at expiration is zero.

CHAPTER 21

Corporate Restructuring: Combinations and Divestitures

Orientation: Corporate restructuring comes through combining assets (mergers and acquisitions) and uncombining assets (divestitures).

I. There are two principal ways by which a firm may grow:

   A. Internally, through the acquisition of specific assets which are financed by the retention of earnings and/or external financing, or

   B. Externally, through the combination with another company. We turn now to a discussion of external growth through mergers with, and the acquisition of, other firms.

II. There have been four identifiable time periods where the number and amount of mergers and acquisitions were particularly accentuated.

   A. End of the 19th century and beginning of the 20th century. During this time, many industries were merged into near monopolies, such as U.S. Steel, American Tobacco, and Standard Oil.

   B. The decade of the 1920s. This merger wave was closely related to the creation of oligopolies (industries dominated by a few firms), such as IBM, General Foods, and Allied Chemical. During this time, the developments in transportation, communications, and merchandising fostered the growth.

C. Between the 1950s and the 1970s. No longer permitted by the Federal Trade Commission to acquire firms in their own industry, companies actively began acquiring companies outside their own industries. The bringing together of these dissimilar firms into one corporate entity came to be known as the conglomerate.

   1. The creation of a conglomerate was thought to be an efficient way of monitoring individual businesses by subjecting them to regular quantitative evaluations by the central office.

   2. With hindsight we now see that conglomerate acquisitions have, for the most part, proven unsuccessful.

D. The 1980s. In this period, the pattern became that of acquiring a conglomerate, breaking it up into its individual business units, and selling off the segments to large corporations in the same businesses. The 1980s merger activity came to an end, however, largely because the huge amounts of debt financing used to fund many of the acquisitions dried up.

E. The 1990's. Consolidation of financial services (banking) and telecommunications firms have dominated the greatest merger wave in history.

III. Why mergers create value. For a merger to create wealth it would have to provide shareholders with something they could not get for free by merely holding the individual shares of the two firms. Such benefits might include:

A. Tax benefits: If a merger were to result in a reduction of taxes that is not otherwise possible, then wealth is created by the merger. This can be the case with a firm that has lost money and thus generated tax credits, but does not currently have a level of earnings sufficient to utilize those tax credits.

B.	Reduction of agency costs: An agency problem is a result of the separation of management and the ownership in the firm. A merger, particularly when it results in a holding company or conglomerate organizational form may reduce the significance of this problem, because top management is created to monitor the management of the individual companies making up the conglomerate. Alternatively, it can be argued that the creation of a conglomerate might result in increased agency costs. This might occur as shareholders in conglomerates feel they have less control over the firm's mangers, as a result of the additional layers of management between them and the decision makers.

C.	The release of free cash flows to the owners: A merger can create wealth by allowing the new management to distribute the free cash flow out to the shareholders, thus allowing them to earn a higher return on these cash flows than would have been earned by the firm.

D.	Economies of scale: Wealth can be created in a merger through economies of scale.

E.	Unused debt potential: Assuming the firm has unused debt capacity, a new management can increase debt financing, and reap the tax benefits associated with the increased debt.

F.	Complementary in financial slack: It may be possible to create wealth by combining cash-rich bidders and cash-poor targets, with wealth being created as a result of the positive NPV projects taken by the merged firm that the cash-poor firm would have passed up.

G.	Removal of ineffective management: If a firm with ineffective management can be acquired, it may be possible to replace the current management with a more efficient management team, and thereby create wealth,

H.	Increased market power: The merger of two firms can result in an increase in the market or monopoly power of the two firms. While this can result in increased wealth, it may also be illegal.

21-3

I.   Reduction in bankruptcy costs: Presuming that bankruptcy costs exist, a merger that reduces the possibility of bankruptcy creates wealth.

J.   The creation of the "chop shop" value: It may be less expensive to purchase assets through an acquisition than it is to obtain those assets in any other way.

IV.   Determining a firm's value

     A.   The value of a firm depends not only on its earnings capabilities but also on the operating and financial characteristics of the acquiring firm. To determine an acceptable price of a corporation, a number of factors must be carefully evaluated. The final objective of this valuation process is to maximize the stockholders' wealth (stock price) of both firms.

     B.   The value of a firm may be represented in a number of ways including (1) book value, (2) appraisal value, (3) chop-shop value, and (4) the free cash flow value.

           1.   The book value of a firm's net worth is the depreciated value of the company's assets less its outstanding liabilities. Book value alone is not a significant measure of the worth of a company but should be used as a starting point to be compared with other analyses.

           2.   Appraisal value, acquired from an independent appraisal firm, may be useful in conjunction with other methods. Advantages include

                  a.   The reduction of accounting goodwill by increasing the recognized worth of specific assets

                  b.   A test of the reasonableness of results obtained through other evaluation methods

                  c.   The discovery of strengths and weaknesses that otherwise might not be recognized

3. The "chop shop" approach to valuation attempts to identify multi-industry companies that are undervalued and would be worth more if separated into their parts. As such, this approach encompasses the idea of attempting to buy assets below their replacement cost.

4. The free cash-flow or "going concern" approach to merger valuation requires that we estimate the incremental net cash flows available to the bidding firm as a result of the merger or acquisition. The present value of these cash flows will then be determined, and this will be the maximum amount that should be paid for the target firm. The initial outlay can then be subtracted out to calculate the net present value from the merger.

V. Divestitures

A. Divestitures, or a "reverse merger," have become an important factor in restructuring corporations.

B. A successful divestiture allows the firm's assets to be used more efficiently, and therefore, be assigned a higher value by the market forces.

C. The different types of divestitures may be summarized as follows:

1. <u>Selloff</u>. A selloff is the sale of a subsidiary, division, or product line by one company to another.

2. <u>Spinoff</u>. A spinoff involves the separation of a subsidiary from its parent, with no change in the equity ownership.

3. <u>Liquidation</u>. A liquidation in this context is not a decision to shut down or abandon an asset. Rather, the assets are sold to another company and the proceeds are distributed to the stockholders.

4. Going private. Going private results when a company, whose stock is traded publicly, is purchased by a small group of investors and the stock is no longer bought and sold on a public exchange.

5. Leveraged buyout. The leveraged buyout is a special case of going private. The existing shareholders sell their shares to a small group of investors. The purchasers of the stock use the firm's unused debt capacity to borrow the funds to pay for the stock.

Study Problems

Two types of problems are developed in the chapter. Both types are demonstrated in the self-test problems in the text. Also, the worked-out solutions for these two problem types are shown at the end of this presentation. Thus, we have not repeated these problems here.

Self-Tests

TRUE-FALSE

_____ 1. Synergism results where the whole is greater than the sum of the parts.

_____ 2. The higher the P/E ratio of the acquiring company in relation to that of the company being acquired and the larger the earnings of the acquired company in relation to those of the acquiring company, the greater the increase in earnings per share of the acquiring company.

_____ 3. It is a mistake to only examine the effect on EPS of an acquisition as the basis for analyzing the merger, since the effects of synergism may play an important role in determining the attractiveness of the proposed acquisition.

_____ 4. Goodwill arises in mergers and increases the merging firm's tax liability.

_____ 5. Conglomerates are the most popular form of corporate merger because of the extremely favorable accounting treatment of mergers.

MULTIPLE CHOICE

1. The value of a firm:

   a. Depends on the firm's earnings potential.
   b. Depends on the financial characteristics of the acquiring firm.
   c. Is a range of value economically feasible to the prospective buyer within which a final price is negotiated.
   d. All of the above.
   e. None of the above.

2. The two factors considered most important by business people in estimating a firm's worth is:

   I. The book value of the firm being considered for acquisition.
   II. The appraisal value of the firm being considered for acquisition.
   III. The stock market value of the common shares of the firm being considered for acquisition.
   IV. The after-merger earnings per share of the acquiring company's stockholders.

   a. I, II.
   b. I, III.
   c. II, III.
   d. I, IV.
   e. III, IV.

CHAPTER 22

International Business Finance

Orientation: This chapter introduces some of the financial techniques and strategies necessary to the efficient operations of an international business. Problems inherent to these firms include multiple currencies, differing legal and political environments, differing economic and capital markets, and internal control problems. The difficulties arising from multiple currencies are stressed here, including the dimensions of foreign exchange risk and strategies for reducing this risk. We also cover working capital management and direct foreign investment for international firms.

I.   The globalization of product and financial markets

    A.   World trade has grown faster over the last few decades than has aggregate world GNP.

    B.   In less-developed countries, long-run overseas investments of the United States' companies have yielded high returns.

    C.   Many American multinational corporations (MNC) have significant assets, sales, and profits attributable to foreign investments.

    D.   Many foreign MNCs have significant operations in the United States.

    E.   Many firms, investment companies, and individuals invest in the capital markets of foreign companies to receive

        1.   Higher returns than those available in domestic capital markets

        2.   Reduced portfolio risk through international diversification

    F.   Companies are increasingly turning to the Eurodollar market to raise funds.

II. Exchange rates

    A. Recent history of exchange rates

        1. Exchange rates between the major currencies were fixed from 1949 and 1970.

        2. Countries were required to set a <u>parity</u> <u>rate</u> with the U.S. dollar, around which the daily exchange rate could narrowly fluctuate.

        3. In order to effect a major adjustment, a currency either had to undergo a <u>devaluation</u> (reducing the cost relative to the dollar) or an <u>up-valuation/revaluation</u> (increasing the cost relative to the U.S. dollar).

        4. Since 1973, a <u>floating</u> <u>rate</u> international currency system has operated, wherein the currencies are allowed to fluctuate freely.

        5. Two major types of transactions now occur in the foreign exchange markets: <u>spot</u> and <u>forward</u> <u>transactions</u>.

    B. Spot exchange rates

        1. The rate at which one currency can be immediately exchanged for another currency

        2. <u>Direct</u> <u>quote</u> expresses the exchange rate in the units of home currency required to buy one unit of foreign currency. For example, 1.4845 U.S. dollars per pound.

        3. <u>Indirect</u> <u>Quotes</u> indicate the number of foreign currency units needed to purchase one unit of home currency. For example, .6691 pounds per U.S. dollar.

        EXAMPLE

        Using the rates listed above, how many dollars would a U.S. manufacturer pay for a part costing 250 pounds?

        250 (pounds) x 1.4845 ($/pound) = $371.13

4.	The direct and indirect quotes should have a reciprocal relationship. In formula

$$\text{Direct Quote} = \frac{1}{\text{Indirect Quote}}$$

or

$$\text{Indirect Quote} = \frac{1}{\text{Direct Quote}}$$

5.	When these quotes are not equal, _arbitrage_ will occur, where a trader (or arbitrageur) makes a riskless profit, by exchanging currency in two markets.

6.	The _asked rate_ is the rate which the bank or foreign exchange trader "asks" the buyer to pay for the foreign currency.

7.	The _bid rate_ is the rate which the bank or foreign exchange trader buys the foreign currency from the customer.

8.	The _spread_ is the difference in the bid and the asked rates.

9.	The narrower the spread, the greater is the efficiency in the spot exchange market.

10.	A _cross rate_ is the result of an indirect computation of one currency's exchange rate from the exchange rate of two other currencies. For example, the calculation of marks per pound from U.S. dollars per pound and marks per U.S. dollars.

11.	Triangular arbitrage will occur when the cross rates calculated are not equal to the exchange rates offered.

C.	Forward exchange rates

1.	A _forward exchange rate_ specifies _today_ the rate at which currencies will be exchanged at in the future, usually 30, 90, or 180 days from today.

2.	Rates are quoted in both the direct and indirect form.

3. Forward rates are often quoted at a <u>premium</u> or a <u>discount</u> to the existing spot rate. This is also referred to as the forward-spot differential.

4. These differentials may be stated either in absolute terms or as an annualized percent premium or discount.

5. The use of forward contracts allows for risk reduction in that future cash outlays are known with certainty.

III. The interest parity theory

A. Theorem states that the forward premium or discount should be equal and opposite in sign to the difference in the national interest rates for securities of the same maturity (except for the effects of small transaction costs).

IV. Purchasing power parity

A. According to purchasing power parity, exchange rates will adjust over time so that the currencies of different countries will have the same purchasing power. The exchange rates will adjust to cover the inflation rate differential between the two countries.

EXAMPLE

The inflation rate in Great Britain is 6% and in the United States it is 10?%. The current spot rate of the pound is $2.00. According to purchasing power parity, what will be the expected value of the pound at the end of the year?

$$S = \$2.00 \ (1 + .10)/(1 + .06)$$

$$= \$2.00 \ (1.0377)$$

$$= \$2.075$$

C.   The law of one price

The law of one price underlies purchasing power parity. This law suggests that where there are no transportation costs or barriers to trade, the same good sold in different countries should sell for the same price if all the different prices are expressed in terms of the same currency.

D.   International Fisher effect

    1.   According to the Fisher effect, interest rates reflect not only the real rate of return but the expected inflation rate.

    2.   The Fisher effect can be expressed as

    the nominal interest rate =

        the real rate of return + the expected inflation rate +

        (the real rate of return)(the expected inflation rate)

    3.   The international Fisher effect suggests that the exchange rate adjusts to cover the interest rate differential between two countries.

    4.   This theory suggests that in efficient markets, with rational expectations, the forward rate is an unbiased forecast of the future spot rate.

IV.   Exchange Rate Risk

A.   Risk arises from not knowing the value of the future spot rate today.

B.   Types of exchange risk

    1.   Risk in international trade contracts -- when an agreement exists to purchase some good at a future date in foreign currency, uncertainty exists as to the future cash outlay.

2. Risk in foreign portfolios -- because of exchange rate fluctuations in foreign securities the returns are more variable and thus more risky than investment in domestic securities.

3. Risk in direct foreign investment (DFI) -- the balance sheet and income statement are dominated in foreign currency. Thus, for the parent company, risk arises from both the fluctuations in the asset's value and the profit streams.

C. Exposure to exchange rate risk

1. Transaction exposure refers to the net total foreign currency transactions whose monetary value was fixed at a time different from when the transactions are actually completed. Examples of transactions exposed to this kind of risk are receivables, payables, and fixed price sales or purchase contracts. Fluctuations in exchange rates can affect the value of these assets and liabilities.

2. Translation exposure is actually a paper gain or loss. Translation exposure refers to gains or losses caused by the translation of foreign currency assets and liabilities into the currency of the parent company for accounting purposes.

3. Economic exposure refers to the extent to which the economic value of a company can decline due to exchange rate changes. It is the overall impact of exchange rate changes on the value of the firm. A decline in value can be attributed to an exchange rate induced decline in the level of expected cash flows and/or by an increase in the riskiness of these cash flows.

D. Hedging strategies

1. The standard procedure to hedge is to match the amount and the duration of the asset (liability) position.

2. The money market hedge offsets the exposed position in a foreign currency by borrowing or lending in the foreign and domestic money markets. This may be costly for small or infrequent users.

3. The <u>forward market hedge</u> matches the asset (liability) position with an offsetting forward contract of equal value and maturity. Generally, this is less costly than the money market hedge.

4. Foreign currency futures contracts and foreign currency options are two relatively new instruments used for hedging. Futures contracts are similar to forward contracts in that they provide a fixed price for the required delivery. Options, on the other hand, <u>permit</u> a fixed price anytime before their expiration date. Options and futures both differ from forward contracts in that they are traded in standardized amounts with standardized maturity dates and are traded through organized exchanges and individual dealers. The difference between the futures contract and the currency option is that the option requires delivery only if it is exercised. The option can be exercised any time before its maturity date; this can provide additional flexibility for a company.

V. Multinational working capital management

A. The MNC must be careful to make decisions concerning working capital management that are optimal for the corporation as a whole and not just the best for the individual entities.

B. <u>Leading</u> and <u>lagging</u> are important risk reduction techniques for a MNC's working capital management.

1. When holding an <u>asset</u> in a:

a. Strong (appreciating) currency, we should lag (delay) conversion to the domestic currency.

b. Weak (depreciating) currency, we should lead (expedite) conversion to the domestic currency.

2. When holding a <u>liability</u> in a:

a. Strong currency, we should lead (expedite) payment of the liability.

b. Weak currency, we should lag (delay) payment of the liability.

C. Cash management

    1. A MNC may wish to position funds in a specific subsidiary in another country such that the foreign exchange exposure and the tax liability of the MNC are minimized as a whole. This strategy may not, however, be the optimal strategy for the specific subsidiary.

    2. The transfer of funds is effected by royalties, fees, and transfer-pricing. The transfer price is the price charged for goods or services transferred from a subsidiary or parent company to another subsidiary.

VI. International Financing Decisions

  A. A multinational corporation (MNC) may have a lower cost of capital than a domestic firm due to its ability to tap a larger number of financial markets.

    1. A multinational company has access to financing sources in the countries in which it operates.

    2. Host countries often provide access to low-cost subsidized financing to attract foreign investment.

    3. A MNC may enjoy preferential credit treatment due to its size and investor preference for its home currency.

    4. A MNC may be able to access third country capital markets.

    5. A MNC has access to external currency markets variously known as Eurodollar, Eurocurrency, or Asiandollar markets. These markets are unregulated and because of their lower spread, can offer attractive rates for financing and investment.

  B. To increase their visibility in foreign capital markets, MNCs are increasingly listing their stocks in the foreign capital markets.

  C. A MNC's capital structure should reflect its wider access to financial markets, the ability to diversify economic and political risks, and several of its other advantages over domestic firms.

VII. Direct foreign investment

    A.   Risk in international capital budgeting

        1.   Political risk arises from operating a business in a different and possibly less stable business climate than the United States.

        2.   Exchange risk incorporates changes in the future earnings stream because of currency fluctuations, possibly in both foreign and domestic currencies.

        3.   Business risk is affected by the response of business and the MNC to economic conditions within the foreign country.

        4.   Financial risk arises from the financial structure of the firm and its effect on the profit stream.

    B.   Cash flows must be estimated considering the potential effects of exchange rate changes, governmental policy, and other items that determine product demand and sales.

    C.   A foreign investment can be evaluated from either a parent or a local firm perspective. If a firm uses a local perspective the initial investment and all of its cash flows should be discounted at a rate that reflects the local inflation rate and the riskiness of the project. When using the parent company perspective, the discount rate should reflect the expected inflation rate in the parent currency and foreign currency cash flows should be converted to the parent currency cash flows using projected exchange rates.

    D.   The net present value (NPV) must be calculated using the above factors.

        1.   If NPV is greater than zero, generally accept direct foreign investments.

        2.   If NPV is less than zero, the MNC may decide to

            a.   Reject direct foreign investment.

            b.   Establish a sales office in the foreign country.

            c.   License a local company to manufacture the product, where the MNC receives royalty payments.

Study Problems

1. An American manufacturer owes 5000 marks to a German supplier. How much does he owe in U.S. dollars, using the exchange rates of .3846 U.S. dollar per mark?

    SOLUTION

    5000 (marks) x .3846 (U.S. dollar/mark) = 1923 U.S. dollars

2. A fashion designer in France owes $65,000, due in 30 days, to a counterpart in the U.S. How much is the foreign liability today using the 30-day forward exchange rate of 8.0451 francs per U.S. dollar?

    SOLUTION

    65,000 ($) x 8.0451 (francs per U.S. dollar) = 522,931.5 francs

3. You own $20,000. The dollar rate in London is .6501 pounds/U.S. dollar. The indirect New York rate is .6691 pounds/U.S. dollar pound rate. Are arbitrage profits possible? Set up an arbitrage scheme with your capital. What is the gain (loss) in dollars?

    SOLUTION

    Assuming no transaction costs, the rates between London and New York are out of line. Arbitrage profits are possible.

    Pounds are cheaper in New York. Buy pounds in New York with the $20,000.

    20,000 ($) x .6691 (pounds/dollars) = 13,382 pounds.

    Sell pounds in London.
    13,382 (pounds) ÷ .6501 (pounds/U.S. dollars) = $20,584.52.

    Your net gain is $20,584.52 - $20,000 = $584.52.

TRUE-FALSE

_____ 1. One of the most difficult aspects of operating a business in a foreign country is the problem of multiple currencies.

_____ 2. International business affairs affect very few firms, and therefore is of little concern to most businesses.

_____ 3. Exchange rates are fixed according to the U.S. dollar and must be maintained within the narrow margins unless a major adjustment is enacted.

_____ 4. The forward contract states the exchange rate to be used in the spot market on a specific date in the near future.

_____ 5. A narrow spread between the bid and asked rates indicates an efficient spot market.

_____ 6. The interest rate parity theorem states that (except for the effect of transaction costs) the forward premium or discount should be equal and opposite in sign to the difference in the respective country's interest rates for securities of the same maturities.

_____ 7. Extensive profit opportunities exist for arbitrageurs in the foreign exchange markets.

_____ 8. Exchange rate risk constitutes only a small portion of the risk associated with international business.

_____ 9. An investor with foreign currency liabilities may want to hedge against exchange rate changes in the money markets.

_____ 10. Leading and lagging are strategies for optimal working capital management.

_____ 11. In general, a multinational firm faces more risks than a firm that does not deal globally.

_____ 12. Purchasing power parity suggests that exchange rates in countries with high inflation rates tend to decline.

_____ 13. Translation exposure results in exchange rate related losses or gains that have little or no impact on taxable income.

_____ 14. Futures contracts are customized with regard to the amount and maturity date of the contract.

_____ 15. Receivables and payables are subject to transaction exposure.

_____ 16. The objective of a hedging strategy is to have a positive net asset position in the foreign currency.

MULTIPLE CHOICE

1. A direct 30-day forward quote of 1.4957 U.S dollars per pound is equivalent to what 30-day indirect quote?

   a. .6686 U.S dollars per pound.
   b. .6671 pounds per U.S. dollar.
   c. 1.4957 U.S. dollars per pound.
   d. .6686 pounds per U.S. dollar.
   e. .6671 pounds per U.S. dollar.

2. An example of a cross rate, when the exchange rates are given in U.S. dollars, would be:

   a. marks per U.S. dollar.
   b. pounds per yen.
   c. yen per mark.
   d. U.S. dollars per yen.
   e. both b and c.

3. Forward rate contracts are used in international transactions to:

   a. reduce the risk for the buyer.
   b. reduce the risk for the seller.
   c. both a and b.
   d. neither a nor b.

4. If an investor noticed a discrepancy in the exchange rates of two countries and acted upon it, he would be engaging in:

   a. money market hedging.
   b. forward hedging.
   c. arbitrage.
   d. sabotage.
   e. leading strategies.

5. If your firm held liabilities in a strong currency, it would be wise to _____.

   a. lead.
   b. lag.
   c. engage in money market hedging.
   d. engage in forward hedging.
   e. all of the above.

6. Direct foreign investment involves:

   a. political risk.
   b. business risk.
   c. financial risk.
   d. exchange rate risk.
   e. all of the above.

7. If the net present value of a direct foreign investment project for a MNC is less than zero, they should:

   a. reject it.
   b. open a sales office.
   c. license a foreign company.
   d. accept it.
   e. a, b, and c are all possibilities.

8. If the U.S. experiences a 7% inflation rate while France is experiencing a 4% inflation rate, then according to purchasing power parity:

   a. The value of the U.S. dollar should increase by approximately 3% against the French Franc.
   b. The U.S. dollar should decline against the French Franc by 3%.
   c. The French Franc would decline by 3% against the U.S. dollar.
   d. There would be no change in either currency.

9. A paper loss/gain best describes which type of risk:

   a. economic.
   b. transaction.
   c. interest rate.
   d. translation.

10. Which of the following do not provide a hedge against some risk:

    a. forward contract.
    b. money market hedge.
    c. currency options.
    d. futures contracts.
    e. all are forms of hedging.

SOLUTIONS TO SELECTED SET B PROBLEMS (See text for problems.)

22-1B.

    (a)   15,000 (Canadian $) x .8439 (U.S. $/Canadian $) = $12,659

    (b)   1,500,000 (Yen) x .004680 ($/Yen) = $ 7,020

    (c)   55,000 (Swiss-franc) x .5140 ($/Swiss franc) = $28,270.

22-3B.

Recall that the indirect quote = (1/Direct Quote). The results are tabulated below:

			Foreign Currency/$
Canadian - dollar		Spot	1.1850
	30 day		1.1891
	90 day		1.1919
Japan - Yen		Spot	213.6752
	30 day		211.8644
	90 day		208.8991
Swiss - franc		Spot	1.9455
	30 day		1.9309
	90 day		1.8744

22-5B.

The Tokyo rate is 216.6752 Yen/$
The (indirect) New York rate is 1/.004680 = 213.6752 Yen/$.

Assuming no transaction costs, the rate between Tokyo and New York are in line. Arbitrage profits are not possible.

Buy Yen for $10,000.

$10,000 x 216.6752 = 2,136,752 Y.

Sell the Yen in New York at the prevailing rate.

2,136,752 x .004680 = $10,149.02

Your net gain is $9,999.99 - $10,000 = <u>$.01</u>

USING THE CALCULATOR TO COMPUTE TABLE VALUES

Note: See that the memory is cleared; you are in the correct mode for financial calculations; and have adequate decimal places.

Appendix B (Compound sum of $1): $FVIF_{i,n} = \$1(1 + i)^n$

Hewlett-Packard HP-12C

1 [CHS] [PV] $\left(\begin{array}{c}\text{No. of periods}\\\text{(Days, mths., or yrs.)}\end{array}\right)$ [n] $\left(\begin{array}{c}\text{Interest rate}\\\text{per period}\end{array}\right)$ [i] 0 [PMT] [FV] $\rightarrow$ ANSWER

Hewlett-Packard HP-17B II, HP-19B II

1 [+/-] [PV] $\left(\begin{array}{c}\text{No. of periods}\\\text{(Days, mths., or yrs.)}\end{array}\right)$ [N] $\left(\begin{array}{c}\text{Interest rate}\\\text{per period}\end{array}\right)$ [I%YR] 0 [PMT] [FV] $\rightarrow$ ANSWER

Texas Instruments BA-35

1 [+/-] [PV] $\left(\begin{array}{c}\text{No. of periods}\\\text{(Days, mths., or yrs.)}\end{array}\right)$ [N] $\left(\begin{array}{c}\text{Interest rate}\\\text{per period}\end{array}\right)$ [%i] 0 [PMT] [CPT] [FV] $\rightarrow$ ANSWER

Texas Instruments BAII

1 [+/-] [PV] $\left(\begin{array}{c}\text{No. of periods}\\\text{(Days, mths., or yrs.)}\end{array}\right)$ [N] $\left(\begin{array}{c}\text{Interest rate}\\\text{per period}\end{array}\right)$ [%i] 0 [PMT] [2nd] [FV] $\rightarrow$ ANSWER

Texas Instruments BAII Plus

1 [+/-] [PV] $\left(\begin{array}{c}\text{No. of periods}\\\text{(Days, mths., or yrs.)}\end{array}\right)$ [N] $\left(\begin{array}{c}\text{Interest rate}\\\text{per period}\end{array}\right)$ [I/Y] 0 [PMT] [CPT] [FV] $\rightarrow$ ANSWER

Appendix C (Present value of $1): $PVIF_{i,n} = \dfrac{\$1}{(1 + i)^n}$

Hewlett-Packard HP-12C

1 [CHS] [FV] $\left(\begin{array}{c}\text{No. of periods}\\\text{(Days, mths., or yrs.)}\end{array}\right)$ [n] $\left(\begin{array}{c}\text{Interest rate}\\\text{per period}\end{array}\right)$ [i] 0 [PMT] [PV] $\rightarrow$ ANSWER

Hewlett-Packard HP-17B II, HP-19B II

1 [+/-] [FV] $\left(\begin{array}{c}\text{No. of periods}\\\text{(Days, mths., or yrs.)}\end{array}\right)$ [N] $\left(\begin{array}{c}\text{Interest rate}\\\text{per period}\end{array}\right)$ [I%YR] 0 [PMT] [PV] $\rightarrow$ ANSWER

Texas Instruments BA-35

1 [+/-] [FV] $\left(\begin{array}{c}\text{No. of periods}\\\text{(Days, mths., or yrs.)}\end{array}\right)$ [N] $\left(\begin{array}{c}\text{Interest rate}\\\text{per period}\end{array}\right)$ [%i] 0 [PMT] [CPT] [PV] $\rightarrow$ ANSWER

Texas Instruments BAII

1 [+/-] [FV] $\left(\begin{array}{c}\text{No. of periods}\\\text{(Days, mths., or yrs.)}\end{array}\right)$ [N] $\left(\begin{array}{c}\text{Interest rate}\\\text{per period}\end{array}\right)$ [%i] 0 [PMT] [2nd] [PV] $\rightarrow$ ANSWER

Texas Instruments BAII Plus

1 [+/-] [FV] $\left(\begin{array}{c}\text{No. of periods}\\\text{(Days, mths., or yrs.)}\end{array}\right)$ [N] $\left(\begin{array}{c}\text{Interest rate}\\\text{per period}\end{array}\right)$ [I/Y] 0 [PMT] [CPT] [PV] $\rightarrow$ ANSWER

Appendix D (Sum of an annuity of $1): $FVIFA_{i,n} = \$1 \sum_{t=0}^{n-1} (1+i)^t$

Hewlett-Packard HP-12C

1 [CHS] [PMT] (No. of periods (Days, mths., or yrs.)) [n] (Interest rate per period) [i] 0 [PV] [FV] → ANSWER

Hewlett-Packard HP-17B II, HP-19B II

1 [+/-] [PMT] (No. of periods (Days, mths., or yrs.)) [N] (Interest rate per period) [I%YR] 0 [PV] [FV] → ANSWER

Texas Instruments BA-35

1 [+/-] [PMT] (No. of periods (Days, mths., or yrs.)) [N] (Interest rate per period) [%i] 0 [PV] [CPT] [FV] → ANSWER

Texas Instruments BAII

1 [+/-] [PMT] (No. of periods (Days, mths., or yrs.)) [N] (Interest rate per period) [%i] 0 [PV] [2nd] [FV] → ANSWER

Texas Instruments BAII Plus

1 [+/-] [PMT] (No. of periods (Days, mths., or yrs.)) [N] (Interest rate per period) [I/Y] 0 [PV] [CPT] [FV] → ANSWER

Appendix E (Present value of an annuity of $1): $PVIFA_{i,n} = \left(\sum_{t=1}^{n} \frac{\$1}{(1+i)^t} \right)$

Hewlett-Packard HP-12C

1 [CHS] [PMT] (No. of periods (Days, mths., or yrs.)) [n] (Interest rate per period) [i] 0 [FV] [PV] → ANSWER

Hewlett-Packard HP-17B II, HP-19B II

1 [+/-] [PMT] (No. of periods (Days, mths., or yrs.)) [N] (Interest rate per period) [I%YR] 0 [FV] [PV] → ANSWER

Texas Instruments BA-35

1 [+/-] [PMT] (No. of periods (Days, mths., or yrs.)) [N] (Interest rate per period) [%i] 0 [FV] [CPT] [PV] → ANSWER

Texas Instruments BAII

1 [+/-] [PMT] (No. of periods (Days, mths., or yrs.)) [N] (Interest rate per period) [%i] 0 [FV] [2nd] [PV] → ANSWER

Texas Instruments BAII Plus

1 [+/-] [PMT] (No. of periods (Days, mths., or yrs.)) [N] (Interest rate per period) [I/Y] 0 [FV] [CPT] [PV] → ANSWER

APPENDIX B: COMPOUND SUM OF $1

n	1%	2%	3%	4%	5%	6%	7%	8%	9%	10%
1	1.010	1.020	1.030	1.040	1.050	1.060	1.070	1.080	1.090	1.100
2	1.020	1.040	1.061	1.082	1.103	1.124	1.145	1.166	1.188	1.210
3	1.030	1.061	1.093	1.125	1.158	1.191	1.225	1.260	1.295	1.331
4	1.041	1.082	1.126	1.170	1.216	1.262	1.311	1.360	1.412	1.464
5	1.051	1.104	1.159	1.217	1.276	1.338	1.403	1.469	1.539	1.611
6	1.062	1.126	1.194	1.265	1.340	1.419	1.501	1.587	1.677	1.772
7	1.072	1.149	1.230	1.316	1.407	1.504	1.606	1.714	1.828	1.949
8	1.083	1.172	1.267	1.369	1.477	1.594	1.718	1.851	1.993	2.144
9	1.094	1.195	1.305	1.423	1.551	1.689	1.838	1.999	2.172	2.358
10	1.105	1.219	1.344	1.480	1.629	1.791	1.967	2.159	2.367	2.594
11	1.116	1.243	1.384	1.539	1.710	1.898	2.105	2.332	2.580	2.853
12	1.127	1.268	1.426	1.601	1.796	2.012	2.252	2.518	2.813	3.138
13	1.138	1.294	1.469	1.665	1.886	2.133	2.410	2.720	3.066	3.452
14	1.149	1.319	1.513	1.732	1.980	2.261	2.579	2.937	3.342	3.797
15	1.161	1.346	1.558	1.801	2.079	2.397	2.759	3.172	3.642	4.177
16	1.173	1.373	1.605	1.873	2.183	2.540	2.952	3.426	3.970	4.595
17	1.184	1.400	1.653	1.948	2.292	2.693	3.159	3.700	4.328	5.054
18	1.196	1.428	1.702	2.026	2.407	2.854	3.380	3.996	4.717	5.560
19	1.208	1.457	1.754	2.107	2.527	3.026	3.617	4.316	5.142	6.116
20	1.220	1.486	1.806	2.191	2.653	3.207	3.870	4.661	5.604	6.727
21	1.232	1.516	1.860	2.279	2.786	3.400	4.141	5.034	6.109	7.400
22	1.245	1.546	1.916	2.370	2.925	3.604	4.430	5.437	6.659	8.140
23	1.257	1.577	1.974	2.465	3.072	3.820	4.741	5.871	7.258	8.954
24	1.270	1.608	2.033	2.563	3.225	4.049	5.072	6.341	7.911	9.850
25	1.282	1.641	2.094	2.666	3.386	4.292	5.427	6.848	8.623	10.835
30	1.348	1.811	2.427	3.243	4.322	5.743	7.612	10.063	13.268	17.449
40	1.489	2.208	3.262	4.801	7.040	10.286	14.974	21.725	31.409	45.259
50	1.645	2.692	4.384	7.107	11.467	18.420	29.457	46.902	74.358	117.391

APPENDIX B: COMPOUND SUM OF $1 (Continued)

n	11%	12%	13%	14%	15%	16%	17%	18%	19%	20%
1	1.110	1.120	1.130	1.140	1.150	1.160	1.170	1.180	1.190	1.200
2	1.232	1.254	1.277	1.300	1.323	1.346	1.369	1.392	1.416	1.440
3	1.368	1.405	1.443	1.482	1.521	1.561	1.602	1.643	1.685	1.728
4	1.518	1.574	1.630	1.689	1.749	1.811	1.874	1.939	2.005	2.074
5	1.685	1.762	1.842	1.925	2.011	2.100	2.192	2.288	2.386	2.488
6	1.870	1.974	2.082	2.195	2.313	2.436	2.565	2.700	2.840	2.986
7	2.076	2.211	2.353	2.502	2.660	2.826	3.001	3.185	3.379	3.583
8	2.305	2.476	2.658	2.853	3.059	3.278	3.511	3.759	4.021	4.300
9	2.558	2.773	3.004	3.252	3.518	3.803	4.108	4.435	4.785	5.160
10	2.839	3.106	3.395	3.707	4.046	4.411	4.807	5.234	5.695	6.192
11	3.152	3.479	3.836	4.226	4.652	5.117	5.624	6.176	6.777	7.430
12	3.498	3.896	4.335	4.818	5.350	5.936	6.580	7.288	8.064	8.916
13	3.883	4.363	4.898	5.492	6.153	6.886	7.699	8.599	9.596	10.699
14	4.310	4.887	5.535	6.261	7.076	7.988	9.007	10.147	11.420	12.839
15	4.785	5.474	6.254	7.138	8.137	9.266	10.539	11.974	13.590	15.407
16	5.311	6.130	7.067	8.137	9.358	10.748	12.330	14.129	16.172	18.488
17	5.895	6.866	7.986	9.276	10.761	12.468	14.426	16.672	19.244	22.186
18	6.544	7.690	9.024	10.575	12.375	14.463	16.879	19.673	22.901	26.623
19	7.263	8.613	10.197	12.056	14.232	16.777	19.748	23.214	27.252	31.948
20	8.062	9.646	11.523	13.743	16.367	19.461	23.106	27.393	32.429	38.338
21	8.949	10.804	13.021	15.668	18.822	22.574	27.034	32.324	38.591	46.005
22	9.934	12.100	14.714	17.861	21.645	26.186	31.629	38.142	45.923	55.206
23	11.026	13.552	16.627	20.362	24.891	30.376	37.006	45.008	54.649	66.247
24	12.239	15.179	18.788	23.212	28.625	35.236	43.297	53.109	65.032	79.497
25	13.585	17.000	21.231	26.462	32.919	40.874	50.658	62.669	77.388	95.396
30	22.892	29.960	39.116	50.950	66.212	85.850	111.065	143.371	184.675	237.376
40	65.001	93.051	132.782	188.884	267.864	378.721	533.869	750.378	1051.668	1469.772
50	184.565	289.002	450.736	700.233	1083.657	1670.704	2566.215	3927.357	5988.914	9100.438

APPENDIX B: COMPOUND SUM OF $1 (Continued)

n	21%	22%	23%	24%	25%	26%	27%	28%	29%	30%
1	1.210	1.220	1.230	1.240	1.250	1.260	1.270	1.280	1.290	1.300
2	1.464	1.488	1.513	1.538	1.563	1.588	1.613	1.638	1.664	1.690
3	1.772	1.816	1.861	1.907	1.953	2.000	2.048	2.097	2.147	2.197
4	2.144	2.215	2.289	2.364	2.441	2.520	2.601	2.684	2.769	2.856
5	2.594	2.703	2.815	2.932	3.052	3.176	3.304	3.436	3.572	3.713
6	3.138	3.297	3.463	3.635	3.815	4.002	4.196	4.398	4.608	4.827
7	3.797	4.023	4.259	4.508	4.768	5.042	5.329	5.629	5.945	6.275
8	4.595	4.908	5.239	5.590	5.960	6.353	6.768	7.206	7.669	8.157
9	5.560	5.987	6.444	6.931	7.451	8.005	8.595	9.223	9.893	10.604
10	6.727	7.305	7.926	8.594	9.313	10.086	10.915	11.806	12.761	13.786
11	8.140	8.912	9.749	10.657	11.642	12.708	13.862	15.112	16.462	17.922
12	9.850	10.872	11.991	13.215	14.552	16.012	17.605	19.343	21.236	23.298
13	11.918	13.264	14.749	16.386	18.190	20.175	22.359	24.759	27.395	30.288
14	14.421	16.182	18.141	20.319	22.737	25.421	28.396	31.691	35.339	39.374
15	17.449	19.742	22.314	25.196	28.422	32.030	36.062	40.565	45.587	51.186
16	21.114	24.086	27.446	31.243	35.527	40.358	45.799	51.923	58.808	66.542
17	25.548	29.384	33.759	38.741	44.409	50.851	58.165	66.461	75.862	86.504
18	30.913	35.849	41.523	48.039	55.511	64.072	73.870	85.071	97.862	112.455
19	37.404	43.736	51.074	59.568	69.389	80.731	93.815	108.890	126.242	146.192
20	45.259	53.358	62.821	73.864	86.736	101.721	119.145	139.380	162.852	190.050
21	54.764	65.096	77.269	91.592	108.420	128.169	151.314	178.406	210.080	247.065
22	66.264	79.418	95.041	113.574	135.525	161.492	192.168	228.360	271.003	321.184
23	80.180	96.889	116.901	140.831	169.407	203.480	244.054	292.300	349.593	417.539
24	97.017	118.205	143.788	174.631	211.758	256.385	309.948	374.144	450.976	542.801
25	117.391	144.210	176.859	216.542	264.698	323.045	393.634	478.905	581.759	705.641
30	304.482	389.758	497.913	634.820	807.794	1025.927	1300.504	1645.505	2078.219	2619.996
40	2048.400	2847.038	3946.430	5455.913	7523.164	10347.175	14195.439	19426.689	26520.909	36118.865
50	13780.612	20796.561	31279.195	46890.435	70064.923	104358.362	154948.026	229349.862	338442.984	497929.223

APPENDIX B: COMPOUND SUM OF $1 (Continued)

n	31%	32%	33%	34%	35%	36%	37%	38%	39%	40%
1	1.310	1.320	1.330	1.340	1.350	1.360	1.370	1.380	1.390	1.400
2	1.716	1.742	1.769	1.796	1.823	1.850	1.877	1.904	1.932	1.960
3	2.248	2.300	2.353	2.406	2.460	2.515	2.571	2.628	2.686	2.744
4	2.945	3.036	3.129	3.224	3.322	3.421	3.523	3.627	3.733	3.842
5	3.858	4.007	4.162	4.320	4.484	4.653	4.826	5.005	5.189	5.378
6	5.054	5.290	5.535	5.789	6.053	6.328	6.612	6.907	7.213	7.530
7	6.621	6.983	7.361	7.758	8.172	8.605	9.058	9.531	10.025	10.541
8	8.673	9.217	9.791	10.395	11.032	11.703	12.410	13.153	13.935	14.758
9	11.362	12.166	13.022	13.930	14.894	15.917	17.001	18.151	19.370	20.661
10	14.884	16.060	17.319	18.666	20.107	21.647	23.292	25.049	26.925	28.925
11	19.498	21.199	23.034	25.012	27.144	29.439	31.910	34.568	37.425	40.496
12	25.542	27.983	30.635	33.516	36.644	40.037	43.717	47.703	52.021	56.694
13	33.460	36.937	40.745	44.912	49.470	54.451	59.892	65.831	72.309	79.371
14	43.833	48.757	54.190	60.182	66.784	74.053	82.052	90.846	100.510	111.120
15	57.421	64.359	72.073	80.644	90.158	100.713	112.411	125.368	139.708	155.568
16	75.221	84.954	95.858	108.063	121.714	136.969	154.003	173.008	194.194	217.795
17	98.540	112.139	127.491	144.804	164.314	186.278	210.984	238.751	269.930	304.913
18	129.087	148.024	169.562	194.038	221.824	253.338	289.048	329.476	375.203	426.879
19	169.104	195.391	225.518	260.011	299.462	344.540	395.996	454.677	521.532	597.630
20	221.527	257.916	299.939	348.414	404.274	468.574	542.514	627.454	724.930	836.683
21	290.200	340.449	398.919	466.875	545.769	637.261	743.245	865.886	1007.653	1171.356
22	380.162	449.393	530.562	625.613	736.789	866.674	1018.245	1194.923	1400.637	1639.898
23	498.012	593.199	705.647	838.321	994.665	1178.677	1394.996	1648.994	1946.885	2295.857
24	652.396	783.023	938.511	1123.350	1342.797	1603.001	1911.145	2275.611	2706.171	3214.200
25	854.638	1033.590	1248.220	1505.289	1812.776	2180.081	2618.268	3140.344	3761.577	4499.880
30	3297.151	4142.075	5194.566	6503.452	8128.550	10143.019	12636.215	15717.106	19518.391	24201.432
40	49074.042	66520.767	89963.354	121392.522	163437.135	219561.574	294321.973	393698.224	525523.341	700037.697
50	730406.758	1068308.196	1558052.359	2265895.716	3286157.879	4752754.903	6855329.878	9861757.523	14149464.787	20248916.240

APPENDIX C: PRESENT VALUE OF $1

n	1%	2%	3%	4%	5%	6%	7%	8%	9%	10%
1	0.990	0.980	0.971	0.962	0.952	0.943	0.935	0.926	0.917	0.909
2	0.980	0.961	0.943	0.925	0.907	0.890	0.873	0.857	0.842	0.826
3	0.971	0.942	0.915	0.889	0.864	0.840	0.816	0.794	0.772	0.751
4	0.961	0.924	0.888	0.855	0.823	0.792	0.763	0.735	0.708	0.683
5	0.951	0.906	0.863	0.822	0.784	0.747	0.713	0.681	0.650	0.621
6	0.942	0.888	0.837	0.790	0.746	0.705	0.666	0.630	0.596	0.564
7	0.933	0.871	0.813	0.760	0.711	0.665	0.623	0.583	0.547	0.513
8	0.923	0.853	0.789	0.731	0.677	0.627	0.582	0.540	0.502	0.467
9	0.914	0.837	0.766	0.703	0.645	0.592	0.544	0.500	0.460	0.424
10	0.905	0.820	0.744	0.676	0.614	0.558	0.508	0.463	0.422	0.386
11	0.896	0.804	0.722	0.650	0.585	0.527	0.475	0.429	0.388	0.350
12	0.887	0.788	0.701	0.625	0.557	0.497	0.444	0.397	0.356	0.319
13	0.879	0.773	0.681	0.601	0.530	0.469	0.415	0.368	0.326	0.290
14	0.870	0.758	0.661	0.577	0.505	0.442	0.388	0.340	0.299	0.263
15	0.861	0.743	0.642	0.555	0.481	0.417	0.362	0.315	0.275	0.239
16	0.853	0.728	0.623	0.534	0.458	0.394	0.339	0.292	0.252	0.218
17	0.844	0.714	0.605	0.513	0.436	0.371	0.317	0.270	0.231	0.198
18	0.836	0.700	0.587	0.494	0.416	0.350	0.296	0.250	0.212	0.180
19	0.828	0.686	0.570	0.475	0.396	0.331	0.277	0.232	0.194	0.164
20	0.820	0.673	0.554	0.456	0.377	0.312	0.258	0.215	0.178	0.149
21	0.811	0.660	0.538	0.439	0.359	0.294	0.242	0.199	0.164	0.135
22	0.803	0.647	0.522	0.422	0.342	0.278	0.226	0.184	0.150	0.123
23	0.795	0.634	0.507	0.406	0.326	0.262	0.211	0.170	0.138	0.112
24	0.788	0.622	0.492	0.390	0.310	0.247	0.197	0.158	0.126	0.102
25	0.780	0.610	0.478	0.375	0.295	0.233	0.184	0.146	0.116	0.092
30	0.742	0.552	0.412	0.308	0.231	0.174	0.131	0.099	0.075	0.057
40	0.672	0.453	0.307	0.208	0.142	0.097	0.067	0.046	0.032	0.022
50	0.608	0.372	0.228	0.141	0.087	0.054	0.034	0.021	0.013	0.009

C-1

APPENDIX C: PRESENT VALUE OF $1 (Continued)

n	11%	12%	13%	14%	15%	16%	17%	18%	19%	20%
1	0.901	0.893	0.885	0.877	0.870	0.862	0.855	0.847	0.840	0.833
2	0.812	0.797	0.783	0.769	0.756	0.743	0.731	0.718	0.706	0.694
3	0.731	0.712	0.693	0.675	0.658	0.641	0.624	0.609	0.593	0.579
4	0.659	0.636	0.613	0.592	0.572	0.552	0.534	0.516	0.499	0.482
5	0.593	0.567	0.543	0.519	0.497	0.476	0.456	0.437	0.419	0.402
6	0.535	0.507	0.480	0.456	0.432	0.410	0.390	0.370	0.352	0.335
7	0.482	0.452	0.425	0.400	0.376	0.354	0.333	0.314	0.296	0.279
8	0.434	0.404	0.376	0.351	0.327	0.305	0.285	0.266	0.249	0.233
9	0.391	0.361	0.333	0.308	0.284	0.263	0.243	0.225	0.209	0.194
10	0.352	0.322	0.295	0.270	0.247	0.227	0.208	0.191	0.176	0.162
11	0.317	0.287	0.261	0.237	0.215	0.195	0.178	0.162	0.148	0.135
12	0.286	0.257	0.231	0.208	0.187	0.168	0.152	0.137	0.124	0.112
13	0.258	0.229	0.204	0.182	0.163	0.145	0.130	0.116	0.104	0.093
14	0.232	0.205	0.181	0.160	0.141	0.125	0.111	0.099	0.088	0.078
15	0.209	0.183	0.160	0.140	0.123	0.108	0.095	0.084	0.074	0.065
16	0.188	0.163	0.141	0.123	0.107	0.093	0.081	0.071	0.062	0.054
17	0.170	0.146	0.125	0.108	0.093	0.080	0.069	0.060	0.052	0.045
18	0.153	0.130	0.111	0.095	0.081	0.069	0.059	0.051	0.044	0.038
19	0.138	0.116	0.098	0.083	0.070	0.060	0.051	0.043	0.037	0.031
20	0.124	0.104	0.087	0.073	0.061	0.051	0.043	0.037	0.031	0.026
21	0.112	0.093	0.077	0.064	0.053	0.044	0.037	0.031	0.026	0.022
22	0.101	0.083	0.068	0.056	0.046	0.038	0.032	0.026	0.022	0.018
23	0.091	0.074	0.060	0.049	0.040	0.033	0.027	0.022	0.018	0.015
24	0.082	0.066	0.053	0.043	0.035	0.028	0.023	0.019	0.015	0.013
25	0.074	0.059	0.047	0.038	0.030	0.024	0.020	0.016	0.013	0.010
30	0.044	0.033	0.026	0.020	0.015	0.012	0.009	0.007	0.005	0.004
40	0.015	0.011	0.008	0.005	0.004	0.003	0.002	0.001	0.001	0.001
50	0.005	0.003	0.002	0.001	0.001	0.001	0.000	0.000	0.000	0.000

APPENDIX C: PRESENT VALUE OF $1 (Continued)

n	21%	22%	23%	24%	25%	26%	27%	28%	29%	30%
1	0.826	0.820	0.813	0.806	0.800	0.794	0.787	0.781	0.775	0.769
2	0.683	0.672	0.661	0.650	0.640	0.630	0.620	0.610	0.601	0.592
3	0.564	0.551	0.537	0.524	0.512	0.500	0.488	0.477	0.466	0.455
4	0.467	0.451	0.437	0.423	0.410	0.397	0.384	0.373	0.361	0.350
5	0.386	0.370	0.355	0.341	0.328	0.315	0.303	0.291	0.280	0.269
6	0.319	0.303	0.289	0.275	0.262	0.250	0.238	0.227	0.217	0.207
7	0.263	0.249	0.235	0.222	0.210	0.198	0.188	0.178	0.168	0.159
8	0.218	0.204	0.191	0.179	0.168	0.157	0.148	0.139	0.130	0.123
9	0.180	0.167	0.155	0.144	0.134	0.125	0.116	0.108	0.101	0.094
10	0.149	0.137	0.126	0.116	0.107	0.099	0.092	0.085	0.078	0.073
11	0.123	0.112	0.103	0.094	0.086	0.079	0.072	0.066	0.061	0.056
12	0.102	0.092	0.083	0.076	0.069	0.062	0.057	0.052	0.047	0.043
13	0.084	0.075	0.068	0.061	0.055	0.050	0.045	0.040	0.037	0.033
14	0.069	0.062	0.055	0.049	0.044	0.039	0.035	0.032	0.028	0.025
15	0.057	0.051	0.045	0.040	0.035	0.031	0.028	0.025	0.022	0.020
16	0.047	0.042	0.036	0.032	0.028	0.025	0.022	0.019	0.017	0.015
17	0.039	0.034	0.030	0.026	0.023	0.020	0.017	0.015	0.013	0.012
18	0.032	0.028	0.024	0.021	0.018	0.016	0.014	0.012	0.010	0.009
19	0.027	0.023	0.020	0.017	0.014	0.012	0.011	0.009	0.008	0.007
20	0.022	0.019	0.016	0.014	0.012	0.010	0.008	0.007	0.006	0.005
21	0.018	0.015	0.013	0.011	0.009	0.008	0.007	0.006	0.005	0.004
22	0.015	0.013	0.011	0.009	0.007	0.006	0.005	0.004	0.004	0.003
23	0.012	0.010	0.009	0.007	0.006	0.005	0.004	0.003	0.003	0.002
24	0.010	0.008	0.007	0.006	0.005	0.004	0.003	0.003	0.002	0.002
25	0.009	0.007	0.006	0.005	0.004	0.003	0.003	0.002	0.002	0.001
30	0.003	0.003	0.002	0.002	0.001	0.001	0.001	0.001	0.000	0.000
40	0.000	0.000	0.000	0.000	0.000	0.000	0.000	0.000	0.000	0.000
50	0.000	0.000	0.000	0.000	0.000	0.000	0.000	0.000	0.000	0.000

APPENDIX C: PRESENT VALUE OF $1 (Continued)

n	31%	32%	33%	34%	35%	36%	37%	38%	39%	40%
1	0.763	0.758	0.752	0.746	0.741	0.735	0.730	0.725	0.719	0.714
2	0.583	0.574	0.565	0.557	0.549	0.541	0.533	0.525	0.518	0.510
3	0.445	0.435	0.425	0.416	0.406	0.398	0.389	0.381	0.372	0.364
4	0.340	0.329	0.320	0.310	0.301	0.292	0.284	0.276	0.268	0.260
5	0.259	0.250	0.240	0.231	0.223	0.215	0.207	0.200	0.193	0.186
6	0.198	0.189	0.181	0.173	0.165	0.158	0.151	0.145	0.139	0.133
7	0.151	0.143	0.136	0.129	0.122	0.116	0.110	0.105	0.100	0.095
8	0.115	0.108	0.102	0.096	0.091	0.085	0.081	0.076	0.072	0.068
9	0.088	0.082	0.077	0.072	0.067	0.063	0.059	0.055	0.052	0.048
10	0.067	0.062	0.058	0.054	0.050	0.046	0.043	0.040	0.037	0.035
11	0.051	0.047	0.043	0.040	0.037	0.034	0.031	0.029	0.027	0.025
12	0.039	0.036	0.033	0.030	0.027	0.025	0.023	0.021	0.019	0.018
13	0.030	0.027	0.025	0.022	0.020	0.018	0.017	0.015	0.014	0.013
14	0.023	0.021	0.018	0.017	0.015	0.014	0.012	0.011	0.010	0.009
15	0.017	0.016	0.014	0.012	0.011	0.010	0.009	0.008	0.007	0.006
16	0.013	0.012	0.010	0.009	0.008	0.007	0.006	0.006	0.005	0.005
17	0.010	0.009	0.008	0.007	0.006	0.005	0.005	0.004	0.004	0.003
18	0.008	0.007	0.006	0.005	0.005	0.004	0.003	0.003	0.003	0.002
19	0.006	0.005	0.004	0.004	0.003	0.003	0.003	0.002	0.002	0.002
20	0.005	0.004	0.003	0.003	0.002	0.002	0.002	0.002	0.001	0.001
21	0.003	0.003	0.003	0.002	0.002	0.002	0.001	0.001	0.001	0.001
22	0.003	0.002	0.002	0.002	0.001	0.001	0.001	0.001	0.001	0.001
23	0.002	0.002	0.001	0.001	0.001	0.001	0.001	0.001	0.001	0.000
24	0.002	0.001	0.001	0.001	0.001	0.001	0.001	0.000	0.000	0.000
25	0.001	0.001	0.001	0.001	0.001	0.000	0.000	0.000	0.000	0.000
30	0.000	0.000	0.000	0.000	0.000	0.000	0.000	0.000	0.000	0.000
40	0.000	0.000	0.000	0.000	0.000	0.000	0.000	0.000	0.000	0.000
50	0.000	0.000	0.000	0.000	0.000	0.000	0.000	0.000	0.000	0.000

APPENDIX D: SUM OF AN ANNUITY OF $1 FOR N PERIODS

n	1%	2%	3%	4%	5%	6%	7%	8%	9%	10%
1	1.000	1.000	1.000	1.000	1.000	1.000	1.000	1.000	1.000	1.000
2	2.010	2.020	2.030	2.040	2.050	2.060	2.070	2.080	2.090	2.100
3	3.030	3.060	3.091	3.122	3.153	3.184	3.215	3.246	3.278	3.310
4	4.060	4.122	4.184	4.246	4.310	4.375	4.440	4.506	4.573	4.641
5	5.101	5.204	5.309	5.416	5.526	5.637	5.751	5.867	5.985	6.105
6	6.152	6.308	6.468	6.633	6.802	6.975	7.153	7.336	7.523	7.716
7	7.214	7.434	7.662	7.898	8.142	8.394	8.654	8.923	9.200	9.487
8	8.286	8.583	8.892	9.214	9.549	9.897	10.260	10.637	11.028	11.436
9	9.369	9.755	10.159	10.583	11.027	11.491	11.978	12.488	13.021	13.579
10	10.462	10.950	11.464	12.006	12.578	13.181	13.816	14.487	15.193	15.937
11	11.567	12.169	12.808	13.486	14.207	14.972	15.784	16.645	17.560	18.531
12	12.683	13.412	14.192	15.026	15.917	16.870	17.888	18.977	20.141	21.384
13	13.809	14.680	15.618	16.627	17.713	18.882	20.141	21.495	22.953	24.523
14	14.947	15.974	17.086	18.292	19.599	21.015	22.550	24.215	26.019	27.975
15	16.097	17.293	18.599	20.024	21.579	23.276	25.129	27.152	29.361	31.772
16	17.258	18.639	20.157	21.825	23.657	25.673	27.888	30.324	33.003	35.950
17	18.430	20.012	21.762	23.698	25.840	28.213	30.840	33.750	36.974	40.545
18	19.615	21.412	23.414	25.645	28.132	30.906	33.999	37.450	41.301	45.599
19	20.811	22.841	25.117	27.671	30.539	33.760	37.379	41.446	46.018	51.159
20	22.019	24.297	26.870	29.778	33.066	36.786	40.995	45.762	51.160	57.275
21	23.239	25.783	28.676	31.969	35.719	39.993	44.865	50.423	56.765	64.002
22	24.472	27.299	30.537	34.248	38.505	43.392	49.006	55.457	62.873	71.403
23	25.716	28.845	32.453	36.618	41.430	46.996	53.436	60.893	69.532	79.543
24	26.973	30.422	34.426	39.083	44.502	50.816	58.177	66.765	76.790	88.497
25	28.243	32.030	36.459	41.646	47.727	54.865	63.249	73.106	84.701	98.347
30	34.785	40.568	47.575	56.085	66.439	79.058	94.461	113.283	136.308	164.494
40	48.886	60.402	75.401	95.026	120.800	154.762	199.635	259.057	337.882	442.593
50	64.463	84.579	112.797	152.667	209.348	290.336	406.529	573.770	815.084	1163.909

APPENDIX D: SUM OF AN ANNUITY OF $1 FOR N PERIODS (Continued)

n	11%	12%	13%	14%	15%	16%	17%	18%	19%	20%
1	1.000	1.000	1.000	1.000	1.000	1.000	1.000	1.000	1.000	1.000
2	2.110	2.120	2.130	2.140	2.150	2.160	2.170	2.180	2.190	2.200
3	3.342	3.374	3.407	3.440	3.473	3.506	3.539	3.572	3.606	3.640
4	4.710	4.779	4.850	4.921	4.993	5.066	5.141	5.215	5.291	5.368
5	6.228	6.353	6.480	6.610	6.742	6.877	7.014	7.154	7.297	7.442
6	7.913	8.115	8.323	8.536	8.754	8.977	9.207	9.442	9.683	9.930
7	9.783	10.089	10.405	10.730	11.067	11.414	11.772	12.142	12.523	12.916
8	11.859	12.300	12.757	13.233	13.727	14.240	14.773	15.327	15.902	16.499
9	14.164	14.776	15.416	16.085	16.786	17.519	18.285	19.086	19.923	20.799
10	16.722	17.549	18.420	19.337	20.304	21.321	22.393	23.521	24.709	25.959
11	19.561	20.655	21.814	23.045	24.349	25.733	27.200	28.755	30.404	32.150
12	22.713	24.133	25.650	27.271	29.002	30.850	32.824	34.931	37.180	39.581
13	26.212	28.029	29.985	32.089	34.352	36.786	39.404	42.219	45.244	48.497
14	30.095	32.393	34.883	37.581	40.505	43.672	47.103	50.818	54.841	59.196
15	34.405	37.280	40.417	43.842	47.580	51.660	56.110	60.965	66.261	72.035
16	39.190	42.753	46.672	50.980	55.717	60.925	66.649	72.939	79.850	87.442
17	44.501	48.884	53.739	59.118	65.075	71.673	78.979	87.068	96.022	105.931
18	50.396	55.750	61.725	68.394	75.836	84.141	93.406	103.740	115.266	128.117
19	56.939	63.440	70.749	78.969	88.212	98.603	110.285	123.414	138.166	154.740
20	64.203	72.052	80.947	91.025	102.444	115.380	130.033	146.628	165.418	186.688
21	72.265	81.699	92.470	104.768	118.810	134.841	153.139	174.021	197.847	225.026
22	81.214	92.503	105.491	120.436	137.632	157.415	180.172	206.345	236.438	271.031
23	91.148	104.603	120.205	138.297	159.276	183.601	211.801	244.487	282.362	326.237
24	102.174	118.155	136.831	158.659	184.168	213.978	248.808	289.494	337.010	392.484
25	114.413	133.334	155.620	181.871	212.793	249.214	292.105	342.603	402.042	471.981
30	199.021	241.333	293.199	356.787	434.745	530.312	647.439	790.948	966.712	1181.882
40	581.826	767.091	1013.704	1342.025	1779.090	2360.757	3134.522	4163.213	5529.829	7343.858
50	1668.771	2400.018	3459.507	4994.521	7217.716	10435.649	15089.502	21813.094	31515.336	45497.191

APPENDIX D: SUM OF AN ANNUITY OF $1 FOR N PERIODS (Continued)

n	21%	22%	23%	24%	25%	26%	27%	28%	29%	30%
1	1.000	1.000	1.000	1.000	1.000	1.000	1.000	1.000	1.000	1.000
2	2.210	2.220	2.230	2.240	2.250	2.260	2.270	2.280	2.290	2.300
3	3.674	3.708	3.743	3.778	3.813	3.848	3.883	3.918	3.954	3.990
4	5.446	5.524	5.604	5.684	5.766	5.848	5.931	6.016	6.101	6.187
5	7.589	7.740	7.893	8.048	8.207	8.368	8.533	8.700	8.870	9.043
6	10.183	10.442	10.708	10.980	11.259	11.544	11.837	12.136	12.442	12.756
7	13.321	13.740	14.171	14.615	15.073	15.546	16.032	16.534	17.051	17.583
8	17.119	17.762	18.430	19.123	19.842	20.588	21.361	22.163	22.995	23.858
9	21.714	22.670	23.669	24.712	25.802	26.940	28.129	29.369	30.664	32.015
10	27.274	28.657	30.113	31.643	33.253	34.945	36.723	38.593	40.556	42.619
11	34.001	35.962	38.039	40.238	42.566	45.031	47.639	50.398	53.318	56.405
12	42.142	44.874	47.788	50.895	54.208	57.739	61.501	65.510	69.780	74.327
13	51.991	55.746	59.779	64.110	68.760	73.751	79.107	84.853	91.016	97.625
14	63.909	69.010	74.528	80.496	86.949	93.926	101.465	109.612	118.411	127.913
15	78.330	85.192	92.669	100.815	109.687	119.347	129.861	141.303	153.750	167.286
16	95.780	104.935	114.983	126.011	138.109	151.377	165.924	181.868	199.337	218.472
17	116.894	129.020	142.430	157.253	173.636	191.735	211.723	233.791	258.145	285.014
18	142.441	158.405	176.188	195.994	218.045	242.585	269.888	300.252	334.007	371.518
19	173.354	194.254	217.712	244.033	273.556	306.658	343.758	385.323	431.870	483.973
20	210.758	237.989	268.785	303.601	342.945	387.389	437.573	494.213	558.112	630.165
21	256.018	291.347	331.606	377.465	429.681	489.110	556.717	633.593	720.964	820.215
22	310.781	356.443	408.875	469.056	538.101	617.278	708.031	811.999	931.044	1067.280
23	377.045	435.861	503.917	582.630	673.626	778.771	900.199	1040.358	1202.047	1388.464
24	457.225	532.750	620.817	723.461	843.033	982.251	1144.253	1332.659	1551.640	1806.003
25	554.242	650.955	764.605	898.092	1054.791	1238.636	1454.201	1706.803	2002.616	2348.803
30	1445.151	1767.081	2160.491	2640.916	3227.174	3942.026	4812.977	5873.231	7162.824	8729.985
40	9749.525	12936.535	17154.046	22728.803	30088.655	39792.982	52571.998	69377.460	91447.963	120392.883
50	65617.202	94525.279	135992.154	195372.644	280255.693	401374.471	573877.874	819103.077	1167041.323	1659760.743

APPENDIX D: SUM OF AN ANNUITY OF $1 FOR N PERIODS (Continued)

n	31%	32%	33%	34%	35%	36%	37%	38%	39%	40%
1	1.000	1.000	1.000	1.000	1.000	1.000	1.000	1.000	1.000	1.000
2	2.310	2.320	2.330	2.340	2.350	2.360	2.370	2.380	2.390	2.400
3	4.026	4.062	4.099	4.136	4.173	4.210	4.247	4.284	4.322	4.360
4	6.274	6.362	6.452	6.542	6.633	6.725	6.818	6.912	7.008	7.104
5	9.219	9.398	9.581	9.766	9.954	10.146	10.341	10.539	10.741	10.946
6	13.077	13.406	13.742	14.086	14.438	14.799	15.167	15.544	15.930	16.324
7	18.131	18.696	19.277	19.876	20.492	21.126	21.779	22.451	23.142	23.853
8	24.752	25.678	26.638	27.633	28.664	29.732	30.837	31.982	33.168	34.395
9	33.425	34.895	36.429	38.029	39.696	41.435	43.247	45.135	47.103	49.153
10	44.786	47.062	49.451	51.958	54.590	57.352	60.248	63.287	66.473	69.814
11	59.670	63.122	66.769	70.624	74.697	78.998	83.540	88.336	93.398	98.739
12	79.168	84.320	89.803	95.637	101.841	108.437	115.450	122.904	130.823	139.235
13	104.710	112.303	120.439	129.153	138.485	148.475	159.167	170.607	182.844	195.929
14	138.170	149.240	161.183	174.065	187.954	202.926	219.059	236.438	255.153	275.300
15	182.003	197.997	215.374	234.247	254.738	276.979	301.111	327.284	355.662	386.420
16	239.423	262.356	287.447	314.891	344.897	377.692	413.522	452.652	495.370	541.988
17	314.645	347.309	383.305	422.954	466.611	514.661	567.524	625.659	689.565	759.784
18	413.185	459.449	510.795	567.758	630.925	700.939	778.509	864.410	959.495	1064.697
19	542.272	607.472	680.358	761.796	852.748	954.277	1067.557	1193.886	1334.698	1491.576
20	711.376	802.863	905.876	1021.807	1152.210	1298.817	1463.553	1648.563	1856.230	2089.206
21	932.903	1060.779	1205.814	1370.221	1556.484	1767.391	2006.067	2276.016	2581.160	2925.889
22	1223.103	1401.229	1604.733	1837.096	2102.253	2404.651	2749.312	3141.902	3588.813	4097.245
23	1603.264	1850.622	2135.295	2462.709	2839.042	3271.326	3767.557	4336.825	4989.450	5737.142
24	2101.276	2443.821	2840.943	3301.030	3833.706	4450.003	5162.554	5985.819	6936.335	8032.999
25	2753.672	3226.844	3779.454	4424.380	5176.504	6053.004	7073.699	8261.430	9642.506	11247.199
30	10632.746	12940.859	15738.077	19124.859	23221.570	28172.276	34149.230	41358.175	50044.592	60501.081
40	158300.134	207874.272	272613.194	357033.889	466960.385	609890.482	795462.089	1036045.327	1347493.183	1750091.741
50	#######	#######	#######	#######	#######	#######	#######	#######	#######	#######

D-4

APPENDIX E: PRESENT VALUE OF AN ANNUITY OF $1 FOR N PERIODS

n	1%	2%	3%	4%	5%	6%	7%	8%	9%	10%
1	0.990	0.980	0.971	0.962	0.952	0.943	0.935	0.926	0.917	0.909
2	1.970	1.942	1.913	1.886	1.859	1.833	1.808	1.783	1.759	1.736
3	2.941	2.884	2.829	2.775	2.723	2.673	2.624	2.577	2.531	2.487
4	3.902	3.808	3.717	3.630	3.546	3.465	3.387	3.312	3.240	3.170
5	4.853	4.713	4.580	4.452	4.329	4.212	4.100	3.993	3.890	3.791
6	5.795	5.601	5.417	5.242	5.076	4.917	4.767	4.623	4.486	4.355
7	6.728	6.472	6.230	6.002	5.786	5.582	5.389	5.206	5.033	4.868
8	7.652	7.325	7.020	6.733	6.463	6.210	5.971	5.747	5.535	5.335
9	8.566	8.162	7.786	7.435	7.108	6.802	6.515	6.247	5.995	5.759
10	9.471	8.983	8.530	8.111	7.722	7.360	7.024	6.710	6.418	6.145
11	10.368	9.787	9.253	8.760	8.306	7.887	7.499	7.139	6.805	6.495
12	11.255	10.575	9.954	9.385	8.863	8.384	7.943	7.536	7.161	6.814
13	12.134	11.348	10.635	9.986	9.394	8.853	8.358	7.904	7.487	7.103
14	13.004	12.106	11.296	10.563	9.899	9.295	8.745	8.244	7.786	7.367
15	13.865	12.849	11.938	11.118	10.380	9.712	9.108	8.559	8.061	7.606
16	14.718	13.578	12.561	11.652	10.838	10.106	9.447	8.851	8.313	7.824
17	15.562	14.292	13.166	12.166	11.274	10.477	9.763	9.122	8.544	8.022
18	16.398	14.992	13.754	12.659	11.690	10.828	10.059	9.372	8.756	8.201
19	17.226	15.678	14.324	13.134	12.085	11.158	10.336	9.604	8.950	8.365
20	18.046	16.351	14.877	13.590	12.462	11.470	10.594	9.818	9.129	8.514
21	18.857	17.011	15.415	14.029	12.821	11.764	10.836	10.017	9.292	8.649
22	19.660	17.658	15.937	14.451	13.163	12.042	11.061	10.201	9.442	8.772
23	20.456	18.292	16.444	14.857	13.489	12.303	11.272	10.371	9.580	8.883
24	21.243	18.914	16.936	15.247	13.799	12.550	11.469	10.529	9.707	8.985
25	22.023	19.523	17.413	15.622	14.094	12.783	11.654	10.675	9.823	9.077
30	25.808	22.396	19.600	17.292	15.372	13.765	12.409	11.258	10.274	9.427
40	32.835	27.355	23.115	19.793	17.159	15.046	13.332	11.925	10.757	9.779
50	39.196	31.424	25.730	21.482	18.256	15.762	13.801	12.233	10.962	9.915

APPENDIX E: PRESENT VALUE OF AN ANNUITY OF $1 FOR N PERIODS (Cont.)

n	11%	12%	13%	14%	15%	16%	17%	18%	19%	20%
1	0.901	0.893	0.885	0.877	0.870	0.862	0.855	0.847	0.840	0.833
2	1.713	1.690	1.668	1.647	1.626	1.605	1.585	1.566	1.547	1.528
3	2.444	2.402	2.361	2.322	2.283	2.246	2.210	2.174	2.140	2.106
4	3.102	3.037	2.974	2.914	2.855	2.798	2.743	2.690	2.639	2.589
5	3.696	3.605	3.517	3.433	3.352	3.274	3.199	3.127	3.058	2.991
6	4.231	4.111	3.998	3.889	3.784	3.685	3.589	3.498	3.410	3.326
7	4.712	4.564	4.423	4.288	4.160	4.039	3.922	3.812	3.706	3.605
8	5.146	4.968	4.799	4.639	4.487	4.344	4.207	4.078	3.954	3.837
9	5.537	5.328	5.132	4.946	4.772	4.607	4.451	4.303	4.163	4.031
10	5.889	5.650	5.426	5.216	5.019	4.833	4.659	4.494	4.339	4.192
11	6.207	5.938	5.687	5.453	5.234	5.029	4.836	4.656	4.486	4.327
12	6.492	6.194	5.918	5.660	5.421	5.197	4.988	4.793	4.611	4.439
13	6.750	6.424	6.122	5.842	5.583	5.342	5.118	4.910	4.715	4.533
14	6.982	6.628	6.302	6.002	5.724	5.468	5.229	5.008	4.802	4.611
15	7.191	6.811	6.462	6.142	5.847	5.575	5.324	5.092	4.876	4.675
16	7.379	6.974	6.604	6.265	5.954	5.668	5.405	5.162	4.938	4.730
17	7.549	7.120	6.729	6.373	6.047	5.749	5.475	5.222	4.990	4.775
18	7.702	7.250	6.840	6.467	6.128	5.818	5.534	5.273	5.033	4.812
19	7.839	7.366	6.938	6.550	6.198	5.877	5.584	5.316	5.070	4.843
20	7.963	7.469	7.025	6.623	6.259	5.929	5.628	5.353	5.101	4.870
21	8.075	7.562	7.102	6.687	6.312	5.973	5.665	5.384	5.127	4.891
22	8.176	7.645	7.170	6.743	6.359	6.011	5.696	5.410	5.149	4.909
23	8.266	7.718	7.230	6.792	6.399	6.044	5.723	5.432	5.167	4.925
24	8.348	7.784	7.283	6.835	6.434	6.073	5.746	5.451	5.182	4.937
25	8.422	7.843	7.330	6.873	6.464	6.097	5.766	5.467	5.195	4.948
30	8.694	8.055	7.496	7.003	6.566	6.177	5.829	5.517	5.235	4.979
40	8.951	8.244	7.634	7.105	6.642	6.233	5.871	5.548	5.258	4.997
50	9.042	8.304	7.675	7.133	6.661	6.246	5.880	5.554	5.262	4.999

APPENDIX E: PRESENT VALUE OF AN ANNUITY OF $1 FOR N PERIODS (Cont.)

n	21%	22%	23%	24%	25%	26%	27%	28%	29%	30%
1	0.826	0.820	0.813	0.806	0.800	0.794	0.787	0.781	0.775	0.769
2	1.509	1.492	1.474	1.457	1.440	1.424	1.407	1.392	1.376	1.361
3	2.074	2.042	2.011	1.981	1.952	1.923	1.896	1.868	1.842	1.816
4	2.540	2.494	2.448	2.404	2.362	2.320	2.280	2.241	2.203	2.166
5	2.926	2.864	2.803	2.745	2.689	2.635	2.583	2.532	2.483	2.436
6	3.245	3.167	3.092	3.020	2.951	2.885	2.821	2.759	2.700	2.643
7	3.508	3.416	3.327	3.242	3.161	3.083	3.009	2.937	2.868	2.802
8	3.726	3.619	3.518	3.421	3.329	3.241	3.156	3.076	2.999	2.925
9	3.905	3.786	3.673	3.566	3.463	3.366	3.273	3.184	3.100	3.019
10	4.054	3.923	3.799	3.682	3.571	3.465	3.364	3.269	3.178	3.092
11	4.177	4.035	3.902	3.776	3.656	3.543	3.437	3.335	3.239	3.147
12	4.278	4.127	3.985	3.851	3.725	3.606	3.493	3.387	3.286	3.190
13	4.362	4.203	4.053	3.912	3.780	3.656	3.538	3.427	3.322	3.223
14	4.432	4.265	4.108	3.962	3.824	3.695	3.573	3.459	3.351	3.249
15	4.489	4.315	4.153	4.001	3.859	3.726	3.601	3.483	3.373	3.268
16	4.536	4.357	4.189	4.033	3.887	3.751	3.623	3.503	3.390	3.283
17	4.576	4.391	4.219	4.059	3.910	3.771	3.640	3.518	3.403	3.295
18	4.608	4.419	4.243	4.080	3.928	3.786	3.654	3.529	3.413	3.304
19	4.635	4.442	4.263	4.097	3.942	3.799	3.664	3.539	3.421	3.311
20	4.657	4.460	4.279	4.110	3.954	3.808	3.673	3.546	3.427	3.316
21	4.675	4.476	4.292	4.121	3.963	3.816	3.679	3.551	3.432	3.320
22	4.690	4.488	4.302	4.130	3.970	3.822	3.684	3.556	3.436	3.323
23	4.703	4.499	4.311	4.137	3.976	3.827	3.689	3.559	3.438	3.325
24	4.713	4.507	4.318	4.143	3.981	3.831	3.692	3.562	3.441	3.327
25	4.721	4.514	4.323	4.147	3.985	3.834	3.694	3.564	3.442	3.329
30	4.746	4.534	4.339	4.160	3.995	3.842	3.701	3.569	3.447	3.332
40	4.760	4.544	4.347	4.166	3.999	3.846	3.703	3.571	3.448	3.333
50	4.762	4.545	4.348	4.167	4.000	3.846	3.704	3.571	3.448	3.333

APPENDIX E: PRESENT VALUE OF AN ANNUITY OF $1 FOR N PERIODS (Cont.)

n	31%	32%	33%	34%	35%	36%	37%	38%	39%	40%
1	0.763	0.758	0.752	0.746	0.741	0.735	0.730	0.725	0.719	0.714
2	1.346	1.331	1.317	1.303	1.289	1.276	1.263	1.250	1.237	1.224
3	1.791	1.766	1.742	1.719	1.696	1.673	1.652	1.630	1.609	1.589
4	2.130	2.096	2.062	2.029	1.997	1.966	1.935	1.906	1.877	1.849
5	2.390	2.345	2.302	2.260	2.220	2.181	2.143	2.106	2.070	2.035
6	2.588	2.534	2.483	2.433	2.385	2.339	2.294	2.251	2.209	2.168
7	2.739	2.677	2.619	2.562	2.508	2.455	2.404	2.355	2.308	2.263
8	2.854	2.786	2.721	2.658	2.598	2.540	2.485	2.432	2.380	2.331
9	2.942	2.868	2.798	2.730	2.665	2.603	2.544	2.487	2.432	2.379
10	3.009	2.930	2.855	2.784	2.715	2.649	2.587	2.527	2.469	2.414
11	3.060	2.978	2.899	2.824	2.752	2.683	2.618	2.555	2.496	2.438
12	3.100	3.013	2.931	2.853	2.779	2.708	2.641	2.576	2.515	2.456
13	3.129	3.040	2.956	2.876	2.799	2.727	2.658	2.592	2.529	2.469
14	3.152	3.061	2.974	2.892	2.814	2.740	2.670	2.603	2.539	2.478
15	3.170	3.076	2.988	2.905	2.825	2.750	2.679	2.611	2.546	2.484
16	3.183	3.088	2.999	2.914	2.834	2.757	2.685	2.616	2.551	2.489
17	3.193	3.097	3.007	2.921	2.840	2.763	2.690	2.621	2.555	2.492
18	3.201	3.104	3.012	2.926	2.844	2.767	2.693	2.624	2.557	2.494
19	3.207	3.109	3.017	2.930	2.848	2.770	2.696	2.626	2.559	2.496
20	3.211	3.113	3.020	2.933	2.850	2.772	2.698	2.627	2.561	2.497
21	3.215	3.116	3.023	2.935	2.852	2.773	2.699	2.629	2.562	2.498
22	3.217	3.118	3.025	2.936	2.853	2.775	2.700	2.629	2.562	2.498
23	3.219	3.120	3.026	2.938	2.854	2.775	2.701	2.630	2.563	2.499
24	3.221	3.121	3.027	2.939	2.855	2.776	2.701	2.630	2.563	2.499
25	3.222	3.122	3.028	2.939	2.856	2.777	2.702	2.631	2.563	2.499
30	3.225	3.124	3.030	2.941	2.857	2.778	2.702	2.631	2.564	2.500
40	3.226	3.125	3.030	2.941	2.857	2.778	2.703	2.632	2.564	2.500
50	3.226	3.125	3.030	2.941	2.857	2.778	2.703	2.632	2.564	2.500

Self Teaching Supplement:
Capital Budgeting Techniques

I.   Net Present Value and Profitability Index Methods

In making investment decisions regarding fixed assets, the analyst compares the benefits of projects with their associated costs. Unfortunately, this comparison is complicated by the fact that the benefits and costs accruing from a given project usually do not occur in the same time period and thus are not directly comparable. This incomparability is a result of the time value of money (i.e., a dollar received today is worth more than a dollar received in the future). This comes about because a dollar today can be put into the bank and earn interest, resulting in a larger sum in the future. In economic terms, we refer to the time value of money as its opportunity cost.

A.   Using the net present value and profitability index

In this section we compare the present value of a project's benefits with the present value of its cost. The difference in these present values is referred to as the net present value, and the ratio of benefits to cost is called the profitability index. Definitionally, then

$$\text{net present value} = \left(\begin{array}{c}\text{present value of}\\ \text{future net cash flows}\end{array}\right) - \left(\begin{array}{c}\text{initial}\\ \text{cash outlay}\end{array}\right)$$

$$\text{profitability index} = \frac{\left(\begin{array}{c}\text{present value of}\\ \text{future net cash flows}\end{array}\right)}{\left(\begin{array}{c}\text{initial}\\ \text{cash outlay}\end{array}\right)}$$

Although both capital-budgeting techniques provide us with the same accept-reject decision, they may rank two or more projects differently. This difference results because the net-present-value criterion measures the total dollar value of a project, while the profitability index measures its value relative to project cost. The decision criteria used in applying these decision tools are:

	NPV	PI
Accept	≥ 0	≥ 1
Reject	< 0	< 1

SOLVED PROBLEMS

EXERCISE 1

The initial cash outlay of a project is $100; the present value of the cash flows is $75. Compute the project's net present value and its profitability index. Should it be accepted?

SOLUTION

$$\text{net present value} = \left(\begin{array}{c} \text{present value of} \\ \text{future net cash flows} \end{array} \right) - \left(\begin{array}{c} \text{initial} \\ \text{cash outlay} \end{array} \right)$$

$$= \$75 - \$100 = -\$25$$

$$\text{profitability index} = \frac{\left(\begin{array}{c} \text{present value of} \\ \text{future net cash flows} \end{array} \right)}{\left(\begin{array}{c} \text{initial} \\ \text{cash outlay} \end{array} \right)}$$

$$= \frac{\$75}{\$100} = 0.75$$

Thus, the project should be rejected because its net present value is negative and its profitability index is less than 1.

EXERCISE 2

The present value of a project's future net cash flow is $580 and the initial cash outlay is $500. What is the project's net present value and what is its profitability index? Should the project be accepted?

SOLUTION

NPV = $580 - $500 = $80

PI = $\dfrac{\$580}{\$500}$ = 1.16

This project should be accepted because the project's net present value is positive and its profitability index is greater than 1.0.

EXERCISE 3

A project's net present value is $300, the initial outlay is $500. What is the present value of the project's net cash flows?

SOLUTION

NPV = PV of project's net cash flows - initial outlay

$300 = PV of project's net cash flows - $500

$800 = PV of project's net cash flows

EXERCISE 4

A project's profitability index is 1.5, and the present value of its net cash flows is $450. What is the project's initial cash outlay?

SOLUTION

$$P = \frac{\left(\begin{array}{c}\text{present value of}\\\text{future net cash flows}\end{array}\right)}{\left(\begin{array}{c}\text{initial}\\\text{cash outlay}\end{array}\right)}$$

1.5 = $\dfrac{\$450}{X}$

X = $300

EXERCISE 5

If either the net-present-value criterion or the profitability index gives an accept signal, will the other criteria give a similar signal?

SOLUTION

Yes. The net-present-value and profitability index will always give similar accept-reject signals. Any time the present value of future net cash flows is greater than the initial outlay, the net-present-value criterion will be positive, signaling accept, and the profitability index will be greater than 1.0, signaling accept. However, because of size differences in projects, a small project, which is relatively more profitable than a project requiring a larger initial outlay, may have a smaller net present value. In this case, unless there is a limit on the amount of funds that is allocated, the net-present-value criterion should be used.

B. **Compounding and Discounting: Single Cash Flows**

To determine the present value of future cash flows, it is necessary to discount those cash flows back to the present. As demonstrated in Chapter 3 of the text, discounting cash flows back to the present is merely the reverse of compounding. For example, if we put $100 (P) in the bank, earning a rate of 10% (i) annually, at the end of 1 year (n) we would have $110 ($FV_1$):

$$FV_1 \quad = \quad PV\,(1+i)$$

$$\$110 \quad = \quad \$100\,(1+0.10)$$

Correspondingly, at the end of 3 years we would have $133.10:

$$\$133.10 \quad = \quad \$100\,(1+0.10)^3$$

On the other hand, with an opportunity rate of 10%, the present value (PV) of $110 to be received in 1 year can be found as follows:

$$\$110 \quad = \quad \$100\,(1+0.10)$$

$$PV \quad = \quad \$110 \left(\frac{1}{(1+0.10)} \right)$$

$$= \quad \$100$$

The present value of $133.10 to be received in 3 years is found similarly:

$$\$100 \quad = \quad \$133.10 \left(\frac{1}{(1+0.10)^3} \right)$$

SOLVED PROBLEMS

EXERCISE 1

What is the present value of $300 to be received in 3 years discounted at:

(a)   10% per annum?
(b)   5% per annum?
(c)   100% per annum?

SOLUTION

(a) PV $= FV_n \left(\frac{1}{(1+i)^n} \right)$

$$= \quad \$300 \left(\frac{1}{(1+0.10)^3} \right)$$

$$= \quad \frac{\$300}{1.331} \quad = \quad \$225.39$$

(b)   PV $= \$300 \left(\frac{1}{(1+0.05)^3} \right)$

$$= \quad \frac{\$300}{1.157625} = \quad \$259.15$$

(c)   PV $= \$300 \left(\dfrac{1}{(1+01.0)^3} \right)$

$\quad\quad\quad = \dfrac{\$300}{8} = \$37.50$

EXERCISE 2

If the appropriate discount rate is 8%, what is the present value of $300 to be received in:

(a)   5 years?
(b)   10 years?
(c)   25 years?

SOLUTION

(a)   PV $= FV_n \left(\dfrac{1}{(1+i)^n} \right)$

$\quad\quad\quad = \$300 \left(\dfrac{1}{(1+0.08)^5} \right)$

$\quad\quad\quad = \dfrac{\$300}{1.4693} = \$204.18$

(b)   PV $= \$300 \left(\dfrac{1}{(1+0.08)^{10}} \right)$

$\quad\quad\quad = \dfrac{\$300}{2.15189} = \$138.96$

(c) $\quad$ PV $\quad = \$300 \left(\dfrac{1}{(1+0.08)^{25}} \right)$

$$= \dfrac{\$300}{6.8485} = \$43.81$$

Fortunately, it is not necessary to do the individual calculation for $1/(1 + i)^n$ because in the table in Appendix C (hereafter referred to as Table C with the table values being referred to as $PVIF_{i,n}$) of the text the results of these calculations are presented for a large number of combinations of i and n. Thus, in order to determine the value of $1/(1 + 0.08)^5$ we need only look in the row of Table C corresponding to the fifth period and the 8% column to find an appropriate value of 0.681. Similarly, in Appendix B a table is provided (hereafter referred to as Table B with the table values being referred to as $FVIF_{i,n}$) which gives the value of $(1 + i)^n$ for various combinations of i and n. This table can be used in compounding.

SELF-TEST 1

1. What is the present value of $250 to be received in 10 years if the appropriate discount rate is 8%?

2. How much must I put in the bank compounded annually at 6% to have $5,000 at the end of 10 years?

3. If a new machine costs $5,000 and will return $3,000 the first year, $4,000 the second year, $2,000 the third year, and my opportunity rate on money is 8%, what is the project's profitability index?

4. What is the NPV for the project in question 3? Should it be accepted?

5. If a new tractor costs $10,000 and will return $3,000 the first year, $5,000 the second year, and $4,000 the third year, calculate the net present value and profitability index using a 10% discount rate. Should the project be accepted?

6. Calculate the net present value and profitability index for the following. Assume a 12% discount rate:

Year	Benefit (+) or Cost (-)
0	$-8,000
1	+3,000
2	+6,000
3	+2,000
4	+1,000
5	-1,000

7. What is the net present value of a bond that pays $100 per year in interest at the end of each year for 10 years, and additionally at the end of 10 years will pay the $1,000 par value if the appropriate discount rate is 8% and the bond costs $1,093?

C. Compounding and Discounting: Annuities

Problem 7 of Self Test 1 was actually an annuity problem. An annuity is simply a series of fixed payments for a specified number of years. This situation comes up frequently in finance, and in order to make the calculation of the present value of an annuity easier, you are provided with the present value of an annuity table (hereafter referred to as Table E with the table values being referred to as $PVIFA_{i,n}$) in Appendix E of the text, which gives present-value factors for an annuity. In addition, a compound annuity or sum of an annuity of $1 for n periods table (hereafter referred to as Table D with the table values referred to as $FVIFA_{i,n}$) is provided in Appendix D of the text. Now, in order to determine the present value of $1,000 received at the end of each year for 5 years, discounted back to present at 7%, you have two alternatives. You could use Table C and discount each one of the five $1,000 flows individually as follows:

$$FV_n \left(\frac{1}{(1+0.07)^1} \right) = \$1,000 \, (0.935) = \$935.00$$

$$FV_n \left(\frac{1}{(1+0.07)^2} \right) = \$1,000 \, (0.873) = \$873.00$$

F-8

$$FV_n\left(\frac{1}{(1+0.07)^3}\right) \quad = \quad \$1,000\,(0.816) \quad = \quad \$816.00$$

$$FV_n\left(\frac{1}{(1+0.07)^4}\right) \quad = \quad \$1,000\,(0.763) \quad = \quad \$763.00$$

$$FV_n\left(\frac{1}{(1+0.07)^5}\right) \quad = \quad \$1,000\,(0.713) \quad = \quad \underline{\$713.00}$$

$$\underline{\$4,100.00}$$

Alternatively, you could look up the annuity discount factor in Table E. The annuity factor for 5 years at 7% is 4.100; multiplying this times $1,000 gives $4,100 - the same answer you got using Table C. This is because you really only have one table, Table C, the values of which have been summed to form Table E. Thus, the annuity discount factor for 5 years at 7% in Table E is equal to the sum of the discount factors for years 1 through 5 at 7% as found in Table C. Therefore, the annuity table value for n years at i% is equal to:

$$PVIFA_{i,n} \quad = \quad \left(\sum_{t=1}^{n} \frac{1}{(1-i)^t}\right) \quad = \quad \sum_{t=1}^{n} \left(PVIF_{i,n}\right)$$

SOLVED PROBLEMS

EXERCISE 1

Pick any number in Table E; note the number of years (call it n) and the discount rate (call it i). Now look in Table C and add up the table values in the i discount rate column for the first n years. What do you find?

SOLUTION

The value found in Table E is equal (except perhaps for minor rounding errors) to the value found from summing the values in Table C.

EXERCISE 2

What is the present value of $50 to be received each year for 5 years if the appropriate discount rate is 8%? Solve this problem by using Table C.

SOLUTION

Present value

$$= \$50\,(PVIF_{8\%,\ 1\ yr.}) + \$50\,(PVIF_{8\%,\ 2\ yr.})$$
$$+ \$50\,(PVIF_{8\%,\ 3\ yr.}) + \$50\,(PVIF_{8\%,\ 4\ yr.})$$
$$+ \$50\,(PVIF_{8\%,\ 5\ yr.})$$

$$= \$50(0.926) + \$50(0.857) + \$50(0.794) + \$50(0.735) + \$50(0.681)$$

$$= \$46.30 + \$42.85 + \$39.70 + \$36.75 + \$34.05$$

$$= \$199.65$$

EXERCISE 3

Solve Exercise 2 using Table E.

SOLUTION

$$\text{Present value} \quad = \quad \$50(PVIFA_{8\%,\ 5\ yr.}) \ = \ \$50\,(3.993)$$

$$= \quad \$199.65$$

EXERCISE 4

What is the NPV of a bond that yields $80 per year in interest at the end of each year for the next 15 years and matures in 15 years, at which time it pays an additional $1,000; it is currently selling for $800 and your discount rate is 10%?

SOLUTION

$$NPV \ = \ \$\text{-}800 + \$80(PVIFA_{10\%,\ 15\ yr.}) + \$1,000(PVIF_{10\%,\ 15\ yr.})$$

$$= \ \$\text{-}800 + \$80(7.606) + \$1,000(0.239)$$

$$= \ \$-800 + \$608.48 + \$239.00$$

$$= \ \$47.48$$

EXERCISE 5

What is the profitability index for the bond described in Exercise 4?

SOLUTION

$$PI \ = \ \frac{\$847.48}{\$800} \ = \ 1.059$$

EXERCISE 6

Given the following cash flows:

Year	Cash Flow
0	$-10,000
1	+ 5,000
2	+ 5,000
3	+ 5,000
4	+ 5,000
5	+ 5,000
6	+ 5,000
7	+10,000

What is the NPV of this project given an appropriate discount rate of

(a)   5%?
(b)   10%?
(c)   30%?

SOLUTION

(a)   NPV = $-10,000 + \$5,000(PVIFA_{5\%, \, 6 \, yr.}) + \$10,000(PVIF_{5\%, \, 7 \, yr.})$
       = $-10,000 + \$5,000(5.076) + \$10,000(0.711)$
       = $-10,000 + \$25,380 + \$7,110$
       = $22,490$

(b) NPV $=$ $-10,000 + \$5,000(\text{PVIFA}_{10\%, \, 6 \, yr.}) + \$10,000(\text{PVIF}_{10\%, \, 7 \, yr.})$
     $=$ $-10,000 + \$5,000(4.355) + \$10,000(0.513)$
     $=$ $-10,000 + \$21,775 + \$5,130$
     $=$ $16,905$

(c) NPV $=$ $-10,000 + \$5,000(\text{PVIFA}_{30\%, \, 6 \, yr.}) + \$10,000(\text{PVIF}_{30\%, \, 7 \, yr.})$
     $=$ $-10,000 + \$5,000(2.643) + \$10,000(0.159)$
     $=$ $-10,000 + \$13,215 + \$1,590$
     $=$ $4,805$

SELF-TEST 2

1. What is the NPV of the following cash flows if the appropriate discount rate is 20%?

Year	Cash Flow
0	$-15,000
1	+ 2,000
2	+ 2,000
3	+ 4,000
4	+ 5,000
5	+ 6,000

What is the profitability index? Should the project be accepted?

2. For how many years must $1,000 compound at 8% to accumulate to $2,000?

3. At what rate must $1,000 compound to accumulate to $3,000 in 7 years?

4. How much must you put in the bank compounded annually at 8% to accumulate to $3,000 at the end of 10 years?

5. What is the present value of $100 to be received at the end of each of the next 10 years discounted back to the present at

    (a)   5%?
    (b)   10%?
    (c)   20%?
    (d)   30%?

6.   How much is $50 worth if it is to be received at the end of 4 years if the appropriate discount rate is

(a)   10%?
(b)   20%?
(c)   0%?
(d)   100%?

7.   What is the future value of $100 if it is placed in the bank for 5 years and compounded at 16%?

(a)   Annually?
(b)   Semiannually?
(c)   Quarterly?

8.   A company is examining a new machine to replace an existing machine that currently has a book value of $5,000 and can be sold for $2,000. The old machine has 5 years of expected life left, is being depreciated on a simplified straight-line basis, and will have a salvage value of zero in 5 years. The new machine will perform the same task but more efficiently, resulting in cash benefits before depreciation and taxes of $10,000. The expected life of the new machine is 5 years; it costs $20,000 and has no salvage value at the end of the fifth year. Assuming simplified straight-line depreciation, a 40% tax rate, and an appropriate discount rate of 14%, find the NPV and profitability index of the project.

II.   The Internal-Rate-of-Return Method

In the previous section we made capital-budgeting decisions through the use of the profitability index and net present-value criteria, by comparing the present value of the benefits of the project with the present value of its costs either through division (determining the profitability index) or subtraction (determining a net present value). In each case you were supplied with an appropriate discount rate or cost of capital with which to determine the present value of future flows. You will now examine a method of evaluating projects that does not rely on an input discount rate but determines the discount rate that would make the project's NPV = 0, or, alternatively, makes its profitability index = 1.0. With the PI and NPV criteria we have a measure of the relative profitability and absolute profitability of the project, with all flows adjusted for the time value of money. The next criterion we examine, the internal rate of return, can be thought of as a rate of return or yield on the

F-13

project. The decision rules on this criterion can be stated as follows: If the IRR is greater than or equal to the required rate of return or hurdle rate, the project should be accepted; otherwise, the project should be rejected. Although this seems quite straightforward and easy to understand, one finds that the solution process is often complex and time-consuming.

A. The Internal Rate of Return: The Case of a Single Cash inflow

The internal rate of return is defined as that rate, IRR, which equates the present value of a project's anticipated cash inflows with the present value of the relevant cash outflows. Where ACF_t is the cash flow for period t, whether it be positive (an inflow) or negative (an outflow), and n is the last period in which any cash flow is expected, the internal rate of return is represented by IRR in equation (A.1):

$$\sum_{t=0}^{n} \frac{ACF_t}{(1 + IRR)^t} = 0 \qquad (A.1)$$

A solution to this problem becomes quite simple in the case in which the only outlay occurs in time period 0 (the initial outlay, IO) and <u>only one</u> cash inflow occurs, say in time period t:

$$IO = \frac{ACF_t}{(1 + IRR)^t}$$

Since you can determine a numerical value for IO/ACF_t and you know that Table C in the text gives you values for $1/(1 + IRR)$, we can easily solve for IRR. All we have to do is look in Table C in the nth row (corresponding to the number of years until the cash inflow) until we find the value IO/ACF_t; the column that gives this value indicates the appropriate value of IRR.

SOLVED PROBLEMS

EXERCISE 1

What is the internal rate of return on a project with an initial outlay of $6,000 which in the ninth year will produce one cash inflow of $18,000?

SOLUTION

$$\$6{,}000 = \frac{\$18{,}000}{(1+\text{IRR})^9}$$

$$\frac{\$6{,}000}{\$18{,}000} = \frac{1}{(1+\text{IRR})^9}$$

$$0.333 = \frac{1}{(1+\text{IRR})^9}$$

The value of 0.333 is found in the 9-year row of Table C in the 13% column; thus, 13% is the project's internal rate of return.

EXERCISE 2

Given the following cash flows, what is the project's internal rate of return?

Year	Cash Flow
0	$-10,000
5	+40,000

SOLUTION

$$\frac{\$10{,}000}{\$40{,}000} = \frac{1}{(1+\text{IRR})^5}$$

$$0.25 = \frac{1}{(1+\text{IRR})^5}$$

Looking in Table C, IRR = 32%

EXERCISE 3

If a project requires an initial outlay of $6,000 and will return $10,000 in year 13, what is its internal rate of return?

SOLUTION

$$\frac{\$6{,}000}{\$10{,}000} \quad = \quad \frac{1}{(1+IRR)^{13}}$$

$$0.6 \quad = \quad \frac{1}{(1+IRR)^{13}}$$

Looking in Table C, IRR = 4%

The accept-reject criteria for the internal-rate of-return method states that if the project's internal rate of return is greater than the required rate of return or hurdle rate, the project should be accepted; otherwise, the project should be rejected. In other words,

IRR ($\geq$) required rate of return, Accept

IRR < required rate of return, Reject

Thus, if the required rate of return in Exercises 1 through 3 were 10%, the projects examined in Exercises 1 and 2 would be accepted, and the project in Exercise 3 would be rejected.

B.   The Internal Rate of Return: Multiple and Equal Cash Inflows

In the case in which there is more than one cash inflow resulting from a project's acceptance, and the cash inflows form an annuity, a similar approach to that just outlined but using Table E instead of Table C will result in a correct solution. In this case the simplification proceeds as follows:

$$IO \quad = \quad \sum_{t=0}^{T} \frac{ACFt}{(1+IRR)^{t}}$$

If all the ACF values are equal and occur periodically (e. g., annually),we have an annuity. The value of the annuity discount factor,

$\sum_{t=0}^{T} 1/(1+IRR)^{t}$, can be found in Table E. Since we know the term of

the annuity, n years, when solving for IRR we need merely look in the

T-year row until we find the value IO/ACF$_t$; then looking to the column heading yields the internal rate of return.

SOLVED PROBLEMS

EXERCISE 1

What is the internal rate of return on a project with an initial outlay of $24,000 which will produce cash inflows of $6,000 for each of the next 15 years?

SOLUTION

$$\$24,000 \quad = \quad \sum_{t=0}^{15} \frac{\$6,000}{(1+\mathrm{IRR})^t}$$

$$4.0 \quad = \quad \sum_{t=0}^{15} \frac{1}{(1+\mathrm{IRR})^t}$$

Looking in Table E, IRR = 24%.

EXERCISE 2

What is the internal rate of return on a project with an initial outlay of $18,000 which will produce cash inflows of $3,000 for each year for the next 9 years?

SOLUTION

$$\$18,000 \quad = \quad \sum_{t=0}^{9} \frac{\$3,000}{(1+\mathrm{IRR})^t}$$

$$6.0 \quad = \quad \sum_{t=0}^{9} \frac{1}{(1+\mathrm{IRR})^t}$$

Looking in Table E, IRR = 9%.

EXERCISE 3

Given the following cash flows, what is this project's internal rate of return?

Year	Cash Flow
0	$20,000
1	5,000
2	5,000
3	5,000
4	5,000
5	5,000

SOLUTION

$$\$20,000 = \sum_{t=0}^{5} \frac{\$5,000}{(1+IRR)^t}$$

$$4.0 = \sum_{t=0}^{5} \frac{1}{(1+IRR)^t}$$

Looking in Table E, IRR = 8%.

For Exercises 1 through 3, if the required rate of return were 10%, the project in Exercise 1 would be accepted and the projects in Exercises 2 and 3 would be rejected.

C.   **The Internal Rate of Return: Multiple and Unequal Cash Flows**

The solution using the internal-rate-of-return criterion becomes more complex when there are unequal cash inflows resulting from a project's acceptance. In this case, the solution can only be found by trial and error, or with the use of a good financial calculator, or an even not so good calculator. Without the calculator, we first arbitrarily pick a return and solve the problem; then, depending on the result, raise or lower that rate until the present value of the inflows equals the present value of the outflows.

SOLVED PROBLEMS

EXERCISE 1

What is the internal rate of return on a project that costs $20,000 and returns $3,000 per year for the first 4 years and $5,000 per year in years 5 through 8?

SOLUTION

$$\$20{,}000 \;=\; \sum_{t=1}^{4} \frac{\$3{,}000}{(1+\text{IRR})^t} \;+\; \sum_{t=5}^{8} \frac{\$5{,}000}{(1+\text{IRR})^t}$$

First, solve the problem using a discount rate picked arbitrarily. Try 20%. In this case this equation reduces to

$$\$20{,}000 \;=\; \$3{,}000(2.589) + \$7{,}000(3.837 - 2.589)$$

$$=\; \$7{,}767 + \$8{,}736$$

$$\neq\; \$16{,}503$$

Thus, 20% is not this project's internal rate of return. If it were the internal rate of return, the present value of the inflows would equal the present value of the outflows; but the present value of the inflows is much less than the present value of the outflows. Since all the inflows occur in the future, the present value of these flows will increase as the discount rate is lowered, so here you should try a lower discount rate. If you try 13%, this equation becomes

$$\$20{,}000 \;=\; \$3{,}000(2.974) + \$7{,}000(4.799 - 2.974)$$

$$=\; \$8{,}922 + \$21{,}775$$

$$\neq\; \$21{,}697$$

This time the present value of the inflows is less than the present value of the outflows. In order to raise the present value of the inflows, the discount rate must be lowered. This time try 15%.

$$\$20,000 \ = \ \$3,000(2.855) + \$7,000(4.487 - 2.855)$$

$$= \ \$8,565 + \$11,424$$

$$\approx \ \$19,989$$

Now the present value of the inflows is approximately equal to the present value of the outflows using a discount rate of 15%; the project's internal rate of return is very close to 15%.

EXERCISE 2

Given the following cash flows, what is the project's IRR?

Year	Cash Flow
0	$-12,000
1	+ 4,000
2	+ 4,000
3	+ 4,000
4	+ 4,000
5	+ 4,000
6	+ 2,000

SOLUTION

First, try 30%:

$$\$12,000 \ = \ \$4,000(2.436) + \$2,000(0.207)$$

$$= \ \$9,744 + \$414$$

$$\neq \ \$10,158$$

Since the present value of the cash inflows is too low, you must lower the discount rate and try again. This time, try 23%:

$$\$12,000 \ = \ \$4,000(2.689) + \$2,000(0.262)$$

$$= \ \$10,756 + \$524$$

$$\neq \ \$11,280$$

Again, the present value of the cash inflows is too low. Therefore, the discount rate is lowered and the problem is trued again. Next, try 20%:

$$\$12,000 \ = \ \$4,000(2.991) + \$2,000(0.335)$$

$$= \ \$11,964 + \$670$$

$$\neq \ \$12,634$$

Since the present value of the cash inflows is too high, the discount rate must be raised. We arbitrarily raise it to 23%:

$$\$12,000 \ = \ \$4,000(2.803) + \$2,000(0.289)$$

$$= \ \$11,212 + \$578$$

$$\neq \ \$11,790$$

This time the present value of the inflows is too low; thus, the discount rate is lowered. We now try 22%:

$$\$12,000 \ = \ \$4,000(2.864) + \$2,000(0.303)$$

$$= \ \$11,456 + \$606$$

$$\approx \ \$12,062$$

Thus, the IRR for this problem is between 22% and 23%, and closer to 22%.

EXERCISE 3

What is the IRR associated with this project?

Year	Cash Flow
0	$-10,000
1	+ 3,000
2	+ 6,000
3	+ 9,000

SOLUTION

Try 20%:

$$\$10,000 = \$3,000(0.833) + \$6,000(0.694) \\ + \$9,000 (0.579)$$

$$= \$2,499 + \$4,164 + \$5,211$$

$$\neq \$11,874$$

The present value of the cash inflows is too large; therefore, the discount rate must be raised. Try 30%:

$$\$10,000 = \$3,000(0.769) + \$6,000(0.592) \\ + \$9,000(0.455)$$

$$= \$2,307 + \$3,552 + \$4,095$$

$$\neq \$9,954$$

Now it is too small; so try 29%:

$$\$10,000 = \$3,000(0.775) + \$6,000(0.601) \\ + \$9,000(0.466)$$

$$= \$2,325 + \$3,606 + \$4,194$$

$$\neq \$10,125$$

Thus, this project's IRR is just under 30%.

As you can see by now, calculating the IRR can become quite time-consuming when a trial-and-error search is necessitated. If it is necessary, remember the following guidelines:

1. Always try a larger discount rate (or trial IRR) when the present value of the cash inflows is larger than the initial outlay.

2. Always try a smaller discount rate (or trial IRR) when the present value of the cash inflows is smaller than the initial cash outlay.

SELF-TEST 3

1.   What is the internal rate of return on a project that requires an initial outlay of $10,000 and returns $14,000 at the end of the fifth year?

2.   What is the internal rate of return on a project that requires an initial outlay of $700 and returns $1,857 at the end of the twentieth year?

3.   What is the internal rate of return on a project that requires a $30,000 outlay and returns $6,000 at the end of each of the next 10 years?

4.   What is the internal rate of return on a project that requires an initial outlay of $20,000 and returns $3,928 at the end of each year for the next 15 years?

5.   Given the following cash flows, determine an internal rate of return.

Year	Cash Flow
0	$-40,000
1	+10,000
2	+10,000
3	+10,000
4	+10,000
5	+10,000
6	+15,000

6.   Given the following cash flows, determine an internal rate of return.

Year	Cash Flow
0	$-61,630
1	+10,000
2	+10,000
3	+10,000
4	+10,000
5	+10,000
6	+10,000
7	+70,000

7. Given the following cash flows, determine an internal rate of return.

Year	Cash Flow
0	$-2,992
1	+700
2	+1,400
3	+3,000

8. Given the following cash flows, determine an internal rate of return.

Year	Cash Flow
0	$5,492
1	2,000
2	2,000
3	4,000
4	3,000

9. What is the internal rate of return on a project that requires an initial outlay of $1,000 and returns $4,000 at the end of the second year?

APPENDIX A

SELF-TEST 1

1. $250(\text{PVIF}_{8\%, \text{10 yr.}})$

   $250(0.463) = \$115.75$

2. $P = \text{FV}_{10}(\text{PVIF}_{6\%, \text{10 yr.}})$

   $= \$5,000(.558)$

   $= \$2,790$

3   Profitability index $= \dfrac{\left(\begin{array}{c}\text{present value of} \\ \text{future net cash flows}\end{array}\right)}{\left(\begin{array}{c}\text{initial} \\ \text{cash outlay}\end{array}\right)}$

Present value of future net cash flows

$= \$3,000 \ (PVIF_{8\%, \ 1 \ yr.}) + \$4,000(PVIF_{8\%, \ 2 \ yr.})$
$\quad + \$2,000(PVIF_{8\%, \ 3 \ yr.})$

$= \$3,000(0.926) + \$4,000(0.857) + \$2,000(0.794)$

$= \$2,778 + \$3,428 + \$1,588$

$= \$7,794$

Profitability index

$= F(\$7,794, \$5,000) = 1.5588$

4.   NPV $=$ PV inflows - PV outflows

$= \$7,794 - \$5,000$

$= \$2,794$

Accept the project because its NPV is positive and its PI is greater than 1.0.

5.   NPV $=$ $\$-10,000 + \$3,000(PVIF_{10\%, \ 1 \ yr.})$
$\quad + \$5,000(PVIF_{10\%, \ 2 \ yr.})$
$\quad + \$4,000(PVIF_{10\%, \ 3 \ yr.})$

$= \$-10,000 + \$3,000(0.909) + \$5,000(0.826)$
$\quad + \$4,000(0.751)$

$= \$-10,000 + \$2,727 + \$4,130 + \$3,004$

$= \$-139$

PI $= \dfrac{\$9,861}{\$10,000} = 0\ 9861$

Reject the project because the NPV is negative and the PI is less than 1.0.

6. $\text{NPV} = \$-8,000 + \$3,000 \, (\text{PVIF}_{12\%, \, 1 \, \text{yr.}})$
$+ \$6,000 \, (\text{PVIF}_{12\%, \, 2 \, \text{yr.}})$
$+ \$2,000 \, (\text{PVIF}_{12\%, \, 3 \, \text{yr.}})$
$+ \$1,000 \, (\text{PVIF}_{12\%, \, 4 \, \text{yr.}})$
$- \$1,000 \, (\text{PVIF}_{12\%, \, 5 \, \text{yr.}})$

$= \$-8,000 + \$3,000(0.893) + \$6,000(0.797)$
$+ \$2,000(0.712) + \$1,000(0.636) - \$1,000(0.567)$

$= \$-8,000 + \$2,679 + \$4,782 + \$1,424 + \$636 - \$567$

$= \$954$

$\text{PI} = \dfrac{\$8,954}{\$8,000} = 1.1192$

7. $\text{NPV} = \$-1,093.00 + \$100(\text{PVIF}_{8\%, \, 1 \, \text{yr.}}) + \$100(\text{PVIF}_{8\%, \, 2 \, \text{yr.}})$
$+ \$100(\text{PVIF}_{8\%, \, 3 \, \text{yr.}}) + \$100(\text{PVIF}_{8\%, \, 4 \, \text{yr.}})$
$+ \$100(\text{PVIF}_{8\%, \, 5 \, \text{yr.}}) + \$100(\text{PVIF}_{8\%, \, 6 \, \text{yr.}})$
$+ \$100(\text{PVIF}_{8\%, \, 7 \, \text{yr.}}) + \$100(\text{PVIF}_{8\%, \, 8 \, \text{yr.}})$
$+ \$100(\text{PVIF}_{8\%, \, 9 \, \text{yr.}}) + \$1,100(\text{PVIF}_{8\%, \, 10 \, \text{yr.}})$

$\text{NPV} = \$-1,093.00 + \$100(0.926) + \$100(0.857) + \$100(0.794)$
$+ \$100(0.735) + \$100(0.681) + \$100(0.630)$
$+ \$100(0.583) + \$100(0.540) + \$100(0.500)$
$+ \$1,100(0.463)$

$= \$-1,093.00 + \$92.60 + \$85.70 + \$79.48 + \$73.50$
$+ \$68.10 + \$63.00 + \$58.30 + \$54.00 + \$50.00$
$+ \$509.30$

$= \$40.90$

SELF-TEST 2

1. NPV = $-15,000 + $2,000(PVIFA_{20\%, 2 \text{ yr.}})$ +

    $4,000(PVIF_{20\%, 3 \text{ yr.}}) + $5,000 (PVIF_{20\%, 4 \text{ yr.}})$

    + $6,000 (PVIF_{20\%, 5 \text{ yr.}})$

    = $-15,000 + $2,000(1.528) + $4,000(0.579) +$5,000(0.482) + $6,000(0.402)$

    = $-15,000 + $3,056 + $2,316 + $2,410 + $2,412$

    = $-4,806$

    PI = f($10,194,$15,000) = 0.6796

The project should be rejected because its NPV is negative and the PI is less than 1.0.

2. $1,000 = $2,000(PVIF_{8\%, ? \text{ yr.}})$

    0.500 = $(PVIF_{8\%, ? \text{ yr.}})$

The table value in the 8% column comes closest to 0.500 in the 9-year row. Thus, it will take 9 years for $1,000 to accumulate to $2,000 if it is compounded at 8%.

3. $1,000 = $3,000 (PVIF_{?\%, 7 \text{ yr.}})$

    0.333 = $(PVIF_{?\%, 7 \text{ yr.}})$

The table value in the 7-year row comes closest to 0.333 in the 17% column. Thus, it is necessary to compound $1,000 at 17% for 7 years in order to accumulate $3,000.

4. P = $3,000 (PVIF_{8\%, 10 \text{ yr.}})$

    = $3,000 (0.463)$

    = $1,389$

5.   a.   P $= \$100 \ (\text{PVIFA}_{8\%, \ 10 \ \text{yr.}})$

                    $= \$100 \ (7.722)$

                    $= \$772.20$

   b.   P $= \$100 \ (\text{PVIFA}_{10\%, \ 10 \ \text{yr.}})$

                    $= \$100(6.145)$

                    $= \$614.50$

   c.   P $= \$100 \ (\text{PVIFA}_{20\%, \ 10 \ \text{yr.}})$

                    $= \$100(4.192)$

                    $= \$419.20$

   d.   P $= \$100 \ (\text{PVIFA}_{20\%, \ 10 \ \text{yr.}})$

                    $= \$100(3.092)$

                    $= \$309 \ 20$

6.   a.   P $= \$50 \ (\text{PVIF}_{10\%, \ 4 \ \text{yr.}})$

                    $= \$50 \ (0.683)$

                    $= \$34.15$

   b.   P $= \$50 \ (\text{PVIF}_{20\%, \ 4 \ \text{yr.}})$

                    $= \$50(0.482)$

                    $= \$24.10$

   c.   P $= \$50 \ \dfrac{1}{(1+0)^4}$

                    $= \$50 \ \left(\dfrac{1}{1}\right)$

                    $= \$50$

d.   P $= \$50 \dfrac{1}{(1+1.0)^4}$

$\hphantom{d. \quad P} = \$50 \left(\dfrac{1}{16}\right)$

$\hphantom{d. \quad P} = \$3.125$

7. a. $FV_5 = \$100\ (FVIF_{16\%,\ 5\ yr.})$

$\hphantom{7. \quad a. \quad FV_5} = \$100\ (2.100)$

$\hphantom{7. \quad a. \quad FV_5} = \$210.00$

b. $FV_{10} = \$100\ (FVIF_{8\%,\ 10\ yr.})$

$\hphantom{b. \quad FV_{10}} = \$100\ (2.159)$

$\hphantom{b. \quad FV_{10}} = \$215.90$

c. $FV_{20} = \$100\ (FVIF_{4\%,\ 20\ yr.})$

$\hphantom{c. \quad FV_{20}} = \$100\ (2.191)$

$\hphantom{c. \quad FV_{20}} = \$219.10$

8. a.   Initial Outlay

New machine	$-20,000
Sale of old machine	+ 2,000
Tax gain	
($5,000 - $2,000) 0.4	<u>+ 1,200</u>
	$-16,800

b.   Annual cash flows

	Book Method	Cash Method
Savings	$10,000	$ 10,000
Change in depreciation	(4,000 - 1,000)	
Taxable increase	7,000	
Taxes	2,800	<u>2,800</u>
Annual net cash flow		<u>$ 7,200</u>

c.   Terminal flow:

Annual cash flow   7,200

d.   Cash-flow diagram

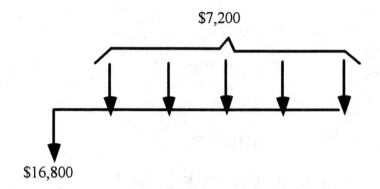

$7,200

$16,800

e.   NPV = $-16, 800 + $7,200 (PVIFA$_{14\%, 5 yr.}$)

= - $16,800 + $7,200 (3.433)

= - $16,800 + $24,717.60

= $7,917.60

PI   = f($24,717.60,$16,800) = = 1.47

SELF-TEST 3

1. $10,000 $= \dfrac{\$14,000}{(1+\text{IRR})^5}$

0.714 $= \dfrac{1}{(1+\text{IRR})^5}$

Therefore, IRR = 7% because the Table C value for 5 years closest to 0. 714 occurs in the 7% column (0. 713).

2. $700 $= \dfrac{\$1,857}{(1+IRR)^{20}}$

   0.377 $= \dfrac{1}{(1+IRR)^{20}}$

In Table C, we see that IRR = 5%

3. $30,000 $= \$6,000 \displaystyle\sum_{t=0}^{10} \dfrac{1}{(1+IRR)^t}$

   5.0 $= \displaystyle\sum_{t=0}^{10} \dfrac{1}{(1+IRR)^t}$

From Table E, IRR = approximately 15%.

4. $20,000 $= \$3,928 \displaystyle\sum_{t=0}^{15} \dfrac{1}{(1+IRR)^t}$

   5.092 $= \displaystyle\sum_{t=0}^{15} \dfrac{1}{(1+IRR)^t}$

From Table E, IRR = 18%.

5. $40,000 $= \$10,000 \displaystyle\sum_{t=1}^{5} \dfrac{\$1}{(1+IRR)^t} + \$15,000 \dfrac{1}{(1+IRR)^6}$

Try 20%

$40,000 = $10,000(2.991) + $15,000(0.335)$

$= $29,910 + $5,025$

$\neq $34,935$

Try 15%:

$40,000 = $10,000(3.352) + $15,000(0.432)$

F-31

$$= \$33,520 + \$6,480$$

$$= \$40,000$$

Thus, 15% is the approximate IRR.

6. $$\$61,630 = \$10,000 \sum_{t=1}^{6} \frac{\$1}{(1+IRR)^t}$$

Try 20%:

$$\$61,630 = \$10,000(3.326) + \$70,000(0.279)$$

$$= \$33,260 + \$19,530$$

$$\neq \$52,790$$

Try 15%:

$$\$61,630 = \$10,000(3.784) + \$70,000(0.376)$$

$$= \$37,840 + \$26,320$$

$$\neq \$64,160$$

Try 16%:

$$\$61,630 = \$100,000(3.685) + \$70,000(0.354)$$

$$= \$36,850 + \$24,780$$

$$= \$61,630$$

Therefore, IRR = 16%.

7. $$\$2,992 = \$700 \frac{\$1}{(1+IRR)} + \$1,400 \frac{1}{(1+IRR)^2} + \$3,000 \frac{1}{(1+IRR)^3}$$

Try 20%:

$$\$2,992 = \$700(0.833) + \$1,400(0.694) + \$3,000(0.579)$$

$$= \$583.10 + \$971.60 + \$1,737.00$$

$\neq$ $3,291.70

Try 25%:

$2,992 $\quad = \quad$ $700(0.800) + $1,400(0.640) + $3,000(0.512)

$\qquad = \quad$ $560 + $896 + $1,536

$\qquad = \quad$ $2,992

Thus, the IRR = 25%.

8. $\quad$ $5,492 $\quad = \quad$ $2,000 \sum_{t=1}^{2} \dfrac{\$1}{(1+\text{IRR})} + $4,000 \dfrac{1}{(1+\text{IRR})^3}$

$\qquad\qquad\qquad + \$3,000 \dfrac{1}{(1+\text{IRR})^4}$

Try 20%:

$5,492 $\quad = \quad$ $2,000(1.528) + $4,000(0.579) + $3,000(0.482)

$\qquad = \quad$ $3,056 + $2,316 + $1,446

$\qquad \neq \quad$ $6,818

Try 30%

$5,492 $\quad = \quad$ $2,000(1.361) + $4,000(0.455) + $3,000(0.350)

$\qquad = \quad$ $2,722 + $1,820 + $1,050

$\qquad \neq \quad$ $5,592

Try 31%

$5,492 $\quad = \quad$ $2,000(1.346) + $4,000(0.445) + $3,000(0.340)

$\qquad = \quad$ $2,692 + $1,780 + $1,020

$\qquad = \quad$ $5,492

Thus, 31% is this project's IRR.

9 . $\$1,000 = \$4,000 \ f(1,(1 + IRR)^2)$

$(1 + IRR)^2 = 4 \ 0$

$1 + IRR = r(4.0)$

$1 + IRR = 2.0$

$IRR = 1.0$, or $IRR = 100\%$

ANSWERS TO SELF TESTS

Chapter 1

True-False		Multiple Choice	
1.	F	1.	d
2.	T	2.	e
3.	F	3.	e
4.	T	4.	e
5.	T	5.	d
6.	F	6.	d
7.	F	7.	c
8.	F	8.	d
9.	T		
10.	F		
11.	T		

Chapter 2

True-False		Multiple Choice	
1.	F	1.	c
2.	T	2.	d
3.	F	3.	e
4.	F	4.	b
5.	F	5.	b
6.	F	6.	a
7.	T	7.	c
8.	T	8.	d
9.	F	9.	c
10.	T	10.	c
11.	T	11.	d
12.	F	12.	b
13.	T	13.	b
14.	F	14.	c
15.	F	15.	c
16.	T	16.	d
17.	T	17.	d
18.	F	18.	b
19.	F	19.	d
20.	T	20.	c
21.	F	21.	c
22.	T	22.	c
23.	F	23.	c
24.	F	24.	b
25.	T		
26.	F		
27.	T		
28.	T		
29.	F		

Chapter 3

True-False		Multiple Choice	
1.	F	1.	d
2.	T	2.	a
3.	F	3.	d
4.	T	4.	d
5.	T	5.	b
6.	F	6.	b
7.	F	7.	c
8.	F	8.	b
9.	F	9.	a
10.	T	10.	d
11.	F		
12.	F		
13.	T		
14.	F		
15.	F		

Chapter 4

True-False		Multiple Choice	
1.	T	1.	c
2.	T	2.	e
3.	F	3.	e
4.	T	4.	c
5.	T	5.	d
6.	T	6.	c
7.	F		
8.	F		
9.	F		
10.	T		

Chapter 5

True-False		Multiple Choice	
1.	T	1.	a
2.	T	2.	c
3.	F	3.	d
4.	T	4.	c
5.	T	5.	c
6.	T	6.	a
7.	T		
8.	F		
9.	T		
10.	F		

Chapter 6

True-False		Multiple Choice	
1.	T	1.	b
2.	T	2.	d
3.	F	3.	c
4.	F	4.	c
5.	F	5.	b
6.	F	6.	d
7.	T	7.	b
8.	F		
9.	T		
10.	F		

Chapter 7

True-False		Multiple Choice	
1.	T	1.	a
2.	T	2.	d
3.	T	3.	e
4.	T	4.	a
5.	F	5.	b
6.	T	6.	b
7.	T	7.	d
8.	T	8.	b
9.	F	9.	a
10.	T		

Chapter 8

True-False		Multiple Choice	
1.	T	1.	a
2.	F	2.	a
3.	T	3.	a
4.	F	4.	d
5.	T	5.	b
6.	F		
7.	F		
8.	F		
9.	T		
10.	F		

Chapter 9

True-False		Multiple Choice	
1.	T	1.	b
2.	T	2.	a
3.	F	3.	d
4.	T	4.	c
		5.	b

Chapter 10

True-False		Multiple Choice	
1.	T	1.	e
2.	T	2.	d
3.	T		
4.	F		
5.	T		

Chapter 11

True-False		Multiple Choice	
1.	F	1.	c
2.	T	2.	d
3.	T	3.	d
4.	F		

Chapter 12

True-False		Multiple Choice	
1.	F	1.	f
2.	T	2.	e
3.	T	3.	c
4.	F	4.	d
5.	F	5.	b
6.	T	6.	a
7.	F	7.	c
8.	F	8.	b
9.	T	9.	b
10.	F		
11.	T		
12.	T		
13.	T		
14.	T		
15.	T		
16.	F		
17.	T		
18.	F		

Chapter 13

True-False		Multiple Choice	
1.	F	1.	c
2.	F	2.	c
3.	T	3.	c
4.	T	4.	c
5.	F	5.	b
6.	T	6.	b
7.	F	7.	b
8.	T	8.	b
9.	F	9.	b
10.	F	10.	d
11.	F	11.	b
12.	F	12.	c
13.	F	13.	a
14.	F	14.	b
15.	T	15.	c
16.	T	16.	d
17.	T	17.	b
18.	T	18.	d
19.	T	19.	c
20.	T	20.	a
21.	F	21.	b
22.	F	22.	b
23.	T	23.	c
24.	F		
25.	F		
26.	T		
27.	T		
28.	T		

Chapter 14

True-False		Multiple Choice	
1.	F	1.	c
2.	T	2.	e
3.	F	3.	b
4.	F	4.	d
5.	T	5.	b
6.	F	6.	b
7.	F	7.	a
8.	F	8.	d
9.	F	9.	b
10.	T	10.	d
11.	T	11.	a
12.	F	12.	c
13.	F	13.	e
14.	F	14.	c
15.	T	15.	c
16.	T	16.	a
17.	T	17.	b
18.	T	18.	e
19.	F	19.	a
20.	F		
21.	T		
22.	F		
23.	F		
24.	T		
25.	F		
26.	F		
27.	T		

Chapter 15

True-False		Multiple Choice	
1.	T	1.	b
2.	F	2.	d
3.	F	3.	d
4.	F	4.	c
5.	T	5.	d
6.	F	6.	d
7.	T	7.	d
8.	T	8.	d
9.	F	9.	e
10.	T	10.	f
11.	T	11.	b
12.	F	12.	b
13.	F	13.	a
14.	F		

Chapter 16

True-False		Multiple Choice	
1.	F	1.	c
2.	F	2.	f
3.	T	3.	c
4.	F	4.	a
5.	T	5.	c
6.	T	6.	e
7.	F	7.	c
8.	T	8.	b
9.	F	9.	a
10.	T	10.	c
11.	F	11.	b
12.	F		
13.	T		
14.	F		
15.	F		
16.	T		
17.	F		
18.	F		
19.	T		

Chapter 17

True-False		Multiple Choice	
1.	F	1.	a
2.	F	2.	d
3.	T	3.	c
4.	F	4.	a
5.	T	5.	d
6.	F	6.	c
7.	T	7.	d
8.	F	8.	e
9.	F	9.	c
10.	F	10.	d
11.	F	11.	e
12.	F	12.	d
13.	F	13.	c
14.	F	14.	b
15.	F	15.	b
16.	F	16.	d
17.	T	17.	c
18.	T	18.	c
19.	F	19.	d
20.	F	20.	e
21.	T		
22.	T		
23.	F		
24.	F		
25.	T		
26.	T		
27.	T		
28.	F		
29.	T		
30.	F		
31.	T		
32.	F		
33.	F		
34.	T		
35.	F		
36.	F		
37.	F		
38.	F		

Chapter 18

True-False		Multiple Choice	
1.	F	1.	c
2.	T	2.	c
3.	T	3.	e
4.	T	4.	d
5.	F	5.	d
6.	T	6.	b
7.	T	7.	a
8.	F	8.	d
9.	T		
10.	F		

Chapter 19

True-False		Multiple Choice	
1.	F	1.	e
2.	T	2.	a
3.	T	3.	a
4.	T	4.	d
5.	F		
6.	T		
7.	F		
8.	F		
9.	T		
10.	T		

Chapter 20

True-False		Multiple Choice	
1.	T	1.	c
2.	F	2.	c
3.	F	3.	d
4.	T	4.	c
5.	T	5.	a
6.	F	6.	a
7.	T	7.	b
8.	T	8.	c
9.	F		

Chapter 21

True-False		Multiple Choice	
1.	T	1.	d
2.	T	2.	e
3.	T		
4.	F		
5.	F		
6.	T		

Chapter 22

True-False		Multiple Choice	
1.	T	1.	d
2.	F	2.	e
3.	F	3.	c
4.	F	4.	c
5.	T	5.	a
6.	T	6.	e
7.	F	7.	e
8.	F	8.	b
9.	T	9.	d
10.	T	10.	e
11.	T		
12.	T		
13.	T		
14.	F		
15.	T		
16.	F		